THE WORLD WAR II U.S. NAVY: 40 Years After Victory

By STEVE EWING

PICTORIAL HISTORIES PUBLISHING COMPANY
MISSOULA, MONTANA

LIBRARY OF CONGRESS
CATALOG CARD NUMBER 86-61528

ISBN 0-933126-79-4

First Printing: November 1986
Second Printing: August 1988

Typography: Arrow Graphics, Missoula, Montana
Layout: Stan Cohen
Cover Design: Artmill, Inc., Missoula, Montana

OTHER BOOKS BY STEVE EWING

American Cruisers of World War II—A Pictorial Encyclopedia (1984)
The Lady Lex and the Blue Ghost (1983)
USS Enterprise: The Most Decorated Ship of World War II (1982)
West Virginia and Appalachia (1977)
Man, Religion and Environment (1975)

PICTORIAL HISTORIES PUBLISHING COMPANY
713 South Third West, Missoula, Montana 59801

TABLE OF CONTENTS

INTRODUCTION

Challenged by the Axis powers in the Atlantic, Pacific and Mediterranean during World War II, the United States Navy emerged in 1945 as the greatest and most powerful naval force in the history of warfare. Forty years after Japan's surrender aboard the USS *Missouri*, very little of history's greatest fleet still exists. In 1985 two support ships, the destroyer tender USS *Prairie* and repair ship USS *Vulcan*, still serve in operational status along with the reactivated battleships *New Jersey* and *Iowa*. Soon, the aging *Missouri* will again commission and the last of the *Iowa*-class battleships, *Wisconsin*, is due to follow. When the *Wisconsin* is recommissioned in the early 1990's, the last aircraft carrier to serve in World War II, the USS *Lexington*, is scheduled to close her half-century of service.

Most of the World War II warships went to the scrap heap within 20 years after the war. Indeed, some ships steamed to the scrap yards under their own power in late 1945 and early 1946. But, many of the major combat ships continued serving either in operational or reserve status until sold.

What remains in memorial status or in museums to remind this and future generations of the victorious World War II U.S. Navy? By 1985 four World War II battle star winning battleships had been memorialized along with two aircraft carriers, four destroyers and 12 submarines. However, no heavy or light cruiser that won battle stars in World War II has been memorialized although two *Brooklyn*-class light cruisers still serve in the navy of Chile. And, regrettably, both memorialized carriers, one of the four destroyers and four of the 12 submarines do not resemble their World War II appearance due to having been modernized to serve in the post-war period.

That which remains in museums and museum exhibits somewhat parallels the preservation experience of memorialized ships in that some museums and exhibits capture the history of the era while some do not. The major problem in museums and with memorialized ships is not what exists; it is what does not exist. Just as there is no World War II era aircraft carrier (*Dedalo*, ex *Cabot* CVL-28 lives on in the navy of Spain) or cruiser in the United States still in original configuration, there are either no exhibits or inadequate exhibits to honor a number of great combat ships such as the battleship *Washington* (one did exist, but it has been removed and placed in storage), the carriers *Essex*, *Franklin* and *Bunker Hill*; cruisers *Atlanta*, *Birmingham* and *Honolulu*; destroyers *Johnston* and *Hoel*; destroyer-escorts *England* and *Samuel B. Roberts*; and the submarine *Tang*.

In view of the above, the major objectives of this book are to highlight the outstanding memories of World War II U.S. Navy warships, and to acknowledge the more significant memorials that have been placed to honor their moments of sacrifice and success. This book is limited to battleships, carriers, cruisers, destroyers and submarines, but this limitation should not be interpreted as an understatement of the critical roles of what are termed "auxiliary" ships. These vessels enjoyed little of the glamor and publicity of the major combatant types, but their successes and sacrifices were equal. They not only fulfilled their respective support roles, but also shot down enemy planes, sank submarines, joined in shore bombardments and on more than one occasion, exchanged gunfire with enemy ships. It is further recognized that these vessels have not received full acclaim for their World War II contributions; hopefully, gaps in naval literature and museum displays will address this in coming days.

In essence this book is intended to be a tribute to the World War II United States Navy. A number of contemporary books emphasize perceived errors in judgment and personal disputes which have diminished the remembrance of certain World War II naval luminaries. Variance of opinion and perhaps some of the personality complaints have their place in the literature, but the reader looking for rust on memorialized ships or negative perspectives on personalities will be disappointed herein.The officers and men of the World War II U.S. Navy got the job done; all tributes to them are inspired, in part, by the hope that those who fight future wars on this country's behalf will know what is required for success and survival.

For nearly three years this writer has been collecting material for this book and in the process has traveled several thousand miles, has been invited to or barged-in on several dozen veterans' reunions and has talked to hundreds of veterans. A number of questions not asked were answered by officers and men who went to war 40 or more years ago. Examples: 1) many veterans believe that current histories do not sufficiently call to attention their conviction that the Allies could have lost the war; 2) many veterans wonder why some of the men who were such a great inspiration to them during the war have since seemingly fallen into historical disrepute; and 3) nearly every veteran believes his ship was the greatest single ship to serve in the war. The last thought was easily the most pervasive offered in personal conversations and initially was a source of some perplexity as awards, battle stars and other documentation seemed to have little or no impact in discussions relating to the respective greatness of ships and crews. On one occasion this writer was told that 17 battle stars were more than 20 (truth, and he was sober). On another occasion, all the evidence available from the National Archives and Navy Historical Center was not sufficient to convince some other veterans that their ship did not sink a certain enemy ship (this even though none of the men were topside during the battle, which was fought at night). These perspectives, as mentioned, were initially somewhat exasperating until I recalled a visit to a ship in the late 1970's at which time a sailor aboard commented that his ship "should be hauled off to the nearest scrap yard." As much as anything, the difference in attitude just related helps explain how the U.S. Navy was successful in World War II. When a man who served on the *Chester*, the *Essex* or the *O'Bannon* said his ship was the best, he meant it. It was not just a floating piece of steel; it was his home. It became as meaningful to him as the brick or wooden frame house he grew up in, and the brotherhood learned at home was transferred to men on board who became members of his new family. Of course there were times when he cursed and complained both about ship and fellow crewmembers, but squabbles are not uncommon in almost any home. A ship personalized? Yes! And, members of the generation that fought the war and the generations that have benefited since can be thankful that they were. When their ship was in trouble, men fought to save their "home" and their "family." Contemporary and future generations should hope that it will never be any different.

One will find very little in the "Memory" sections of the following chapters that is new except for the organization and perhaps the listings of winners of the Presidential Unit Citation and Navy Unit Commendation, and battle star leaders. Battle star totals are those listed in the *Dictionary of American Naval Fighting Ships* although it is known that some challenges to this listing have resulted in changes. Presidential Unit Citation and Navy Unit Commendation awards listed herein are based on the *Navy and Marine Corps Awards Manual.*

Much of what appears in the "Memorials" sections, the heart of this book, is new. No other exclusive treatment of memorialized World War II ships is known,[1] and no exclusive treatment of World War II U.S. Navy ship memorials, museums and museum exhibits is known to exist. Most of the pictures presented in the "Memorials" sections were taken in 1984 and 1985 by this writer, but in the interest of better photography, some pictures taken by others have been used. The willingness of others to supply pictures was especially appreciated when entire rolls from the author's camera returned either undeveloped or ground-up like confetti. Whereas the "Memorials" section in the battleships, cruisers and submarine chapters is relatively lengthy, the "Memorials" section in the carriers and destroyers chapters is not. Battleships were named for states, cruisers mostly were named for cities and submarines – although usually named for fish – are not terribly expensive to set up in memorial status; therefore, memorials are relatively abundant. World War II carriers, often named for ships of the Revolutionary War period, and destroyers – usually named for individuals – lacked a natural sponsor such as a state or city for preservation purposes. Too, carriers are quite expensive to maintain. All this has been stated to call attention to the relative paucity of attention to carrier and destroyer memorials as there simply is not that much to highlight.

In deference to all the veterans who believe that their ship was the greatest to serve in World War II, it must be stated that the ships and submarines that have been memorialized were not saved necessarily because they were the best. In several instances a ship or submarine was memorialized because a city or organization was seeking a ship – any ship – and the request to Washington asked for "what is available?" Many of the more famous and deserving ships with well-documented claims to immortality were dismantled before an interest in preserving the history of the World War II U.S. Navy was manifested. In fact, part of the rush to preserve some of this history was the realization that most of the truly famous ships were already gone and there was a desire to save "something" by which more deserving and/or other deserving ships might be remembered. Still, several of the memorialized ships are deserving of preservation in their own right.

Although an effort has been made to present information and pictures on all the major memorialized combat ships and as many of the major single ship exhibits as possible, surely some exhibits have been missed. Even if all had been located and chronicled, this book would still be dated before the printer's ink was dry because 1) museum exhibits are constantly rotated 2) new exhibits are being placed 3) some previously existing exhibits will have been dismantled (example: USS *Washington*) 4) hundreds of relics from World War II ships are on loan to junior high schools, high schools, ROTC departments, military clubs, VFWs and even college fraternity houses; and 5) many artifacts held in private hands will appear or disappear only after the death of the veteran or person to whom the relic has meaning. Although there may not be a present memorial to a World War II ship, in many instances it is still possible to create a museum exhibit with pictures and relics from the ship. Before being sold for scrap, certain relics are removed and held in storage by the curator of the Navy. A partial list of these relics includes bells, china and silverware, clocks, flags, hand operating wheels, indicators, plaques, planking, tompions and trophies. At the specific request of the curator, the following relics (partial listing) may be removed: anchors, engine-order telegraph, guns, navigational equipment, port-

1. The Naval Institute's small booklet *Historic Naval Ships Association of North America* includes vessels that did not participate in World War II: likewise the excellent, lengthy appendix "Historic Ship Exhibits in the United States" in the *Dictionary of American Naval Fighting Ships*.

hole frames and glass, sidelights, steering stand and voice tubes. Seen alone away from a museum or away from historical context, these relics are little more than junk; but in a museum exhibit these items are often viewed by veterans as being sacred, and they are greatly respected by many who never served on or saw one of the World War II warships that has disappeared into history.

It is not the purpose of this book to worship inorganic steel. However, floating structures of steel housed men who placed their lives in peril for their country. A warship was more than a hull, bulkheads and superstructure; it was a place. It was a place to live, to work, to fellowship, to fight, and for some it would become the final place in life. It was a tangible piece of the American homeland away from home and the closest reminder of all for which one fought. Not only a "home" to defend, it was an instrument by which an enemy might be repelled, a means toward a victorious end, and in the end, it was a conveyance that returned a sailor to his loved ones.

In the twilight of their lives, veterans assemble with regularity to share again a unique period in history when they stood at the center of the world's stage and helped shape the direction and destiny of their generation and future generations. All too soon these men will go the way of history's greatest fleet. But they will have bequeathed inspiring and impelling memories that will be their greatest memorial.

Iron ore
to Newport News, New York and the River Fore
and then off to war.

After victory, bent into a plowshare;
but since enemies yet prepare,
old souls in reborn iron steam forth to bear
the cost of freedoms fare

SE

CHAPTER ONE
BATTLESHIPS

PRESIDENTIAL UNIT CITATION

No Awards

NAVY UNIT COMMENDATION

USS Mississippi	BB-41
USS Pennsylvania	BB-38
USS South Dakota	BB-57
USS Tennessee	BB-43

ULTIMATE SACRIFICE

USS Arizona	BB-39
USS Oklahoma	BB-37

BATTLE STARS

USS North Carolina	BB-55...15*
USS Washington	BB-56...13
USS South Dakota	BB-57...13
USS Massachusetts	BB-59....11
USS Tennessee	BB-43....10
USS Alabama	BB-60.....9
USS Indiana	BB-58.....9
USS Iowa	BB-61.....9
USS New Jersey	BB-62.....9
USS Mississippi	BB-41.....8
USS Pennsylvania	BB-38.....8
USS Colorado	BB-45.....7
USS Maryland	BB-46.....7
USS Idaho	BB-42.....7
USS Nevada	BB-36.....7
USS California	BB-44.....7
USS New Mexico	BB-40.....6
USS West Virginia	BB-48.....5
USS Wisconsin	BB-64.....5
USS Texas	BB-35.....5
USS Arkansas	BB-33.....4
USS New York	BB-34.....3
USS Missouri	BB-63.....3
USS Arizona	BB-39.....1
USS Oklahoma	BB-37.....1

*USS North Carolina was awarded 12 battle stars in the 1948 Naval Awards Manual. A challenge in 1983 resulted in the award of three previously overlooked battle stars.

MEMORIES

Before World War II the battleship reigned supreme in the minds of many naval leaders in the major countries that would engage in the global conflict of 1939-1945. Although the naval aspect of the war would prove to be essentially a carrier and submarine war, the battleship nonetheless affected thinking and strategy from the beginning to near the end.

For the United States war began with the Japanese attack against Battleship Row and other targets at Pearl Harbor. In the Far East the British first felt major losses to the Japanese with the loss of the battleship *Prince of Wales* and the battlecruiser *Repulse* on 11 December 1941. Even into the latter stages of the war, Allied attention in planning strikes into Japanese-held territory took into consideration whether or not the 18.1-inch guns of Japan's two super battleships, the *Yamato* and *Musachi*, might be encountered.

For both the United States and Japan, battleships were used with some hesitancy after the first week of the Pacific war. For the United States the three *New Mexico*-class battleships (*New Mexico, Idaho* and *Mississippi*) were ordered to the Pacific immediately after Pearl Harbor as "insurance." These three and a few quickly repaired battleships damaged at Pearl formed the last line of defense until mid-1943 when the course of the war provided offensive opportunities. At the critical juncture of the battle for Guadalcanal (November 1942) the Japanese committed two battleships, but it was not until the U.S. Navy arrived off the Philippines in late 1944 and Okinawa in early 1945 that the Japanese finally committed their total battleship strength to combat.

In the memories of Americans no event concerning battleships is more often recalled than the attack on Pearl Harbor. On that fateful 7 December the U.S. Navy lost forever the services of the *Arizona* and the *Oklahoma*. The *West Virginia, California* and *Nevada* touched the bottom of the harbor, were raised, and by mid-1944 all three had been repaired, modernized and returned to the war. The *Tennessee, Maryland* and *Pennsylvania* were slightly damaged during the Pearl Harbor raid, but they too needed modernization – especially in anti-aircraft protection – and therefore were not immediately available. However,

World War I veteran *New York* (BB-34) leads *Nevada* (BB-36) and *Oklahoma* (BB-37) during maneuvers in 1932. *Langley* (CV-1) is visible in the background. Battleship tactics perfected before World War II did not find anticipated expression in a war to be greatly influenced by aircraft. *New York* served through World War II only to be sunk 8 July 1948 as a target after surviving both atom bomb tests at Bikini. USN

One of the memorable photos of the "day of infamy." Taken from a Japanese plane just after the torpedo attack but before the dive bombers struck. From left to right are *Nevada* (BB-36), *Vestal* outboard of *Arizona* (BB-39) – which would explode only moments later, *West Virginia* (BB-48) sinking outboard of *Tennessee* (BB-43), *Oklahoma* (BB-37) capsizing outboard of *Maryland* (BB-46). Note oil spreading from torpedoed ships. USN

California (BB-44) listing to port and on her way to the bottom with 98 dead. In the background *Nevada* is seen attempting to escape the harbor. Back in the war by early 1944, *California* lost 44 more men to a kamikaze in January 1945. She was eventually sold for scrap in 1959. NA

USS *Arizona* (BB-39) on 12 December 1941. With 1,104 men lost during the 7 December attack, the hull of the ship is today where it sank 40 years ago. Most of the wrecked superstructure seen in this photo was removed within a year of the attack with the remainder being removed in the late 1950s. Only the barbette for the number three main 14-inch battery (at right with catapult on top) remains above the water today. USN

Of the five battleships sunk at Pearl Harbor, three would be raised, repaired and sent back into the war. *Nevada,* shown here being refloated in February 1942, would be the first of the three to return to the war (May 1943). *Nevada* lost 50 men at Pearl Harbor, 11 to a kamikaze and two to a shore battery off Okinawa before surviving both atomic tests at Bikini. She was finally sunk, again, as a target 31 July 1948. USN

these six ships along with older and newer sisters made their presence felt as the U.S. Navy advanced across the Pacific to the Japanese homeland. Indeed, two of the four battleships awarded the Navy Unit Commendation (*Tennessee* and *Pennsylvania*) were damaged at Pearl Harbor.

Perhaps the second most vivid memory of American battleships is their performance as bombardment and anti-aircraft platforms. These duties are often remembered as routine and relative to some tasks, not very dangerous. However, a look at the record indicates otherwise. Shore bombardment proved dangerous on numerous occasions: *Colorado*, as an example, was hit 22 times off Tinian. And while tied to the beaches off enemy-held islands in the last two years of the war, a dozen American battleships suffered over a thousand casualties from enemy air attacks and shore batteries.

A third popular memory of U.S.Navy battleships in World War II centers on the old battleships and the 25 October 1944 Battle of Surigao Strait, one of the several engagements during the last week of that month that comprised the Battle of Leyte Gulf. The two Japanese battleships sunk in Surigao Strait, the *Fuso* and *Yamashiro*, and their accompanying cruisers and destroyers, had been greatly wounded by U.S. Navy destroyers before they came into range of American cruisers and battleships. But, the battleships (*West Virginia, California, Pennsylvania, Maryland, Tennessee,* and *Mississippi*) and cruisers hit the enemy column hard and ensured the victory that history records as the last occasion on which battleships opposed each other,

Somewhat surprisingly, the one memory that seems to have escaped the attention of some was the first occasion wherein Japanese and American battleships closed each other and fought. On the night of 14-15 November 1942 in the critical and decisive Naval Battle of Guadalcanal, the *South Dakota* and *Washington* engaged the Japanese battleship *Kirishima* and her escorts. Although veterans of the *South Dakota* don't remember it this way, naval records indicate that the major damage to the *Kirishima* was done by the *Washington*. Reconstruction of the battle indicates that the *Kirishima* was so occupied in defending herself from the guns of the *South Dakota* that she did not see *Washington* until it was too late.

The *South Dakota's* role in another battle, the 26 October 1942 Battle of Santa Cruz, is still a favorite debate among some. *South Dakota* gunners claimed 32 enemy planes, the U.S. Navy credited the battleship with 26 and the matter received considerable attention in the press. When the newspaper articles appeared, the *South Dakota* was referred to as "Battleship X" for security reasons. The newspaper articles were good for the morale of American citizens, but gunners on other ships declared that the *South Dakota's* claims and credits were inflated primarily because most of the planes she fired on required deflection shots. Actual numbers will never be known, of course, but it is only fair to note that "Battleship X" was a fighting ship in two critical battles, she was there when she was needed, and she was a target in both the surface battle (Guadalcanal) and air battle (Santa Cruz) wherein she diverted shells, bombs and torpedoes that would have been aimed at some other ship. In both battles she was hit—severely off Guadalcanal—but she gave better than she got, and she will always be remembered as a fighting ship committed to battle when the need was greatest.

40

Opposite top: War for *Oklahoma* (BB-37) and over 400 of her crew lasted only 20 minutes on 7 December 1941, but the remainder of her crew avenged her by transferring their experience to newer ships. Twenty-five years old at the time of her loss, the ship is seen here after her 1927-29 modernization. She was raised in 1943 to clear the harbor and sank again 17 May 1947 while under tow to San Francisco. USN

Opposite middle: *New Mexico* (BB-40), shown here, and her two nearly identical sister ships, *Mississippi* (BB-41) and *Idaho* (BB-42), were in the Atlantic when the Japanese attacked Pearl Harbor. The three ships of this class earned 21 battle stars collectively. *New Mexico* lost 30 men to a kamikaze off the Philippines and 54 off Okinawa by air attack. *Mississippi* lost 48 men in 1924 and 43 more in 1943 in turret explosions and was hit by two kamikazes. *Mississippi* served as a gunnery and missile training ship into 1956, but both *New Mexico* and *Idaho* were sold in 1947. See picture of *Mississippi* in following chapter. USN

Opposite bottom: Of the 10 modern battleships, seven still exist: the four Iowas—either in commission or scheduled to return—and the museum ships *Alabama, Massachusetts* and *North Carolina. South Dakota* (shown here) *Washington* and *Indiana* were scrapped in the early 1960s. Of the three only *South Dakota* is now honored by a large, major exhibit. Two of the old battleships were sunk at Pearl Harbor, eight were scrapped, two were sunk as targets (*New York* and *Nevada*), one was scuttled (*Pennsylvania*) and *Arkansas* was destroyed during the atomic tests at Bikini. USN

North Carolina (BB-55) in 1944. The "Showboat," commissioned 9 April 1941, was the first of the modern battleships. She still exists as a memorial ship in Wilmington, N.C. USN

These two views of *West Virginia* (BB-48) show the ship in her pre-Pearl and rebuilt appearances. The last battleship sunk at Pearl Harbor to return to action (late 1944) BB-48 lost 105 on 7 December 1941 and four more to a kamikaze off Okinawa. "Wee Vee" was sold 24 August 1959. USN and USN

It is regrettable that the *Washington* is not remembered more frequently in books and articles. Perhaps her victory over *Kirishima* was too easy thanks to *South Dakota's* role. Still, *Washington* did not retreat after she lost her escorting destroyers; she pressed on looking for more action. Surprisingly, *Washington* did not receive either the Presidential Unit Citation or Navy Unit Commendation for actually placing the shells into *Kirishima* that resulted in her sinking. And, as will be noted later, even the memorial to the great battleship has also suffered in remembrance.

Although the *Washington's* sister ship *North Carolina* is now a magnificent memorial ship in Wilmington, N.C., her wartime remembrance also has been somewhat unfortunate. Defender of the carrier *Enterprise* in the Battle of the Eastern Solomons, the "Showboat" fared well with nearly a dozen planes shot down and only one man killed by strafing and seven near misses. However, the first modern American battleship to enter the Pacific was hit by a torpedo on 15 September 1942, and she was removed from the battles of Santa Cruz and the Naval Battle of Guadalcanal, where she no doubt would have made considerable contributions. Some have speculated that she might have been able to save the carrier *Hornet* at Santa Cruz with her anti-aircraft fire and attraction as an alternative target. By the time the *North Carolina* was repaired and returned to duty, she was one of several battleships available and her subsequent battles did

When newspapers recounted the exploits of *South Dakota* in the Battle of Santa Cruz, she was named "Battleship X" due to censorship. Her name will endure as a result of her roles off Santa Cruz and the Naval Battle of Guadalcanal. USN

USS *South Dakota* (BB-57) in 1944 appearance. Note similarity of "SoDak" and the rebuilt *West Virginia* in superstructure and 5-inch gun turrets. USN

not provide the singular opportunities afforded in the fall of 1942.

Unquestionably, the most often recalled memory of the *Massachusetts* was her battle with the Vichy French battleship *Jean Bart* while serving as flagship of Operation Torch in November 1942. *Jean Bart* was not totally operational during the battle; in fact she was able to use only one turret and she remained tied to her moorings. However she did offer resistance before the 16-inch guns of the *Massachusetts* disabled her.

Some ships like the *Alabama* may have been somewhat penalized in historical remembrance for being effective and lucky. If a ship was not effective or unlucky, much was written about it. And if ships like the *Indiana* and *Washington* collided, which they did on 1 February 1944, nearly everyone familiar with naval history knows about it. But the *Alabama* was effective and lucky. She did her job well in the Atlantic and Pacific: she fought enemy planes, bombarded enemy-held islands and the Japanese home islands. She did not collide with another ship and was never seriously hurt by enemy action. Her only incident was when one five-inch mount fired accidently into another. None of the booklets sold in the bookstore in

Often reproduced for obvious reasons, this photo shows *Pennsylvania* (BB-38) leading *Colorado* (BB-45), *Louisville* (CA-28), *Portland* (CA-33) and *Columbia* (CL-56) into Lingayen Gulf January 1945. Flagship of the Pacific fleet on 7 December 1941, *Pennsylvania* survived Pearl Harbor (29 killed), a torpedo off Okinawa (20 killed) and the atomic tests before being scuttled off Kwajalein 10 February 1948. USN

front of the now-memorialized ship mention the accident, and former crew members are reluctant to discuss it. Just as the man who rises early, goes to work, does his job well, is law abiding and treats his family well does not make the news, battleships like the *Alabama, Idaho, Arkansas, New York* and *Texas* seldom grabbed the headlines or even made the news, but they did their job well.

Forty years after World War II, articles still appear in naval journals, both popular and professional, discussing what probably would have happened had the members of the *Iowa*-class ever tangled with one or both of Japan's super battleships. Most articles conclude that the *Iowas* would have had an advantage because radar would have allowed them to open fire before they could be seen by either *Yamato* or *Musachi*. Not surprisingly, many articles written by Japanese authors do not concur. Fewer articles debate what might have happened if the French *Jean Bart* had been fully operational in her battle against *Massachusetts*. For the sake of historical interest and debate, perhaps it is best that these questions were not answered during World War II. And if Japanese and some European writers are correct in their assumptions, it was best for the *Iowas* and the *Massachusetts*.

In 1985 all four of the *Iowa*-class battleships existed, two of the *South Dakota*-class remain (*Alabama* and *Massachusetts*) and one of the *North Carolinas* is extant (*North Carolina*). Consequently, only three of the "modern" battleships have been scrapped – *Washington, South Dakota* and *Indiana*. Only one of the 15 old battleships that won at least one battle star in World War II is still intact (*Texas*). Eight old battleships were scrapped. *Pennsylvania, New York* and *Nevada* were sunk as targets or scuttled in the late 1940s after surviving the atomic tests at Bikini; *Arkansas* was sunk during the atomic tests; *Oklahoma* was sunk at Pearl Harbor, raised, and she went under again in 1947 while under tow to California to be dismantled. *Arizona* (and the one-time battleship *Utah*) is an underwater memorial at Pearl Harbor.

Few books or articles relating to Peleliu, Iwo Jima or Okinawa fail to show *Tennessee* (BB-43) sitting majestically offshore pounding enemy targets. Such a sight provided confidence to Marines moving shoreward. Battleships were worth their weight in gold to Marines who benefitted from their shore bombardment and call fire. While off Okinawa *Tennessee* lost 22 men to a kamikaze; five were lost at Pearl Harbor and eight to a shore battery off Tinian. USN

Even when the enemy was not attacking, life at sea during wartime could be perilous. Here *Indiana* (BB-58) and *Washington* (BB-56) show the effects of a collision on 1 February 1944. *Washington* lost 60 feet of her bow; damage to the starboard side of *Indiana* is apparent. Other collisions included *California* and *Tennessee*, and *South Dakota* and *Mahan* (DD-364). USN and USN

New Jersey (BB-62) alongside Japanese battleship *Nagato* shortly after World War II. Now (1985) in her fourth commission, *New Jersey* has fired her guns in anger during World War II, the Korean Conflict, the Vietnam War and off Lebanon. NA

In the European theater *Massachusetts* (BB-59) and *Texas* (BB-35) experienced some of their more notable moments. *Massachusetts* is seen just after disabling the Vichy French battleship *Jean Bart* and two destroyers at Casablanca while *Texas* has just taken a near miss off Normandy. NA and NA

Washington at work. Victor over Japanese battleship *Kirishima* at Guadalcanal in November 1942, BB-56 is pictured here 19 March 1945 providing anti-aircraft protection for carriers. *Washington* and *South Dakota* led battleships in battle stars (13). USN

Another picture appearing consistently in naval books and articles is this view of the *Missouri* BB-63 firing her two forward main batteries. Note 16-inch shells in the air. The other frequently seen photo of *Missouri* is, of course, the occasion of the Japanese surrender. USN

After a commendable performance during the August 1942 Battle of the Eastern Solomons, *North Carolina* was hit by a submarine torpedo on 15 September 1942. Only five were killed but the battlewagon was greatly missed in the following momentous sea battles off Guadalcanal while she was being repaired. USN

Heading for San Francisco and the October 1945 Navy Day celebration are units of the Third Fleet. Photo was taken from the bridge of *Wisconsin* (BB-64) which is scheduled to rejoin the fleet for the third time in the early 1990s. USN

By virtue of being overhauled at Puget Sound and missing the Pearl Harbor attack, *Colorado* (BB-45) retained more of her pre-war appearance than her extensively rebuilt sister ship *West Virginia. Colorado* was hit 22 times by shore batteries off Tinian, lost 19 killed to kamikazes (November 1944) and 18 to accidental gunfire in January 1945. *Colorado* was sold for scrap in July 1959. USN

Commissioned in 1921, *Maryland* (BB-46) was almost 40 years old when this picture was taken in 1960 as she awaited the scrapper's torch. Not greatly damaged at Pearl Harbor, BB-46 was not modified as extensively as her sister ship *West Virginia.* Somewhat ironically, the Japanese hurt *Maryland* more seriously with two kamikaze attacks (31 killed in 1944 and 53 killed in 1945) and an aerial torpedo attack off Saipan in 1944 than when she was a sitting duck 7 December 1941. With Pearl Harbor veterans *West Virginia, Pennsylvania, Tennessee* and *California* plus *Mississippi,* she settled scores at Surigao Strait in October 1944. USN

BATTLESHIP MEMORIALS

Numerous times the "age of the battleship" has been declared over since Gen. Billy Mitchell demonstrated his theories with aerial bombing tests in the 1920s. The battleship did lose her paramount place in late 1941 and early 1942 to the aircraft carrier. Ironically, many now declare the aircraft carrier an anachronism. Britain scrapped her last fleet carrier only a few years before the 1982 war in the Falklands. Unquestionably, that last fleet carrier was greatly missed in that conflict.

Four decades after World War II, two battleships from that era are presently in commission: the *New Jersey* for the fourth time (World War II, Korea, Vietnam and present) and class leader *Iowa* for the third time (World War II, Korea and present). The *Missouri* at the time of this writing is being prepared for her second commissioning (she was not decommissioned after World War II and served on through Korea into 1955) and will have the somewhat unique distinction of moving from museum status back to active duty. When the "Mighty Mo" was moved from Bremerton, Wash. to Long Beach, Calif., citizens of the Bremerton area were quite vocal about the loss of the historic ship upon whose deck the Japanese surrender occurred on 2 September 1945. Although the Bremerton citizenry was not happy to see the ship depart (over 100,000 people visited the ship per year – an obvious tourist attraction), they have already begun to make plans to bring back the ship as a permanent memorial and museum at some future date. The only *Iowa*-class battleship still in mothballs is the *Wisconsin*. She has been in mothballs since 1958 (presently in the Philadelphia Navy Yard), but is tentatively scheduled to be refitted like her three sisters and rejoin the fleet in the early 1990s. By that time all four of the *Iowas* will be over 50 years old and a new president and new congress will be sitting in Washington. In short, the celebrating in Corpus Cristi, Texas, where the *Wisconsin* is to be homeported, may prove to be premature. And, Bremerton may have back her favorite ship sooner than expected. Regardless of when the *Iowas* are finally retired for the last time, undoubtably the "age of the battleship" will have indeed come to an end. It is difficult to imagine a scenario that would inspire the United States or any other country ever to build another dreadnought.

Because the Japanese surrender occurred on the battleship carrying the home state name of the then president of the United States (Harry Truman's daughter, Margaret, christened BB-63 while Mr. Truman was still in the Senate), the *Missouri* will have an excellent chance of being retained as a memorial and museum. The enthusiasm in favor of such an idea in Bremerton will not hurt "Mighty Mo's" possibilities. Some city or group will no doubt make an attempt to obtain the *New Jersey*; her history will enhance her opportunities as will the fact that the state of New Jersey is on the coast. The people of her namesake state and some in Texas may eventually compete for the *Wisconsin*, but inland Iowa may have to follow the lead of South Dakota in honoring their namesake only with meaningful artifacts of BB-61.

The fate of the four *Iowas* being indeterminable, we now survey what remains to remind this and future generations of the World War II battleship. Except for submarines, no other type of World War II combat ship is as well represented for posterity as the battleship. Four are intact – *Texas* near Houston, *North Carolina* at Wilmington, *Alabama* at Mobile and *Massachusetts* at Fall River. Additionally, several other battleships are called to remembrance because they were named for states and their namesake states have placed memorials or constructed museum displays in their honor.

The *Texas*, only 20 minutes east of Houston at the San Jacinto Battleground Park, is a treasure not only for the state of Texas but also for the nation. Commissioned only a few months before the outbreak of World War I in Europe, the *Texas* can offer a visitor some feeling for the state of the art of battleship construction for that period and for the period between the two world wars. The forward tripod mast is quite reminiscent of the battleships' appearance in Pearl Harbor on 7 December 1941. It is similar to the foremast of *Arizona* and when one views the *Texas*, the mind quickly pictures the crumpled, burned mast of the lost battlewagon. All other battleships that fought in World War II which were in service before the first modern battleship was commissioned (*North Carolina* in 1941) have long since been discarded. Therefore, *Texas* is the only living reminder of the battlewagons that captured the imagination of generations before planes, nuclear weapons and missiles rewrote the definition of ultimate weapons.

On the *Texas* one will see 5-inch deck guns arranged in a manner that was abandoned in general practice on battleships during the war. Also, one will find several 1.1-inch anti-aircraft guns. Although the *Texas* did carry the newer and more efficient 40mm guns during World War II, the 1.1s are especially noteworthy since they are now so rare in museum displays: none exist on any of the other memorialized battleships.

A visitor to the *Texas* will notice a slight list to starboard and a noticeable gradient toward the stern as the ship rests in her berth on the Galveston Ship channel. The ship is sitting on the bottom in a cradle she has created, but occasional storms such as Hurricane Carla have caused the still watertight vessel to change position. Also, one quickly notes the concrete deck which replaced the original wood deck. Main deck areas not exposed to weather are still wood.

Seventy-one years old in 1985, the *Texas* served in World War I and World War II before becoming a museum ship in 1948. As the only survivor of the "old" battleships, she has significance beyond her own history. Author's Collection

The problem of a deteriorating wood deck on the *Texas* was solved by covering exposed areas with concrete. Other memorialized ships will have to deal with this same problem in time. Unique to the *Texas* are the several 1.1-inch anti-aircraft guns at right. These weapons, known for their unreliability in combat, preceded the 40mm AA guns which became the standard intermediate anti-aircraft guns for the Navy in World War II. Author's Collection

Deck guns on the *Texas*. The arrangement and type of weapons on BB-35 is a lesson in naval history especially appreciated if one has already visited the newer *North Carolina, Alabama* or *Massachusetts.* Author's Collection

The location for the *Texas* could not be better. The well-marked San Jacinto Battleground provides a quiet and solemn setting, and one perceives that as other visitors come aboard there seems to be a sense of introspection. Perhaps they are carried back to North Africa or Cherbourg where *Texas* was hit twice and near-missed 65 times. Many, of course, do not know as they step aboard that the *Texas* was present for the German Fleet surrender in 1918 or that she distinguished herself off North Africa and Cherbourg. But, they do seem to know they are touching history, and this is evident when one watches another gently place a hand upon a gun or plaque in a sacred manner.

If the dominant impression of visitors to the *Texas* is reverence, the apparent impression that dominates guests of the *North Carolina* is awe. The "Showboat" is big, curvaceous, and clean; indeed, she appears ready to recommission. Close inspection on board only documents the initial impression acquired from shore.

Like the *Texas*, the *North Carolina* sits in a channel carved just for the ship off the Cape Fear River. With abundant foliage on three sides of the ship, the *North Carolina* possesses an environment similar to that of the *Texas*. During the winter of 1985-1986 a new orientation center is scheduled to be constructed to replace the 1950s-style building that has served visitors since the 1960s. Within the new building will be a small theater showing a film on the history of BB-55, and exhibition area, souvenir gift shop and snack area (all of the major museum ships have exhibition areas, gift shops and snack bars; they vary only in size). Plans are to continue as before the sound and light spectacular which is a combination of narrative backed by appropriate music, lighting and sound effects. Presented only from early June to Labor Day, these nightly performances provide the spectator with a perspective of war in the Pacific.

The display areas inside the superstructure along

Although 44 years old in 1985, the battleship *North Carolina* has been so well maintained in appearance that one would believe she was still in commission. At first view one can appreciate the larger size of the *North Carolina* compared to the other three memorialized battleships. Author's Collection

Seen here is a late afternoon view of the *North Carolina* with the Wilmington waterfront in the background. The structure at right is to be replaced during the winter of 1985-1986 by a new orientation center and exhibition building. Author's Collection

the main deck are well done. They are accessible appropriate, meaningful and informative. There is no attempt to tell the story of World War II – just that of the *North Carolina* and her role in the war. The story of the *North Carolina* is told in pictures and print on plexiglass-covered display boards similar to the design found on the *Yorktown* approximately 150 miles south. Numerous photos adequately tell the story of BB-55 in the Battle of the Eastern Solomons, the story of the damaging torpedo attack that nearly cost the ship her life, the story of her role as a fire support platform and, finally, the story of how she was saved for posterity. Although all the pictures and captions are well written and interesting, the story of how close the ship came to being lost on 15 September 1942 lingers long after one has left Wilmington. When struck by I-19 (appropriately, there is a model of this Japanese sub on display) in the same attack that sank the carrier *Wasp* and fatally damaged the destroyer *O'Brien*, the *North Carolina* lost only five men and took a list of only 5½ degrees. The 36-foot by 18-foot hole 20 feet below the waterline and two feet below the bottom of the protective armor was not the main threat. The main threat was the possibility of fire in the forward magazine. Cracks in the side armor are still there; the armor was never replaced.

In the Battleship Memorial Museum, the staff of the ship has done an outstanding job. Lowered ceilings, carpet, new paint and excellent lighting give a more meaningful setting to the display of a large and beautiful silver service, seven-foot model of the ship, commissioning pennant and sponsors cup, war record and builders plaque. The BB-55 Crewmens Association has its own compartment adjacent to the museum with proper remembrances to wartime service, sacrifice and continuing support.

Although the *Alabama* on Battleship Parkway in Mobile is only about 50 feet shorter than the *North Carolina*, it seems even smaller by comparison. Although more compact than the two ships of the *North Carolina*-class, the *South Dakota*-class *Alabama* was slightly faster and her main battery punch (16-inch guns) was identical.

The reverence accorded *Texas* and the awe evident among visitors to the *North Carolina* stands in stark contrast to guests heading up the ramp of the *Alabama*. During World War II the *Alabama* was a happy, effective ship – according to her record and the recollection of her crew – and this same spirit seems to pervade those who walk upon her decks 40 years later. The *Alabama* dispensed considerable pain to the enemy but was never seriously hurt in return. As much as any other reason this may be the answer to the ebullient emotions one sees on BB-60.

The setting of the *Alabama* differs from that of the *Texas* and *North Carolina*. The *Alabama* may be seen on a clear day for a distance of six miles as one drives along Jubilee Parkway (Interstate 10) from the east. The port side of the very well-kept ship looks out onto a large park covered with picnic grounds (a standard for most of the major enshrined ships), tanks, guns, planes – including a B-52 – and the skyline of Mobile. To starboard, in contrast, there is an extensive view of Mobile Bay and one quickly gravitates there for the "at sea" view. Just as quickly, movement is back to port as the always healthy wind off the water creates new hair styles. And, nearly 2,000 roses are visible from the port side much of the year.

Most of BB-60 is open to guests. One can climb up or down according to energy and inclination. On some other enshrined ships, numerous areas high and low are closed. Favorite locations on the *Alabama* are the bridge (great view), display areas along the main deck and lower decks, and the insides of gun turrets and mounts. Frequent visitors – such as this writer – often call at the snack bars, both in the gift shop and aboard,

With nine battle stars, the battleship *Alabama* had a charmed combat life as she was never severely hurt by the enemy. The peaceful setting in Mobile Bay belies the experiences of the battlewagon during World War II. Like many other military parks, here one can find tanks, guns, a World War II submarine (*Drum*), a B-52, gift shop and bookstore. Author's Collection

Visible for six miles on a clear day as one approaches Mobile on Interstate 10 from the east, the *Alabama* provides a more "at sea" feeling than the other three memorialized World War II battleships. This view was taken from the bridge of BB-60 – one of the few bridge sections of memorialized ships open to the public – and shows a portion of Battleship Park. Interstate 10 and U.S. Highway 98 are in the distance. Author's Collection

Self-explanatory photo of 20mm gun on *Alabama*; this message was there during World War II. A close look at the photo presented earlier of the *Massachusetts* – Alabama's sister ship – off Casablanca reveals this same message on a portside 20mm mount. Author's Collection

Baseball fans will find Bob Fellers' bunk on the *Alabama* a point of interest. The photo shows Feller in a late 1940s pose and there is a narrative under the picture concerning the Hall of Fame pitcher. Author's Collection

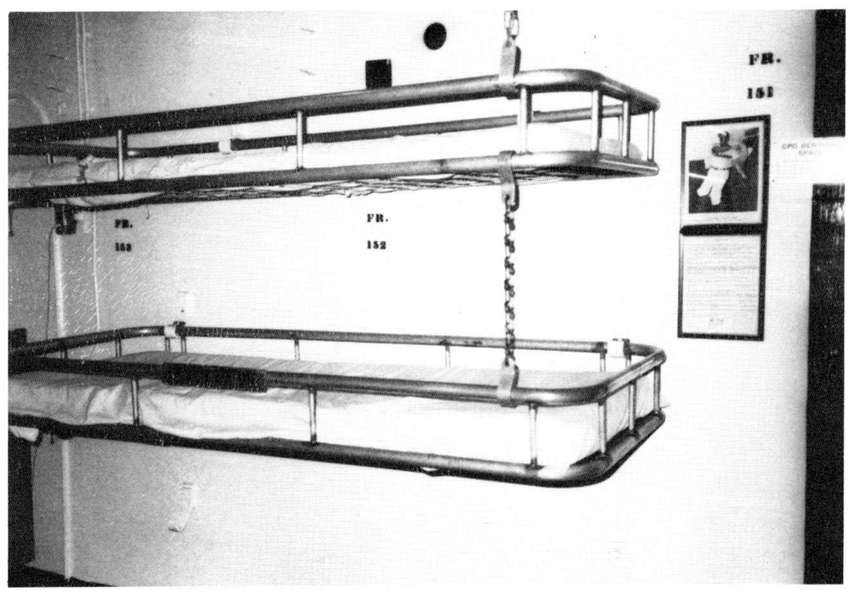

climb high in the superstructure to a favorite isolated spot, enjoy the view, eat, drink and look mean at anyone who approaches to disturb the serenity of it all. Certainly, 40 years ago no one aboard this fighting ship anticipated the day when she would become a place of education, relaxation, enjoyment and a hub of social events. Swords to plowshares, indeed! Still, above the sounds of enjoyment, this ship never loses its aura of dignity. In fact, her commanding presence inspires a never-ending occurrence: as guests pull away from the large parking area and head for the main gate, they slow down and often stop to look back for one last glance. One may have been aboard for most of the day attending a social event, but in that last over-the-shoulder view, *Alabama* is again the warship she was 40 years ago.

The *Massachusetts* at Fall River, Mass., seems larger than her sistership *Alabama*. She isn't, of course, but perhaps the relatively more crowded setting gives the impression. Too, it would seem that a visit to the *Alabama* would be sufficiently instructive and informative, but that impression is erroneous also.

Just as the citizens of Mobile and the state of Alabama are to be lauded for what they have created, so too are the citizens of Fall River and the state of Massachusetts to be congratulated for their efforts. No double take is necessary to know that one is in New England when visiting Battleship Cove. The omnipresent pleasure boats characteristic of the region are much in evidence, and the architecture of commercial buildings and personal dwellings is almost exactly what one equates with traditional and historic New England. The word "quaint" is overused, but here it is most fitting.

The park area around Battleship Cove is not nearly as spacious as what one finds in Mobile, and cer-

The *Massachusetts* is the flagship of Battleship Cove at Fall River, Mass. The World War II veteran, which won 11 battle stars, offers three decks, the first platform (engine room and ordnance exhibit) and superstructure decks to the public. Author's Collection

Part of a shell and fragments are displayed on the *Massachusetts* with a written account of the Battle of Casablanca. Supplementing the written word are hand-held wand devices which provide a narration explaining functions of various sections of the ship and provide historical facts. Author's Collection

Within the *Massachusetts* are several interesting exhibits with a memorial to PT boats rivaling the space and quality of the battleship's own exhibit. Most helpful to the historian, however, are the several signs such as the one seen here that tell where the ship was hit during her battles. Author's Collection

tainly there is not as much water to see, but the scenery is splendid, and there is adequate provision for relaxation between visits to the several historic ships, boats and museum exhibits on board and ashore. The *Massachusetts* is the flagship of Battleship Cove, and she offers three decks, the first platform (engine room and ordnance exhibit) and superstructure decks to the public. Within the ship are several interesting exhibits with a memorial to PT boats rivaling the space and quality of the battleship's own exhibit. Particularly helpful are numerous hand-held wand devices that provide a narration to explain the functions of various sections of the ship. Most helpful to the historian, however, are the several signs that tell where the ship was hit during her battles.

It would not be fair to attempt to compare the *Texas, North Carolina, Alabama* and *Massachusetts* in regard to the quality of their surrounding parks, condition of the ships, value of on board or dockside exhibits or even the quality of hot dogs sold by their snack bars. All are unique and all are worth traveling to see. Dignity is maintained, there is a constant effort to increase the size and quality of exhibits, and there are people responsible for these four ships in 1985 who care as much for them as did the men who served aboard 40 years ago. Overall appearance is somewhat relative as one may visit one of these ships just after it has been painted and then visit another just before it is to be painted. On this subject it must be noted that there is some variance among attitude of curators and others responsible for the appearance of a memorial ship as to whether or not to present it as though she was going back into commission tomorrow or to leave sections of the ship as they were during former operational days. *North Carolina* and *Alabama* show emphasis on being ready for another commissioning date; *Texas* and *Massachusetts* show more emphasis on maintaining portions of the ships in World War II expression. Still, one can touch the past on any of these four historic battleships.

In touching history, no other memorial – battleship or otherwise – is more significant in meaning than the USS *Arizona* Memorial at Pearl Harbor. If only one memorial could be chosen to call remembrance to the U.S. Navy in World War II, it would be this one. As fine a memorial as it may become, the planned Navy Memorial in Washington, D.C., will never elicit the feelings that attend the sunken remains of the *Arizona* and the thousand-plus men still entombed within her.

Unofficially, units of the U.S. Navy rendered honors to the remains of the *Arizona* until March 1950 when Adm. Arthur Radford issued an order for daily color ceremonies aboard the ship. For nearly 12 years the flag was flown over the wreck, but in 1962 the flag was raised over the new permanent memorial that rests over the sunken ship but does not touch any part of it. Designed by Alfred Preis, the memorial structure has the appearance of an enclosed bridge and contains a shrine room where the names of the men killed on 7 December 1941 are inscribed. Also within is a museum and an assembly room.

Not unexpectedly, the elegant memorial is not the focus of attention on one's first visit to this site. The ship itself, partially visible beneath the water, is the attraction. The foundation for the number three turret rises above the water, and probably no other rusted section of steel anywhere in the world is viewed with more frequency or with equivalent sensations. The Pacific war began here; inspiration for the successful prosecution of the war was born here; the sentiment of sadness spawned by the "day of infamy" is still here. If for any reason one wishes to experience the emotions generated by the war, one must come here.

It is not unusual to find portions of the *Arizona* away from her grave. One of her bells has been moved

Foundation for No. 3 Gun Turret, *Arizona* (BB-39), Arizona Memorial, Pearl Harbor, Hawaii. Stan Cohen

This badly rusted steel is mostly without form and one would not know what is in this picture without being told. It is a portion of Arizona's above-water remains resting in a field on Waipio Peninsula (1984). Stan Cohen

several times with one stop on the University of Arizona campus. A hatch removed from the ship is on display at the Nimitz Museum in Fredericksburg, Texas (see Color section) and a considerable portion of her above-water remains presently rests in a field on Waipio Peninsula. The badly rusted steel is mostly without form, and one would not know what he or she was viewing without being told. One might suspect that the apparent "junk" has some worth, however, as someone has written "not for sale" in several places.

Centuries ago it was said that all roads led to Rome. More recently students at a one-time great party school in the South (until the current president decided to get serious about academics) declared that all roads led *from* the campus – to football games in the fall, New Orleans' French Quarter in the winter and the beach in spring. Today, hardly any roads lead to Sioux Falls, S.D., from anywhere. To learn that there is a major memorial to the USS *South Dakota* in Sioux Falls causes one to initially determine that the memorial had better be first class to justify traveling well off the beaten path to see it. The approaches to Sioux Falls are lonely – beautiful country, but lonely. Nevertheless, the trip is worth the time and expense. The state of South Dakota, the city of Sioux Falls and the veterans of BB-57 have established and maintained the single best memorial exhibit of a non-existing ship in the continental United States.

Landlocked South Dakota could not float the famous battleship home so it was decided to bring numerous significant parts of the ship to Sioux Falls as the battlewagon was being dismantled in the early 1960s. Several railroad cars were loaded, but when the Navy informed officials in South Dakota what the costs would be to transport everything that had been saved, the decision was made to transfer only a portion of the artifacts. That is one of the reasons why so

Unique and worth a long journey to see is the *South Dakota* memorial. Shown here is the mast of BB-57 and the green brick museum. Note that the outline of the ship has been recreated. The memorial covers an entire city block. Author's Collection

View of a portion of the interior of the *South Dakota* museum. Numerous parts of the battleship, photographs and memorabilia are on display. The ceiling is covered with wood from the ship's deck. Author's Collection

One of South Dakota's bronze screws rests at the entrance to the Mariners Museum in Newport News, Va. Another of the battleship's screws is on display in the Washington Navy Yard along with a 40mm quad mount and armor plate. Author's Collection

much of the famous battleship is found at memorial parks *outside* South Dakota. Example: one of the *South Dakota's* bronze propellers (screws) stands at the entrance to the Mariners Museum in Newport News, Va.; another propeller is on display in the Washington Navy Yard along with a complete 40mm gun mount and sections of armor plate; a four-foot section of a 16-inch gun barrel is on display at the Buffalo & Erie County Naval & Servicemen's Park in Buffalo, N.Y. while another section rests inside the Mariners Museum. There are, by far, more significant pieces of the USS *South Dakota* remaining than portions of any other World War II battleship that was scrapped.

Four-foot sections of South Dakota's 16-inch guns are found at the memorial in Sioux Falls, inside the Mariner's Museum and outside at the Buffalo & Erie County Naval & Servicemen's Park (seen here). Cruiser *Little Rock* is in the background. Author's Collection

Although many artifacts cut off *South Dakota* did not make it to Sioux Falls, many others did. The BB-57 memorial was created by the combined efforts of the state of South Dakota, the city of Sioux Falls and veterans of the battleship. Located on a busy highway beside a large, well-maintained sports complex, the memorial dedicated in 1969 has continued to grow and develop. In 1976 the main deck configuration of the ship was placed in concrete by the local Naval Reserve and the original lifelines and stanchions were placed on top. The concrete outline rises from two feet to six feet at the bow (see Color section). Near the bow is a flagstaff and an anchor with anchor chain appropriately placed. Located where the superstructure was is a circular, green brick building which houses artifacts and memorabilia. On either side of the building are miniature concrete turrets supporting four-foot sections of the 16-inch main battery guns from the ship. Between the museum building and the aft miniature turret is the ship's mast. Several plaques have been placed including one commemorating the men lost in action aboard BB-57.

The square footage inside the museum is not impressive, but the use of it is. Even an engineer would be pleased with the optimum use of the available space. Certainly, the history buff is gratified because the history of "Battleship X" is here. The bell of the ship hangs near the entrance; and when one looks up to see it, the ceiling covered with planks of wood from the ship's deck cannot be missed. Visitors usually move directly to the large, waterline, Navy model and from there to the numerous artifacts including a binnacle, engine order telegraph, valve wheels, tompions, blinker light, flags, and a model of the ship's powerplant first used to train engineering personnel on BB-57 and later used by Naval ROTC students at the University of Michigan. Portions of the captain's silver service (Capt. Thomas Gatch was very highly respected by his men) are on display as is the ship's christening bottle and models of the destroyer *Preston, Benham, Gwin* and *Porter*—brave ships that served with *SoDak* off Guadalcanal.

Approximately 200 pictures are displayed showing the life of *SoDak* from construction to scrapping. Also shown are photos of the memorial as it was being built. Not all of the pictures and paintings are captioned, but those that aren't are self-explanatory. In short, *SoDak* veterans and the citizens of Sioux Falls have done themselves proud in demonstrating how to preserve the memory of a ship that is no longer intact.

Almost as many parts were saved from the USS *Indiana* (BB-58) as were removed from the *South Dakota*, but not as many large items were saved and what was preserved has not been collected in a single location similar to the memorial in Sioux Falls. There are few junior high and high schools in the state of Indiana that don't have some artifact from the ship. An anchor from *Indiana* has been placed in Fort Wayne, but the most significant memorial to the ship is outside the football stadium at Indiana University.

The academically renowned Indiana University can hold its own with any other university in the country in terms of the beauty of its campus. The old football stadium sits somewhat mysteriously on a hill; the newer stadium is a short distance away. When approaching the stadium, any graduate of the Naval Academy or citizen familiar with the city of Annapolis will be quite surprised: Indiana's football stadium is almost identical to the one in Annapolis. And, they were both constructed at nearly the same time. With this apparent relationship established, a naval history enthusiast visiting the stadium in Bloomington is not surprised to find the mast of BB-58 and two twin 40mm mounts just outside the main gates (see Color section). A plaque on the elevator tower reads:

USS INDIANA The mast of the USS *Indiana* is a gift of the United States Navy to Indiana University. With accompanying armament it stands as a memorial to the sons and daughters of the state of Indiana who have so gallantly served in the armed forces of our nation.

The battleship *Indiana* was commissioned April 30, 1942 and earned nine battle stars in operations and engagements in the war in the Pacific. Her distinguished career closed when she was decommissioned September 11, 1947.

Two 40mm twin mounts, mainmast and dedication plaque honoring the battleship *Indiana* (BB-58) are outside the football stadium at Indiana University in Bloomington. Author's Collection

Outside the state of Indiana, one will find (in 1985) the ship's builders plaque and a 16-inch tompion on display in the Hampton Roads Naval Museum. And, a porthole may be found at the Philadelphia Navy Yard.

With the departure of the *Missouri* from Bremerton, the West Coast is left without a battleship memorial museum, although "Mighty Mo" is to be homeported in San Francisco and will undoubtably host legions of visitors if the Navy decides to allow guests while the battleship is in port. *Missouri* aside, there is at least one ship that should have been retained as a memorial on the West Coast but was not...the USS *Washington* (BB-56).

One wonders why BB-56 did not receive more official acclaim for her performance during the war, and it is surprising that no stronger effort was made to preserve the ship. The state of Washington did see fit to construct a memorial to the famed warship that won 13 battle stars and sank the Japanese battleship *Kirishima* off Guadalcanal in November 1942. However, the experience of the memorial has paralleled the experience of the ship in remembrance. The splendid memorial that once graced the Rotunda of the Legislative Building at Olympia was removed in early 1984. Newspaper accounts of the dedication in 1962 indicated the memorial was to be permanent. Presently, the memorial rests in storage, its former place of honor now occupied by two statues. Perhaps the artifacts of BB-56 will be returned to the Navy Historical Center for display in the World War II exhibit of the Navy Memorial Museum or be placed in some maritime museum in the state of Washington.

The veterans of the *Washington* have in their possession several small parts of their ship and numerous mementoes. However, at this time there is no appropriate location to place the historical objects. A request was made to the Washington's sister ship *North Carolina*, but the commission overseeing the "Showboat" had to decline. As was previously mentioned, the *North Carolina* was set up to honor the veterans of North Carolina and BB-55 exclusively. Certainly if an exception could have been made, it would have been made for *Washington*. Still, the problem remains and portions of naval history will be lost unless a proper location can be found to display artifacts and store archival materials.

The problem of an adequate location for exhibiting memorabilia and storing archival materials is not unique to the *Washington*. It also applies to many of the pre-war battleships. For many, it is already too late as both artifacts and archival materials have been discarded by relatives of deceased veterans. In many instances not only was the value of artifacts and written materials not known to the inheriting generation, but the objects themselves were not recognized for what they were.

As the older, pre-war battleships were broken up relatively soon after the war, not much remains in 1985. Although several of the older battleships earned awards (three of the four Navy Unit Commendations were won by the pre-war battleships), respective states did not rush to acquire major portions of the ships for museum purposes. Perhaps the somewhat embarrassing remembrance of Pearl Harbor diminished interest; perhaps it was just too soon to fully appreciate the historical value of the old battlewagons; or perhaps there was no precedent as to how to establish a large memorial similar to the one established to honor the USS *South Dakota*. As nearly all the pre-war battleships were gone before *South Dakota* was scrapped, the last reason just mentioned may be the most valid in answering why memorials to the older battleships are either relatively small or don't exist.

Memorials that do exist are similar to that erected to honor the USS *West Virginia* (see photo). Located in the Cultural Center on the grounds of the capitol complex in Charleston, W. Va., the USS *West Virginia* display includes a steering wheel, large ship's bell,

Seemingly overlooked for official honors during World War II even though she was the only U.S. Navy battleship to sink a Japanese battleship, *Washington* (BB-56) has not fared much better since. Not saved from the scrap pile by her namesake state as was her sister ship *North Carolina*, the memorial to her in the State Capitol at Olympia was recently removed from display. Rendering by Joe Cason

small model and several small artifacts (mostly instruments). And, like other pre-war battleships, several parts of the *West Virginia* are found away from the statehouse exhibit.

Although the following is by no means complete, a listing of some meaningful artifacts remaining from several pre-war battleships is presented. Again, it must be noted that museum exhibits are constantly rotated and what is on display today may be removed tomorrow only to reappear at a later time. For example, several artifacts including bell, silver service and christening bottle remain from the USS *Nevada*, but in January 1985 only the silver service is on display within the Nevada State Museum in Carson City. And it should be noted that the bell(s), silver service and builder's models of most all pre-war battleships still exist either on display or in storage. Further, some artifacts – especially from the USS *New Mexico* and USS *Idaho* – are held by individuals who wish to remain anonymous.

Seen here is the anchor from the USS *Oklahoma* in downtown Oklahoma City. The inscription beneath the anchor is most appropriate: "Eternal Vigilance is the Price of Liberty." Author's Collection

The "norm" for most old (pre-war) battleships is a small display similar to this one honoring the *West Virginia* (BB-48). Shown here is a small, but excellent, model, a few artifacts, bell and 10-spoke wheel. An identical wheel exists at the Washington Navy Yard Navy Memorial Museum from the *Maryland* and a 12-spoke wheel from the *Oklahoma* is displayed in the Kirkpatrick Center in Oklahoma City. The *Tennessee* is honored with a similar display in Nashville. The bells and wheels of nearly all the old battleships still exist. Author's Collection

BATTLESHIP	ARTIFACT	LOCATION
California BB-44	Memorial Display	State Capitol, Sacramento, Calif.
	Large model, wheel	Navy, Marine Corps, Coast Guard Museum, Treasure Island, San Francisco, Calif.
	Planking	U.S. Naval Academy Chapel, Annapolis, Md.
	Large Model	Museum of Science and Industry, Chicago, Ill.
Maryland BB-46	Exhibit (includes bell and aft steering wheel)	Maryland State Capitol, Annapolis, Md.
	Steering wheel	Navy Memorial Museum, Washington, D.C.
	Planking	U.S. Naval Academy Chapel, Annapolis, Md.
Mississippi BB-41	Silver service	Mississippi State Historical Museum, Jackson, Miss.
Nevada BB-36	Bell, silver service, flags, christening bottle, 3 small models	Nevada State Museum, Carson City, Nev.
Oklahoma BB-37	Anchor	Downtown Oklahoma City, Okla.
	Steering wheel and large model	Kirkpatrick Center, Oklahoma City, Okla.
Pennsylvania BB-38	Bell, minor artifacts	William Penn Mem. Museum, Harrisburg, Pa.
Tennessee BB-43	Exhibit (wheel, annunciator, plaque) large model	Tennessee State Museum (Military Branch)
	Planking	U.S. Naval Academy Chapel, Annapolis, Md.
	Portholes	USS *Massachusetts*, Fall River, Mass.
	Large model	Navy Memorial Museum, Washington, D.C.
West Virginia BB-48	Exhibit (bell, small model, wheel) instruments	State Capitol Complex, Charleston, W.Va.
	Mast	West Virginia University
	Flagstaff	Clarksburg, W.Va.
	72-inch steering wheel lanterns, binnacle, plaques	Hampton Roads Naval Museum, Norfolk, Va.
	Indicator shaft and lanterns	USS *Massachusetts*, Fall River, Mass.

CHAPTER TWO
AIRCRAFT CARRIERS

PRESIDENTIAL UNIT CITATION

Bunker Hill	CV-17
Enterprise	CV-6
Essex	CV-9
Hornet	CV-12
Lexington	CV-16
Yorktown	CV-10
Belleau Wood	CVL-24
Cabot	CVL-28
San Jacinto	CVL-30
Bogue	CVE-9
Card	CVE-11
Fanshaw Bay (2)	CVE-70
Gambier Bay	CVE-73
Guadalcanal	CVE-60
Kalinin Bay	CVE-68
Kitkun Bay	CVE-71
Lunga Point	CVE-94
Natoma Bay	CVE-62
Petrof Bay	CVE-80
Saint Lo	CVE-63
Sangamon	CVE-26
Santee	CVE-29
Savo Island	CVE-78
Suwannee	CVE-27
White Plains	CVE-66

NAVY UNIT COMMENDATION

Enterprise	CV-6
Hancock	CV-19
Wasp	CV-18
Cowpens	CVL-25
Langley	CVL-27
Anzio	CVE-57
Chenango	CVE-28
Hoggatt Bay	CVE-75
Makin Island	CVE-93
Manila Bay	CVE-61
Marcus Island	CVE-77
Wake Island	CVE-65

ULTIMATE SACRIFICE

Lexington	CV-2 (8-5-42)
Yorktown	CV-5 (7-6-42)
Wasp	CV-7 (15-9-42)
Hornet	CV-8 (26-10-42)
Princeton	CVL-23 (24-10-44)
Liscome Bay	CVE-56 (24-11-43)
Block Island	CVE-21 (29-5-44)
Gambier Bay	CVE-73 (25-10-44)
Saint Lo	CVE-63 (25-10-44)
Ommaney Bay	CVE-79 (4-1-45)
Bismarck Sea	CVE-95 (21-2-45)

BATTLE STARS

Enterprise	CV-6....20
Essex	CV-9....13
Yorktown	CV-10....11
Bunker Hill	CV-17....11
Lexington	CV-16....11
Wasp	CV-18....8
Saratoga	CV-3....7
Hornet	CV-12....7
Ticonderoga	CV-14....5
Intrepid	CV-11....5
Franklin	CV-13....4
Hancock	CV-19....4
Hornet	CV-8....4
Yorktown	CV-5....3
Randolph	CV-15....3
Bennington	CV-20....3
Wasp	CV-7....2
Ranger	CV-4....2
Lexington	CV-2....2
Shangri-La	CV-38....2
Langley	CV-1....1
Bon Homme Richard	CV-31....1
Cowpens	CVL-25....12
Belleau Wood	CVL-24....11
Monterey	CVL-26....11
Cabot	CVL-28....9
Princeton	CVL-23....9
Langley	CVL-27....9
Independence	CVL-22....8
San Jacinto	CVL-30....5
Bataan	CVL-29....5
Suwannee	CVE-26....13
Chenango	CVE-28....11
Santee	CVE-29....9
Anzio	CVE-57....9
Manila Bay	CVE-61....8
Sanyamon	CVE-26....8
Natoma Bay	CVE-62....7
Nehenta Bay	CVE-74....7
Kitkun Bay	CVE-71....6
Sargent Bay	CVE-83....6
Steamer Bay	CVE-87....6
Nassau	CVE-16....5
White Plains	CVE-66....5
Kalinin Bay	CVE-68....5
Fanshaw Bay	CVE-70....5
Hoggatt Bay	CVE-75....5
Petrof Bay	CVE-80....5
Rudyerd Bay	CVE-81....5
Saginaw Bay	CVE-82....5
Lunga Point	CVE-94....5
Makin Island	CVE-93....5

(39 others awarded 4 or less)

MEMORIES

In the 1930s students at Japan's Naval Academy (Eta Jima) were asked to write a paper on how they would attack Pearl Harbor. The British proved how effective an air attack could be against battleships and cruisers at anchor on 11 November 1940 when 21 Royal Navy torpedo-bombers struck the Italian Fleet at Taranto. Even U.S. Navy exercises demonstrated the potential of the aircraft carrier as an offensive weapon. The 1932 fleet exercise in which Rear Adm. Harry E. Yarnell "attacked" Pearl Harbor on a Sunday with planes from *Lexington* and *Saratoga* provided evidence to support the potential of naval air power. Still, it was not until the second week of December 1941 that theory became reality and dramatic events in the Pacific proved that the aircraft carrier had become the preeminent combatant upon the seas.

The British were nearly four years ahead of the United States and Japan in developing an aircraft carrier for fleet use, but by late 1941 all three had quality carriers with Japan enjoying a slight numerical advantage. Japan's initial advantage held into mid-1942 and was then smothered both in combat and on the builder's ways. By the end of the war, carrier strength for the United States had risen to nearly 100 fleet, light and escort carriers in commission or building.

It is relatively safe to state that the most often recalled memory of American carriers during World War II is the successful account of *Enterprise, Yorktown* and *Hornet* at Midway in June 1942. Pick up any book concerning the war and this battle, which turned the tide in the Pacific, is recounted. The story is so well known to readers of naval history that more recent stories address the very finest of details. To a lesser degree accounts are rendered of the hit-and-run raids of early 1942; the Battle of the Coral Sea, which was the first battle to be fought between naval forces that never came into view of each other except from the air; the Battle of the Philippine Sea (the Marianas "Turkey Shoot"); the carrier "decoy" battle off Cape Engano during the Battle of Leyte Gulf; the fight-and-flight of the escort carriers of Taffy 3 off Samar (also during the Battle of Leyte Gulf); the air battles off the Eastern Solomons and Santa Cruz in 1942; and the kamikaze attacks against carriers in late 1944 and early 1945.

MEMORIES OF SACRIFICE

During World War II the United States lost four large carriers. Each will be remembered because they were lost, but each also had good moments. *Lexington*, lost during the Battle of the Coral Sea, shared in the sinking of the Japanese carrier *Shoho* with the *Yorktown*, which was sunk the following month off Midway. *Yorktown* is also credited with sinking the Japanese carrier *Soryu* at Midway, and 14 of her planes flew with "Big E" planes from the deck of her sister ship (Enterprise) to fatally damage *Hiryu* in the same battle. Before the *Wasp* was fatally wounded by submarine torpedoes off Guadalcanal, she contributed greatly to the British effort to hold Malta in the Mediterranean. And, *Hornet* (CV-8) was in commission only a year (October 1941-October 1942) but her life was productive and eventful. Doolittle's B-25 bombers flew from her flight deck in April, she fought at Midway in June, and before she was fatally damaged during the October Battle of Santa Cruz, her planes so severely damaged the Japanese fleet carrier *Shokaku* that it was out of service for months.

One of the significant factors in the loss of at least two of the big carriers in 1942 was inadequate damage control, but lessons learned in 1942 helped save other large carriers later in the war. When the U.S. Navy reached the western Pacific, the big carriers became prime targets for land-based planes and few escaped serious injury. As time continues to pass, the most often recalled memory of those dark days are stories and pictures of the *Franklin*. Hit while operating only 55 miles off the Japanese homeland in March 1945, "Big Ben" lost 724 men, a total that far exceeded the casualties of the respective American carriers lost in 1942. Apparently there were more movie cameramen present when *Bunker Hill* was seriously damaged in May 1945 as nearly every film relating to Franklin's experience shows considerable footage of *Bunker Hill*. This is disconcerting to the few who would recognize "the Hollywood touch," but the essence is nonetheless conveyed of the tragic hours aboard these and other ships.

Saratoga and *Intrepid* shared the dubious distinction of the most wounds requiring time away from the combat arena for repairs. The several voyages for repairs help explain the relative paucity of battle stars for the two carriers (seven and five respectively), but these carriers also enjoyed more favorable experiences. During the Battle of the Eastern Solomons, *Saratoga's* air group accounted for the Japanese carrier *Ryujo* while *Intrepid's* air groups carried their weight when in combat.

Several of the more dramatic photos of carriers not sunk but under fire or on fire are presented within these pages. Particularly notable are those of the *Enterprise* with her forward elevator 400 feet up and still rising after a kamikaze hit; a Japanese plane crashing between the *Hancock* and *J.Halsey Powell*; and a crash off the starboard bow of the *Essex*. Not presented in this book but equally instructive in sacrifice are existing pictures of the very large hole in the aft flight deck of the *Randolph*; the kamikaze hit on *Lexington* (CV-16) (often seen in movies as the kamikaze was picked up on film over a thousand feet above the *Lex* and was followed down to impact); the burning *Ticonderoga*

Commissioned in 1922, the *Langley* (CV-1) was the U.S. Navy's first aircraft carrier. Converted from a collier, the "Covered Wagon" served operationally until converted again in 1936 to a seaplane carrier and later to an aircraft transport. While serving as an aircraft transport she was sunk 27 February 1942 while ferrying planes to Java, unable to launch planes in her own defense. USN

Lexington (CV-2) entered the fleet in 1927. Along with sister ship *Saratoga* (CV-3) she was converted from a battlecruiser hull into a carrier. Inadequate damage control was a prime factor in her premature loss in the Coral Sea in May 1942. Most of her crew and air group survived the sinking and went on to newer construction to avenge her loss. The *Essex*-class *Lexington* (CV-16) inherited her name. USN

Saratoga (CV-3), seen here off Hawaii and in the previous picture behind her sister ship *Lexington* (CV-2), survived the war with seven battle stars. Although *Saratoga* and *Lexington* were very fast on a straight power run, neither was very maneuverable. Later large carriers had a turning radius half that of *Lexington* and *Saratoga*. The often-damaged *Saratoga* was expended in the 1946 Bikini atomic bomb tests. USN

The first carrier built from the keel up as an aircraft carrier, *Ranger* (CV-4) saw combat only in the Atlantic during World War II. Commissioned in 1934, the 14,500 ton carrier was scrapped in 1947. USN

Top: At a cost of $19 million each, the *Yorktown* (CV-5) at left and sister ship *Enterprise* (CV-6) were two of the best buys the American public ever got. *Yorktown* is recalled by veterans as the "Cadillac" of carriers as her three-year-plus building time allowed for attention to detail some later carriers would not enjoy. The carrier is seen here at Newport News while fitting out; she was commissioned 30 September 1937. USN

Above: Wasp (CV-7) resembled the *Yorktown*-class carriers but was in fact an improved *Ranger.* Confined to a small geographic area in support of the Guadalcanal operation, she was struck by three submarine torpedoes and sank on 15 September 1942. *Wasp* was sunk by the same Japanese submarine (*I-19*) that damaged the *North Carolina* and fatally wounded *O'Brien* (DD-415). USN

Top: With a wartime-high 20 battle stars, Presidential Unit Citation and Navy Unit Commendation, *Enterprise* (CV-6) earned the unofficial title of "World War II's most decorated ship." One significant factor in the Big E's success was the three-and-one-half year period devoted to training from her 12 May 1938 commissioning date and the outbreak of war. USN

Above: Hornet (CV-8) had an operational life of only one year (commissioned 20 October 1941; lost after the 26 October 1942 Battle of Santa Cruz), but her life was eventful. The launch of Doolittle's bombers was from her deck, and her air group damaged the Japanese carrier *Shokaku* so severely at Santa Cruz that she was unavailable for further combat during the Guadalcanal campaign. USN

and the equally damaged *Hancock* and *Wasp* (CV-18).

Although the *Essex*-class carriers were built to withstand punishment, they were still a pleasant surprise in the amount of damage they could sustain and return to fight on a later day. It could never be calculated, of course, but the sight of broken carriers steaming away from battle under their own power and then returning to challenge the enemy again must have been a great inspiration to all sailors on all ships.

CVs: MEMORIES OF SUCCESS

On balance, the big fleet carriers administered far more punishment than they received and their performance serves as the central memory of naval success for the 1,364 days of war. American submarines cut the industrial foundation from under Japan, but the success of the carrier enabled the offensive push across the Pacific.

The major successes of the lost *Lexington, Yorktown, Wasp, Hornet*, and the often-damaged *Saratoga* have already been recorded; therefore, attention is turned to those that survived the war.

In addition to *Saratoga*, two other pre-war carriers survived combat and shared in the honors rendered to the fleet in the fall of 1945. *Ranger* saw action only in the Atlantic and won only two battle stars. But the first American carrier built from the keel up to be a carrier contributed significantly during the invasion of North Africa in 1942.

The third pre-war carrier to survive the war emerged with more honors than any ship. It is not unusual to hear or see statements that a ship was "the most decorated ship of World War Two," but the only one that can document the claim is the *Enterprise* (CV-6). Despite seven major and several lesser wounds, the "Big E" received more battle stars (20) than any other warship, was the first carrier to be awarded the Presidential Unit Citation, and, among carriers, battleships and cruisers, she was the only one to win this award *and* the Navy Unit Commendation. Her planes flew into the battle over Pearl Harbor; she fought in five of the six fleet carrier battles and was coming up over the horizon when the other battle (Coral Sea) concluded. The "workhorse of the war" did not win her place in history only because of the large number of enemy ships and planes her air groups destroyed. The foundation of her fame was established on *when* she fought, *who* she fought and defeated, and *where* she fought. The year 1942 was the decisive year of the war; even the Japanese say this. In that year *Enterprise* fought the best carriers and the best pilots Japan would produce. After sinking *Akagi*—the Japanese flagship at Pearl Harbor and Midway—*Kaga*, and sharing in the death of *Hiryu* at Midway, the "Big E" was the only American carrier available to meet the last major thrust of the enemy to take Guadalcanal. Although battered and leaking, she nonetheless steamed into battle. The place of the great American carriers that came along later in the war is secure in naval history, but the fact is that the war in the Pacific was 46 percent over and four of the six fleet carrier battles had been fought before the excellent *Essex*-class and *Independence*-class carriers could add their weight to the scales of the struggle.

It was late in the summer of 1943 before the *Essex*-class and *Independence*-class carriers steamed into the Pacific, but when they did arrive the scales tipped immediately and drastically. It is fair to say that *Enterprise* and the other pre-war carriers held the line on defense

Yorktown (CV-5) was the only American carrier lost at Midway, and if she had not been prematurely abandoned she might have lived to continue outstanding service. *Yorktown* had been slowed by bomb hits before being hit with two aerial torpedoes in the attack pictured here. USN

Hornet (CV-8) received several bomb and torpedo hits off Santa Cruz, but could have been towed to safety had not the Japanese been so close. Two enemy pilots crashed their planes on the carrier; one is seen here only a moment before impact. Both American and Japanese (later) destroyer-launched torpedoes were required to finally sink the valiant carrier. USN

while the *Essex*-class carriers were building. It is also fair to say that the newer carriers were the offensive "stars" in the push through the Pacific islands to victory.

No single hull was awaited with more eagerness and interest than *Essex* (CV-9). Sailors, Marines, soldiers and airmen alike watched news releases and the horizon for the approach of the carrier that would give her name to the class that would prove to be one of the most adaptable designs ever, and would prove to be the most successful in combat. That later carriers would improve upon her design and be capable of carrying more devastating payloads does not diminish the place of the *Essex*-class carriers in history. Indeed, they were eminently successful in the era they were built and in two subsequent wars. Forty years after CV-9 was commissioned, some concerned with naval affairs are yet calling for new construction along the lines of the *Essex* in place of the larger nuclear carriers.

By the late summer of 1943 *Essex* was ready to begin the long-awaited and subsequently uninterrupted offensive toward Japan. With her were new sister ships, several carrying names inherited from the carriers lost in 1942. *Essex* was the class leader in more than name. She, the second *Yorktown* (CV-10), the second *Hornet* (CV-12), the second *Lexington* (CV-16) and the *Bunker Hill* (CV-17) recorded outstanding combat records. Each won the Presidential Unit Citation and each scored impressive numbers in enemy planes and ships destroyed.

While *Franklin* will always be remembered primarily for her great personnel losses and structural damage, she too was well on her way to earning a reputation for pain inflicted upon the enemy. Her air groups helped sink the *Musachi* and due to her rapid returns to combat after earlier wounds and the effectiveness of her air groups, she was on the verge of offensive greatness. The afternoon of 19 March 1945 kept "Big Ben" from obtaining the reputation for offensive greatness she was fast approaching, and it kept her from further combat service. However, that same afternoon destined her to greatness of another kind. Memory of "Big Ben" will always be synonymous with courage and devotion to duty as well as sacrifice. *Franklin* did not serve as long as *Enterprise*, did not win nearly as many battle stars and did not win the Presidential Unit Citation or Navy Unit Commendation. But, no ship can claim as many well deserved heroism awards to individuals for a single action as can *Franklin*, and this does not refer to nearly 1,000 purple hearts. And, significantly, these awards for heroism were for *saving* lives instead of taking them.

Except for the tragic events on *Franklin, Bunker Hill, Intrepid, Hancock, Lexington, Wasp, Ticonderoga, Essex, Randolph* and *Yorktown,* the carriers of the *Essex*-class did not experience the singular opportunities in combat that would cause history to remember any of them in a manner similar to the *Enterprise* alone in the Solomons, the first *Lexington* (CV-2) and first *Yorktown* (CV-5) in the Coral Sea or *Hornet* launching Doolittle's Raiders. When the new carriers arrived in late 1943 they usually steamed together in large numbers. Obviously, numbers obscure the heroics of individuals, air groups and ships. Forty years after the battles off the Philippines and Okinawa, conversations with many pilots who helped sink the last enemy carriers, battleships and cruisers that were put to sea reveal that "we don't know exactly who put the bombs or torpedoes into individual ships; there were just too many of us attacking and we were too busy evading anti-aircraft fire to worry about whom to credit."

Although several carriers and air groups duplicated claims – in good faith – the collective accomplishments are beyond question. The big carriers not only overcame the enemy, they overwhelmed him.

When the war ended, service was not over for most of the *Essex*-class carriers. The World War II veterans were represented in the Korean War by *Essex* (four battle stars and a Navy Unit Commendation) and *Bon Homme Richard* (five battle stars). *Bon Homme Richard* also received the Navy Unit Commendation for service off Vietnam as did *Intrepid, Hancock* and *Ticonderoga*. *Hornet, Yorktown* and *Intrepid* received notice for their roles in assisting with the space program and today venerable *Lexington*, the "Blue Ghost" of World War II fame, steams back and forth across the Gulf of Mexico serving as the Navy's training carrier.

No other hull in the history of the U.S. Navy was more eagerly awaited than *Essex* (CV-9). When *Essex* and her sister ships arrived in the Pacific (1943) the character of the war changed dramatically. *Essex* led her class with 13 battle stars and was awarded the Presidential Unit Citation. For service in the Korean War she was credited with four battle stars and the Navy Unit Commendation. USN

Although her designation was CV-16, the second *Lexington* was the second carrier of the *Essex* class to commission. Still serving into 1985 as the Navy's training carrier, the "Blue Ghost" had 11 battle stars and the Presidential Unit Citation for her World War II service. USN

Like the second *Lexington*, the second *Yorktown* (CV-10) is still alive in 1985 as a memorial in Charleston, S.C. In World War II the "Fighting Lady" recorded 11 battle stars and received the Presidential Unit Citation. Activated too late to serve off Korea, the carrier was awarded four battle stars for duty off Vietnam. USN

Exploding anti-aircraft shells and near misses of enemy bombs were a not uncommon experience for ships in the western Pacific. Here, *Essex* takes a near miss off her starboard bow late in the war. USN

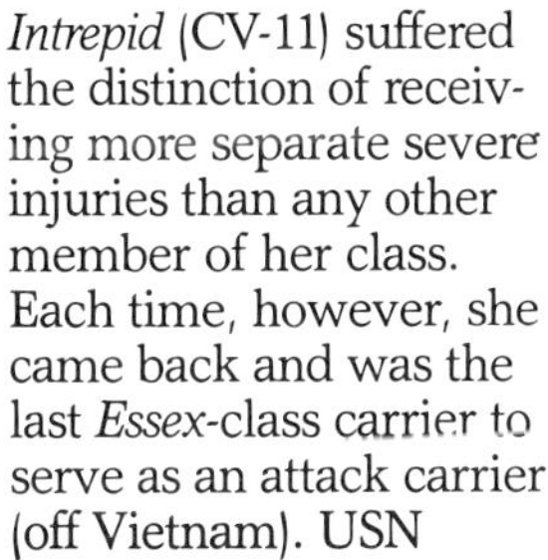

Intrepid (CV-11) suffered the distinction of receiving more separate severe injuries than any other member of her class. Each time, however, she came back and was the last *Essex*-class carrier to serve as an attack carrier (off Vietnam). USN

Below: *Hancock* was hit on 7 April 1945 by a kamikaze (62 killed) and was nearly hit on 20 March 1945 (seen here). However, destroyer *Halsey Powell* received most of the pain in this crash. Like several of her sisters, *Hancock* also suffered casualties from accidents on the flight deck. CV-19 received only four battle stars in World War II, a number inadequate to document casualties sustained and combat experienced. *Hancock* had a distinguished post-World War II career and received a Navy Unit Commendation for service off Vietnam to go with an earlier NUC for World War II. USN

Above: Many pictures of the burning *Bunker Hill* (CV-17) on 11 May 1945 are captioned "running for her life." Indeed, she was. *Bunker Hill* will most likely be remembered for this terrible day, and it is unfortunate that her excellent war record (Presidential Unit Citation and 11 battle stars) is overshadowed in many history books by her encounter with a kamikaze. NA

One of the more memorable pictures of the war is this one showing Enterprise's forward elevator being blown over 400 feet in the air by the explosion resulting from the crash of a kamikaze on 14 May 1945. NA

Opposite: October 30, 1944, was a bad day off the Philippines for carriers. In one of the first kamikaze attacks, *Franklin* (upper left) lost 56 men while *Belleau Wood* (CVL-24) lost 92. Gunners on the *Enterprise* look into the sun for more enemy planes. USN

Opposite: On board the *Enterprise* only moments after the 14 May 1945 kamikaze crash. Note parts of destroyed elevator, the wounded men at the upper left, and at the extreme right, a sailor blown out of a gun tub hangs suspended between fire and water. USN

The extensive damage to *Franklin* (CV-13) is apparent in this picture taken as the carrier steamed to New York for repairs. With 724 killed on 19 March 1945, *Franklin* paid the highest price in lives lost among carriers. In the 30 October 1944 attack she lost 56 killed. Like *Hancock*, her four battle stars are little measure of her war experience. NA

The second *Hornet* (CV-12) won seven battle stars and the Presidential Unit Citation. Still afloat in mothballs at Bremerton, Wash., in 1985, *Hornet* escaped serious battle damage in World War II, but did have a "crushing" experience with a storm. *Bennington* (CV-20) suffered a similar fate as did a post-World War II *Essex*-class carrier, *Valley Forge* (CV-45). These experiences inspired the "hurricane bow" modifications of the *Essex*-class carriers that served in the post-war era. USN

Essex-class carriers served operationally into the 1970s. Only the badly damaged *Franklin* and *Bunker Hill* were not modernized to serve with the post-World War II fleet. Here, *Essex* (CV-9) and the *Forrestal*-class carrier *Saratoga* (CVA-60) honor America in 1960. This photo helps one appreciate the difference in size of the later *Forrestal*-class carriers and the *Essex* class. USN

With 12 battle stars (and the Navy Unit Commendation) *Cowpens* (CVL-25) led the nine cruiser-hull, light carriers in combat experience. The CVLs were fleet carriers and as a class their wartime records were distinguished: 79 battle stars, three Presidential Unit Citations and two Navy Unit Commendations. USN

CVL MEMORIES

The success accorded the *Essex*-class carriers above was shared by the nine light carriers (CVLs) of the *Independence* class. The CVLs arrived in the Pacific at the same time as the new CVs and they steamed into battle in the same formations. In the last two years of the war a common practice was to include two *Essex*-class and one or two *Independence*-class carriers in the same operational group. In trials an *Essex*-class carrier could outrun an *Independence*-class unit, but in combat the CVLs could stay with the larger carriers. Officially the status of the CVL was "fleet carrier" – the same as *Saratoga, Enterprise* and the *Essex*-class carriers.

Inspired by the conversion of *Lexington* (CV-2) and *Saratoga* (CV-3) from battlecruiser hulls to carriers, the U.S. Navy in March 1942 ordered nine *Cleveland*-class cruiser hulls converted into "emergency" fast carriers. By late 1943 all nine were in commission, and by the end of the war the class had received 79 battle stars. Three (*Belleau Wood, Cabot* and *San Jacinto*) won the Presidential Unit Citation and two (*Cowpens* and *Langley*) won the Navy Unit Commendation. As mentioned above, it was often difficult or impossible to determine exactly which air group to credit for a particular sinking, but aviators from *Belleau Wood* did place the fatal hits into the Japanese carrier *Hiyo* during the Battle of the Philippine Sea.

More often recalled than the success of *Belleau Wood* is the sacrifice of the *Princeton*. Only *Princeton* was lost due to enemy action (Battle of Leyte Gulf), but three were damaged: *Belleau Wood* was struck by a kamikaze 20 October 1944 off the Philippines and suffered 92 killed; *Independence* was hit by an aerial torpedo off Tarawa 20 November 1943 and counted 17 killed; and *Cabot* lost 36 killed when she was crashed by a kamikaze off Luzon on 25 November 1944.

Only one of the *Independence*-class carriers fought again after World War II: *Bataan* earned seven battle stars during the Korean War. Still, several units of the class had noteworthy experiences after 1945. *Independence* survived the atomic bomb tests at Bikini in 1946 before being sunk off California in January 1951 in another weapons test. *Belleau Wood* was transferred to France in 1953 for service there, but was returned to the United States, stricken in 1960 and scrapped. *Langley* was also transferred to France in 1951, returned, and sold for scrap in 1963. *Bataan* was sold 1 September 1959, *Cowpens* was stricken 1 November 1959 and scrapped, *San Jacinto* was sold for scrap 15 December 1971 and *Monterey* served as the Navy's training carrier at Pensacola in the early 1950s before being stricken in 1970. *Cabot* still lives at the time of this writing as the helicopter carrier *Dedalo* in Spain.

MEMORIES OF CVEs

Reality is that some ships are glamorous and some are not. Battleships and large carriers are glamorous; cruisers slightly less so. Of combat ships, the escort carrier is perhaps least glamorous. They did not look powerful, did not look fast and did not even look like a warship. Indeed, many were never intended to be warships when they were built. Relative to what one can find in the literature concerning battleships and the larger fast carriers, very little is available to honor the memory of escort carriers.

Despite the comments just recorded, one can't overlook the fact that escort carriers steamed away from the war with more battle stars than all the fast carriers combined, more Presidential Unit Citations and more Navy Unit Commendations. Granted, there were more escort carriers than fast carriers, but as a group they were nearly as late as the fast carriers in getting into the war. Once there, however, they performed beyond expectations and played an extremely significant role in winning the war in both the Pacific and the Atlantic.

Before the *Casablanca* and *Commencement Bay*-class escort carriers were designed and built from the keel up as such, escort carriers were originally merchant ships or tankers (*Sangamon*-class). Top speed was not over 20 knots with a trailing wind, smooth seas and the Japanese Navy in hot pursuit (off Samar). The appearance of the ships inspired concern for safety. With little speed, few guns and no armor, the concern was justified. Certainly, someone in Washington, D.C., knew these carriers were in for trouble: the design of the *Casablanca*-class called for only one 5-inch gun...and it was placed on the fantail.

Even though escort carriers were not expected to withstand significant damage, several such as *Suwanee, Santee, Fanshaw Bay* and *Kalinin Bay* took serious hits and survived. Too often, however, the thin skins of the CVEs were not equal to the punishment inflicted. Perhaps it is surprising that only six were lost. Five of the six that were lost did share at least one characteristic with the five fleet carriers that went down. Specifically, they got in major blows against the enemy before being lost.

Liscome Bay was lost within three days of her first combat mission; the 646 lives lost when she was torpedoed off the Gilbert Islands ranked her second only to *Franklin's* 724 in sacrifice among carriers. The other five lost CVEs, however, made their presence felt before going down.*Block Island*, the only CVE lost in the Atlantic, accounted for two German submarines with her own planes while her escorts sank five including *U-549*, the submarine that placed the fatal torpedoes into CVE-21. *Gambier Bay* and *St. Lo* were lost off Samar during the Battle of Leyte Gulf; *Gambier Bay* sank as a result of gunfire while *St. Lo* was lost later on that same day after being hit by a kamikaze. Before being lost each carrier had received three battle stars; their fourth star and Presidential Unit Citations were awarded for the heroic resistance against overwhelming odds on that memorable October 25th. *Ommaney Bay* received two battle stars before being hit and sunk by a kamikaze off the Philippines 4 January 1945, and *Bismarck Sea* won three before two kamikazes sank her off Iwo Jima 21 February 1945.

The U.S. Navy's escort carriers in World War II served in a multitude of roles including the unenviable but necessary functions of training and plane transport. Early in the war while the carrier shortage was critical, escort carriers were ordered to serve operationally; *Sangamon, Suwannee, Chenango, Santee* and others were so successful in combat air patrol, attack, observation, invasion support, pre-invasion strikes and close air support that CVEs would continue to be used in some of these functions not only throughout the remainder of World War II but into the Korean War as well.

While every function imaginable was assigned to escort carriers in the Pacific, the major function of CVEs in the Atlantic was anti-submarine duty. The hunter-killer groups composed of escort carriers, destroyers and destroyer-escorts completely turned around the war in the Atlantic. Although their strategic role was defensive (to protect convoys), their tactical approach was offensive. The majority of the German submarines lost in World War II were accounted for by the British. Twenty-three percent of the German submarines destroyed were accounted for by American forces with U.S. Navy hunter-killer groups responsible for 65 percent of the American effort.

Several U.S. Navy escort carriers experienced particularly noteworthy successes in the Atlantic. Among these were *Bogue*, one of the U.S. Navy pioneers of the hunter-killer groups, responsible for 13 German submarines sunk by her or her escorts (eight by planes, two shared with her escorts and three by escorts alone); *Card* which scored eight sub kills with her escorts; and *Guadalcanal* which captured *U-505* and brought her home as a prize. The German submarine *U-505* still exists and is on display at the Chicago Museum of Science and Industry. In the Pacific, *Anzio* totaled five Japanese submarines with her planes and escorts.

After World War II many escort carriers were broken up, sold to other countries or returned to the Maritime Commission to be reconverted. Some, however, served on into Korea but none presently operate with the U.S. Navy. Ironically, the first escort carrier, *Long Island* (CVE-1), was one of the last to be utilized. After being decommissioned in 1946 she was sold for scrap, but was instead sold again and served as an immigrant carrier between Europe and Canada. Sold again in 1953, she became a schoolship for the University of the Seven Seas, and, after 13 years of educational service, she was sold to the University of Rotterdam to be used as a floating dormitory.

One of the most dramatic stories of the war was the battle and capture of the German submarine *U-505* by *Guadalcanal* (CVE-60) on 4 June 1944. The prize of *Guadalcanal* is currently on display at the Museum of Science and Industry in Chicago. Note the 40mm and smaller caliber holes in the conning tower of *U-505*. The photo of *U-505* was taken in 1984. NA and Author's Collection

In one of the more unusual photographs of the war, Presidential Unit Citation recipient *Gambier Bay* (CVE-73) is seen under fire by Japanese surface units off Samar during the Battle of Leyte Gulf. Despite heroic resistance, Gambier Bay's fourth battle star was her last and she became the only American carrier in World War II to be lost to enemy gunfire. USN

Card (CVE-11) was also an early arrival in the Atlantic where she and her escorts accounted for eight German submarines. *Card* was awarded the Presidential Unit Citation and three battle stars. USN

Only one light carrier was lost during the war: *Princeton* on 24 October 1944 during the Battle of Leyte Gulf. Not long after this picture was taken, an explosion on the carrier killed 237 men on the attending cruiser *Birmingham* (CL-62). Reunion groups representing both ships remain in contact into 1985. USN

A pioneer of the anti-submarine hunter-killer groups in the Atlantic, *Bogue* (CVE-9) accounted for 13 German submarines (eight by aircraft, five with her escorts). *Bogue*, with a misleading total of only three battle stars for her long service, was one of 16 CVEs to win the Presidential Unit Citation. USN

Suwannee (CVE-27), like her three sisters of the *Sangamon* class, was converted from a tanker into an escort carrier. In the early stages of the war all four served operationally with fleet carriers. Suwannee's planes supported the North African invasion in 1942 and then moved to the Pacific. Two separate kamikaze hits did not sink *Suwannee*, but did end her combat career in which she won 13 battle stars and the Presidential Unit Citation. USN

USS *Bismarck Sea* (CVE-95), the last carrier lost in World War II by the U.S. Navy (21 February 1945 off Iwo Jima; two kamikazes), is seen loading planes and suffering a flight deck crash. The plane that missed the arresting wire disappears over the bow after striking parked torpedo bombers. USN

Two escort carriers ride at anchor with other ships off Manus Island 19 September 1944. Some terms such as "jeep carriers" diminished the appreciation of the outstanding contributions rendered by CVEs; their value toward final victory is well documented. In the foreground is the USS *Mississippi*, one of only four battleships to be awarded the Navy Unit Commendation. USN

AIRCRAFT CARRIER MEMORIALS

When one visits the memorialized battleships *Alabama, North Carolina, Massachusetts* and *Texas*, one has truly touched the World War II era as these ships appear today as they did when Japan surrendered in 1945. It is not so with World War II era aircraft carriers. Only one fleet carrier from the 1941-1945 period still exists with an appearance essentially the same as her original configuration and that carrier – *Dedalo* formerly *Cabot* (CVL-28) – belongs to Spain and probably will be discarded by 1990.

America's best opportunity to preserve a carrier in World War II appearance was lost in the late 1950s. During the ebullient, victory-laden Navy Day celebrations in the fall of 1945, Secretary of the Navy James V. Forrestal wrote in a letter to President Truman that *Enterprise* (CV-6) was "the one ship that most nearly symbolizes the history of the United States Navy in World War II," and he recommended that the "Big E" be preserved as a memorial. Truman endorsed the letter and when *Enterprise* arrived in Boston in early November 1945 for minor conversion to enable her to bring home troops from Europe, the Boston newspapers carried headlines announcing "*Enterprise* to be National Shrine." Twelve years later Congress passed legislation to have *Enterprise* towed up the Potomac and enshrined just below the Washington Monument. President Eisenhower signed the bill, but the responsibility for raising the funds necessary for the project was left to private sources. Efforts by retired Adm. William F. Halsey and others failed and *Enterprise* went to the scrap heap in 1959.

Bunker Hill was the last *Essex*-class carrier in original configuration to go to the scrap yard (1971); for a brief period *Franklin*, the only other World War II *Essex*-class veteran not modernized, was considered as a memorial in the mid-1960s. Consequently, the two World War II era *Essex*-class carriers now serving in memorial status do not resemble their appearance of 40 years ago. With a redesigned island, enclosed bow, angled deck, removal of approximately 100 anti-aircraft barrels and other changes, one strains unsuccessfully to picture *Yorktown, Intrepid* or the other five remaining non-memorialized big carriers as they once were.

Yorktown and *Intrepid* were scheduled to be dismantled, but a series of favorable circumstances saved both. Members of the Yorktown Association had been active since 1948, and soon after the carrier was decommissioned in 1970, CV-10 veterans began working to save their ship. There were some grim days during the endeavor. Efforts to save *Enterprise* as a national shrine had failed; the drive to enshrine *Essex* at Bridgeport, Conn., had terminated; and negotiations between the Yorktown Association and the state of Virginia were not showing positive signs. *Yorktown* veterans believed citizens in the Tidewater region would be interested in CV-10 inasmuch as *Yorktown* carried the name of the Virginia battlefield where the American Revolution was successfully concluded. Just as it became apparent that Virginia officials would decline the opportunity to enshrine "the Fighting Lady," word came that the state of South Carolina was looking for ships to be displayed as part of the Patriots Point Naval and Maritime Museum. Matters moved quickly and in 1975 the state of South Carolina and Yorktown Association entered into a "marriage" that is still in the honeymoon stage and promises to remain.

The World War II veteran *Cabot* (CVL-28) still exists but with a different name. For over a decade the Presidential Unit Citation recipient has served in the navy of Spain as *Dedalo*. She is the last of the World War II straight-deck fleet carriers. USNI

The U.S. Navy's training carrier since 1962, *Lexington* (CV-16), seen here departing Pensacola en route to sea, will most likely not become a memorial. The last *Essex*-class carrier and World War II veteran to serve in the U.S. Navy, *Lexington* is scheduled to serve into the early 1990s. Author's Collection

One of only two World War II carriers serving in memorial status, *Interpid* is presently moored on the Hudson river in New York City where she is a Sea, Air and Space Museum. Not strictly a World War II memorial, *Intrepid* enjoyed extensive post-World War II experience and was a participant in the space program. Courtesy of Marlene Vance

Yorktown (CV-10), located in Charleston, S.C. (Mt. Pleasant, S.C., technically), is the flagship of the Patriots Point Naval and Maritime Museum. "The Fighting Lady" strongly emphasizes World War II history throughout her decks and exhibits, but also acknowledges post-World War II aviation exploits. Author's Collection

Each October the veterans of the *Yorktown* return to their carrier; the picture presented here was snapped during the 1985 reunion. Central among the reunion ceremonies is the induction of new members into the "Carrier Aviation Hall of Fame" and the dedication of plaques for the "Arlington of Carrier Aviation." Author's Collection

Before *Yorktown* is anything else, she is herself. This observation is necessary because the decks of "the Fighting Lady" have been opened to all other carriers, and a very special "red carpet" has been placed inviting all other World War II carriers to have a place of honor and remembrance within her. Before detailing this magnanimous gesture it is necessary to note that veterans of CV-10 have dedicated themselves to restoring as much of the ship's World War II history as possible. Together, and with the considerable help of the state of South Carolina, they have sought World War II combat planes, purchased them and paid for their restoration. At the forward end of the hangar deck, they have built the "Smokey" Stover Memorial Theater. Inside this theater – which was once the forward elevator pit – movies are shown and meetings held. Facing the hangar deck are numerous plaques calling to remembrance several of the more noted officers, men and even civilians whose lives touched CV-10 and either helped "the Fighting Lady" earn her nickname or publicize it. On the second deck the expansive wardroom spaces have been developed into a museum where the history of the *Yorktown*, her air groups and men is preserved.

One naturally expects an association of veterans such as the men of the *Yorktown* to honor their own. What is not expected is the desire and actions to honor other deserving ships and their men. With the cooperation of Patriots Point, the Yorktown Association has endeavored – and continues – to honor other carriers and their men by: 1) establishment of the "Arlington of Naval Aviation"; 2) sponsorship of the Carrier Aviation Hall of Fame; and 3) offering compartments to be converted into museum exhibits for respective carriers.

When aviators, officers and seamen were lost at sea, it was not possible in most cases to return remains

One of the several compartments developed aboard *Yorktown* is the *Ticonderoga* Room. Pictures, maps, artifacts and memorabilia help tell the story of CV-14 which won five battle stars in World War II and served with distinction off Vietnam (three Navy Unit Commendations). Author's Collection

Among World War II era memorialized ships, none has been as magnanimous as *Yorktown* in honoring other ships and their veterans. Nearly 50 plaques have already been dedicated in the "Arlington of Carrier Aviation." Although respective reunion groups usually defray the cost of the plaque and provide the names of men lost during World War II, the CV-10 Association initiated the project and continues to serve as sponsor. Author's Collection

The USS *Saratoga* Room aboard *Yorktown* is quite extensive. Following the "open scrapbook" scheme, the *Saratoga* exhibit succeeds in carrying a visitor back to the World War II era. The history of CV-3 is well told with many pictures and newspaper articles. Seen in these two pictures are memorabilia donated by the family of Vice Adm. Mitscher and a row of photos honoring respective commanding officers of CV-3. Note the photo of Admiral Halsey (fourth from left, third row down). Several items of interest donated by Admiral Halsey's family are also on display. Author's Collection

to a location on land where some marker could designate a final place of rest. The "Arlington of Naval Aviation" aboard the *Yorktown* provides a location where family and friends of those lost may come and find an appropriate setting honoring sacrifice. To date nearly 50 plaques have been placed either by reunion associations or other sponsors and over 3,500 names have been recorded. At the bottom of the plaques are brief statements relating to the life and accomplishments of the ship which was the last home of the departed.

Not all of the plaques found in this solemn place honor the men and ships of World War II: Korea and Vietnam are both represented. As impressive as it is now, it will become even more imposing in the future. In time, someone will research the records in the National Archives and a sponsor or veterans themselves will dedicate plaques to honor men of three prominent carriers presently not represented.

Franklin, with 724 men lost in one attack and 56 in another, will someday have the largest plaque; *Bunker Hill* with 389 men lost in May 1945 will add her other losses to this total and have the second-largest plaque among fleet carriers. One is hesitant to say that a veteran of *Liscome Bay* will step forward to research the names of the 646 officers and men lost aboard her in November 1943 because there were so few survivors: 75 percent of those on board this new escort carrier died with her. Still, it must be done.

The Carrier Aviation Hall of Fame presently honors 30 officers and civilians for their contributions. To date the inductees include 16 flag officers, six civilians and eight officers not of flag rank. All presently included are deserving, and those who will follow in the future will no doubt be deserving. Indeed, several have already been honored who have been overlooked or inadequately treated in some history books. No induction, however, has had any more emotional overtones than the 1985 induction of Capt. Arnold J. Isbell. In the spring of 1945 Captain Isbell received orders to take command of *Yorktown* (CV-10), but a week before reporting aboard, he was among the 724 lost when *Franklin* suffered her tragic afternoon. Forty years and six months later, Captain Isbell was united with the *Yorktown*.

Secure in the knowledge that their ship was famous in her own right and acutely aware that she was nonetheless destined to be dismantled, *Yorktown* veterans have not only been magnanimous but enthusiastic in recruiting other carrier associations to share space aboard. The *Yorktown* has offered compartments below the hangar deck to veterans of carriers so that they might display artifacts and memorabilia to perpetuate special memories of their ships. To date, veterans of the World War II carriers *Saratoga* (CV-3), *Hancock (CV-19)*, *Ticonderoga* (CV-14) and *Monterey* (CVL-26) have constructed displays. In late 1985 negotiations were proceeding between Patriots Point and representatives of *Yorktown* (CV-5), "Taffy 3" (especially *Gambier Bay*), and *Enterprise* (CV-6) regarding possible displays.

Of the displays currently existing, the overall theme – whether intended or not – is the "open scrapbook." Unquestionably it is different from what one would see in the Naval Aviation Museum at Pensacola, the Smithsonian, Hampton Roads Naval Museum or numerous other museums. The several museums just mentioned emphasize aesthetic appeal and each has certain regulations that do not allow the display of certain items: example, ordnance and uniforms are not to be placed on permanent display at Pensacola. Aboard the *Yorktown*, "laissez faire" lives.

The *Hancock* CV-19 Room aboard the *Yorktown* is a fitting tribute to the long-serving carrier that began her illustrious career in the Pacific in 1944. The area of the display shown in this picture is only a fraction of the space devoted to memorializing the carrier. Author's Collection

In 1985 the second *Hornet* (CV-12) is still alive, mothballed at Bremerton. However, she has already been stripped of many artifacts for possible museum use. The scoreboard from CV-12 (shown here) is on display at the Naval Aviation Museum aboard the Pensacola Naval Air Station. Author's Collection

Four World War II Carriers are represented in this picture taken on the grounds of the Naval Aviation Museum at Pensacola. In the distance is an anchor from *Essex* (CV-9), the bell is from *Ranger* (CV-4), the anchor chain from *Enterprise* (CV-6) and closest to the camera is an anchor from *Antietam* (CV-36) which commissioned during World War II but too late to win a battle star. Both *Antietam* and *Essex* served brief stints at Pensacola as the Navy's training carrier. Author's Collection

First, a visitor to the *Yorktown* must keep in mind that CV-10 is an aircraft carrier; the museums listed above are found in buildings. There is the logical policy aboard the *Yorktown* that she not be so completely converted below decks as to lose her own history. Therefore, exhibits are built around hatches, vents, wiring and other protrusions. If someone is over 6 feet, 6 inches tall, it might be advisable to visit only the flight deck and hangar deck. Still, the exhibits aboard CV-10 are excellent in content, and what may be lacking in beauty is more than compensated for in the quality of the history presented.

The *Saratoga* Room(s) requires at least two hours of a visitors time. Approximately two hundred pictures have been placed, and the several newspaper articles from the 1920s, 1930s and 1940s provide very interesting reading. The life of the *Saratoga* is here from construction through World War II to her sinking in the 1946 atomic bomb tests. Some of the more interesting items on display include: uniforms belonging to Admiral Halsey and Admiral Mitscher; a battle flag flown over the carrier during the Battle of the Eastern Solomons; a portion of the flight deck removed while repairing the damage from the February 1945 kamikaze attacks; portions of the Japanese kamikaze planes that hit *Saratoga*, including a metal identification tag belonging to one of the pilots and a partially burned, red sash cord from around the pilot's neck.

The *Hancock* (CV-19) display is more compact than the *Saratoga* Room (the word "room" is sparsely used aboard ships, but Patriots Point and *Yorktown* officials have chosen this term for compartments converted to museum displays). *Hancock* did not have the pre-war history of *Saratoga* but did have a very active life during and after the war, especially off Vietnam. The life of the *Hancock* is told in pictures and several individuals have been highlighted. As in the *Saratoga* display, the commanding officers of CV-19 are presented.

A large wooden nameplate bearing the name "Hancock" greets a visitor in the former air operations offices. The men of the "Fighting Hanna" contributed rarely seen photographs, documents, uniforms, flash gear, flight gear, tin foil strips dropped from carrier planes to foul enemy radar and a battle helmet among other memorabilia. The spaces occupied by the *Hancock* display are compact, which does not allow one to capture much of the large exhibit in one photograph. But, these spaces were not made into museum displays for the sake of photography; they were made to visit.

The *Ticonderoga* Room is mostly a photographic display as much of her surviving memorabilia is located elsewhere: a bell is located in San Diego and there is a small museum in Ticonderoga, N.Y., honoring Capt. Dixie Kieffer and the men of the carrier who gave their lives while serving aboard. Of special interest in "Ti's" display aboard *Yorktown* is a plaque dedicated in 1961 honoring the ship's World War II dead, and a copy of the song sheet about the *Ticonderoga*. Unlike most other displays aboard, the builders plaque is here and a history of the earlier ships carrying the name "Ticonderoga" is presented.

The USS *Monterey* Memorial Ready Room and the Gerald R. Ford Display successfully conveys to the visitor the sights of men preparing for a combat mission. A uniform and other items belonging to the former naval officer aboard CVL-26 and president of the United States are on display. The pictures of the only light carrier memorial presently on board are graphic if not as plentiful as what one finds in other displays.

Located on the Hudson River at 46th Street in New York City, the *Intrepid* (CV-11) was opened in

Like the remains of the battleship *South Dakota*, with whom she fought side-by-side at Santa Cruz in 1942, the *Enterprise's* artifacts are all over the country. A major exhibit exists inside the Naval Aviation Museum at Pensacola, plaques adorn the elevator tower at Annapolis and the hangar deck aboard *Yorktown* and her bell rests in front of Bancroft Hall at the Naval Academy. Shown here are the nameplate cut from the ship in 1959 (at River Vale, N.J.), a plaque under one of the Big E's anchors in the Washington Navy Yard and the memorial to Butch O'Hare – for whom Chicago's O'Hare Airport is named. O'Hare was serving on *Enterprise* when he died in 1943. Courtesy of J.K. Pegues, Author's Collection and Dave Lister

Another artifact associated with the *Enterprise* is the raft in which three CV-6 aviators survived for 34 days after being forced down in early 1942. Their experience formed the basis for the book *The Raft* by Robert Turnbull. Gene Aldrich, A.J. Pastula and H.F. Dixon are seen here receiving medals from Admiral Nimitz on the deck of the Big E. In 1985 the raft itself is on display in the Naval Academy Museum at Annapolis. USN and Author's Collection

1982 as a Sea, Air, and Space Museum. Like *Yorktown*, she is not exclusively a World War II memorial, but her experiences in that war cannot be – and are not – overlooked. Compared to the *Yorktown* there is very little World War II emphasis, but in time that could well change. Certainly all interested in naval history hope that *Intrepid* will have time, and money, to more fully develop exhibits to honor CV-11's World War II history and, perhaps, the history of other carriers. A good start has been made toward these goals, but recent financial problems – well chronicled on other pages outside this book – have delayed plans. *Intrepid* was badly damaged three times during World War II, but each time she came back. After serving off Vietnam she was scheduled for demolition, but she came back from that. Her track record indicates she also will survive her latest challenge.

Somewhat reminiscent to the experience of the battleship *South Dakota*, memorials to the *Enterprise* or parts of her are found in several locations. The largest display is the *Enterprise* Exhibit within the Naval Aviation Museum at Pensacola. Large letters spelling out "CV-6" and other panel boards covered with nearly 200 photos depict the 20 year life of the "Big E." A steering wheel and stand, engine order telegraph, rudder angle indicator, porthole and valve wheel from the carrier are displayed along with parts of the last kamikaze plane to hit the ship and mementoes donated from survivors who flew into the Battle of Midway. Other memorials to the "most decorated ship of World War II" include the nameplate located in a Little League baseball park in River Vale, N.J.; the elevator tower at the football stadium in Annapolis, Md.; the ship's bell at the Naval Academy (rung only when Navy beats Army) and an anchor with appropriate plaque inside the Washington Navy Yard. The wing of a Japanese plane shot down over *Enterprise* is scheduled to be placed in the new World War II exhibit within the Navy Memorial Museum in the Washington Navy Yard.

Beyond what has already been mentioned, little else exists in the manner of major single carrier memorials. There has been consideration of moving the *Shangri-La* (CV-38) from the Philadelphia Navy Yard to Tampa, Fla., as a museum, but at the time of this writing that project is on hold. With *Intrepid* experiencing financial problems in 1985 and *Yorktown* not very far from Tampa, the odds of *Shangri-La* being preserved are not overly great. *Lexington* (CV-16) would be a strong candidate for preservation at Pensacola as a result of her successful service in both war and peace. However, she too would not be far from the *Yorktown* in South Carolina and she would be competing for financial support with the relatively new and still growing Naval Aviation Museum. Consequently, her odds are not good. The three carriers in mothballs at Bremerton – *Hornet, Bennington* and *Bon Homme Richard* – are not being sought as memorials, but the West Coast is far enough away from *Yorktown* and *Intrepid* to justify consideration. Too, the West Coast is particularly lacking in World War II era combat ships.

In 1985, there is only one major, single, World War II aircraft carrier exhibit at the Naval Aviation Museum in Pensacola (*Enterprise* CV-6) and one smaller exhibit (*Gambier Bay* CVE-73). In time there will certainly be a major exhibit honoring *Lexington* (CV-16) as she has been a part of the Pensacola NAS and city of Pensacola since 1962. Veterans of the *Cabot* (CVL-28) are holding their 1986 reunion in Pensacola to consider establishing a major exhibit within the museum. These facts aside, the Naval Aviation Museum already is a mecca for anyone interested in aircraft carriers. All the World War II fleet carriers and escort carriers are honored with listings, pictures

The anchor from *Anzio* (CVE-57), the escort carrier that won nine battle stars and teamed with her escorts to sink five Japanese submarines, is on display outside the main entrance to the Navy Memorial Museum in the Washington Navy Yard, Washington, D.C. Author's Collection

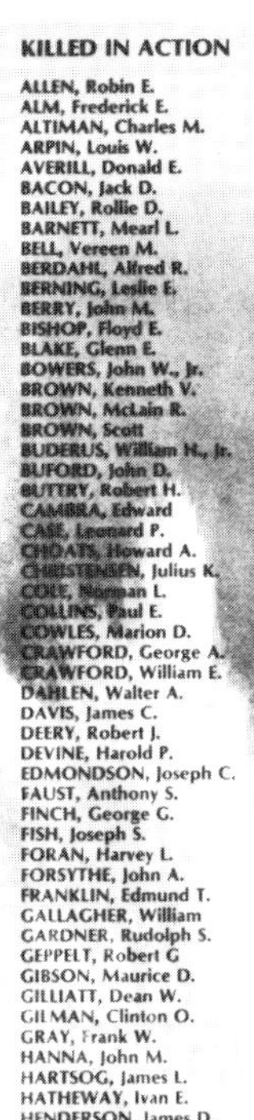

KILLED IN ACTION

ALLEN, Robin E.
ALM, Frederick E.
ALTIMAN, Charles M.
ARPIN, Louis W.
AVERILL, Donald E.
BACON, Jack D.
BAILEY, Rollie D.
BARNETT, Mearl L.
BELL, Vereen M.
BERDAHL, Alfred R.
BERNING, Leslie E.
BERRY, John M.
BISHOP, Floyd E.
BLAKE, Glenn E.
BOWERS, John W., Jr.
BROWN, Kenneth V.
BROWN, McLain R.
BROWN, Scott
BUDERUS, William H., Jr.
BUFORD, John D.
BUTTRY, Robert H.
CAMBRA, Edward
CASE, Leonard P.
CHOATS, Howard A.
CHRISTENSEN, Julius K.
COLE, Norman L.
COLLINS, Paul E.
COWLES, Marion D.
CRAWFORD, George A.
CRAWFORD, William E.
DAHLEN, Walter A.
DAVIS, James C.
DEERY, Robert J.
DEVINE, Harold P.
EDMONDSON, Joseph C.
FAUST, Anthony S.
FINCH, George G.
FISH, Joseph S.
FORAN, Harvey L.
FORSYTHE, John A.
FRANKLIN, Edmund T.
GALLAGHER, William
GARDNER, Rudolph S.
GEPPELT, Robert G
GIBSON, Maurice D.
GILLIATT, Dean W.
GILMAN, Clinton O.
GRAY, Frank W.
HANNA, John M.
HARTSOG, James L.
HATHEWAY, Ivan E.
HENDERSON, James D.
HENRY, Wilfred
HERTENSTEIN, Arthur E.
HOLLAND, James L.
HOLLY, Leonard
HOLT, Leo W.
HOOKS, Carson L.
HORN, William D.
JACKSON, John M.
JARRELL, Harvey, Jr.
JOHNS, Otto J., Jr.
JOHNSON, William
JORDAN, Robert L.
KALBE, Walter H.
KAMATS, Michael T.
KEENAN, John F.
KIMBALL, Sidney C.
KIRK, Robert
KLOTKOWSKI, Henry S.
KNIGHT, Robert W.
KOZLOWSKI, George J.
LARKIN, Joseph B.
LAURN, Alvin B.
LEMAIRE, John R.
LEWIS, Angelo P.
LUCCHESI, Louis L.
MARSHALL, Walter F.
MARTIN, Leonard G.
MAYES, Morrison W.
McDONOUGH, Thomas E.
McLAUGHLIN, Henry A.
MENTLICK, William E.
MILLER, George
MUDD, Raymond L.
MUNTZ, Eugene
MURRAY, Eugene T.
NASLUND, Lage T.
PARMANTJE, John J.
PHIPPS, John S.
PILGRIM, Edward F.
PITTMAN, Everett
PRIBISKI, Mike J.
PROKOP, Edward J.
PRUITT, Forrest W.
RAWLINGS, Cecil A.
RAYMOND, Ralph N.
RICHARDS, James
RICHARDSON, Hubert L.
RIVERS, Howard M.
RIZZO, Charles V.
RUFFIN, Reginald F.
SABOVIK, John D.
SAINTS, George M.
SANDERSON, John P.
SCHNEIDERJAN, Daniel J.
SEYMOUR, Hovey
SHORT, Edward B.
SHRIVER, Warren F.
SICHERMAN, Burton H.
SKAGGS, Ralph L.
SMEHYL, Charles
SMITH, Ernest J.
SMITH, William F.
SMURDA, John R.
STEWART, Wayne H.
STONE, Harold R.
STONER, Lyle T.
STRAITON, James L.
STURDY, William G.
TELLIER, Leslie W.
THOMAS, Harrell A.
TREECE, Otis A.
WALL, Theodore
WEISS, Fred E.
WHITE, Edgar
WHITTED, Raymond C.
WILDER, Paul
WILLIAMS, Junior R.
WOLLAND, Manuel F.
ZANON, William L.

O Eternal God,

Who alone spreads out the heavens and rules the raging of the seas, may this Memorial bring continued remembrance of these men who died defending their country in time of danger, and whose bodies found their last resting place in the waters of the Pacific off the coast of Samar. May it call to mind that they were called by their nation to defend liberties and preserve unity. We do not want those who died to have died in vain. They died that war would end, that an aggressor would be stopped, and peace would come and make the world safe for freedom. May their deaths give to us an enlightened love of peace, justice and righteousness that we may be more dedicated to freedom than to power; more to a resolve of doing justice than maintaining pride; more to service than to strength. In the strong name of our Lord. Amen.

Captain Verner N. Carlsen, Ship's Chaplain
October 25, 1977

REUNION FOR PEACE

U.S.S. GAMBIER BAY

The USS GAMBIER BAY (CVE-73), a WW-II Casablanca class "jeep carrier" was launched on November 22, 1943 and commissioned in Astoria, Oregon on December 28, 1943. Nineteenth of its class, a [illegible] was built in 171 days.

The "baby flat-top" displacement [illegible], length 512 feet, beam [illegible], [illegible] draft [illegible], maximum speed 19 knots, armament one 5-inch and sixteen 40mm guns. [illegible] VC-10, contained eighteen Grumman [illegible] FM-2 "Wildcats" and twelve Grumman Torpedo Bombers TBM-1c "Avengers." The ship's personnel complement was [illegible] men.

In its brief life-span of ten months, its final 130 days were spent in the Pacific combat theater as part of Task Group 77.4.3. For their part in the liberation of Saipan, Tinian, Guam, Yap, Ulithi, and Palaus, CVE-73 and VC-10 earned four battle stars. For their role in diverting a mighty Japanese fleet from counter-attacking General MacArthur's landing force at Leyte, Philippines, the group was awarded the Presidential Unit Citation.

The USS GAMBIER BAY was sunk in the Battle of Leyte Gulf off Samar on October 25, 1944, the only American aircraft carrier in naval history to be sunk by surface gunfire. Of its complement, the survivors were adrift from 45 to 73 hours until rescued, while 20% of its "sailors" are entombed with the gallant ship at the bottom of the Philippine Sea.

WELL DONE!

Probably no other World War II escort carrier will have been memorialized to any greater degree than *Gambier Bay* (CVE-73). Shown here is a display honoring the carrier in the Naval Aviation Museum at Pensacola, and a postcard featuring a drawing of CVE-73 under fire off Samar with a listing of the men lost with the carrier. A memorial plaque already stands in the "Arlington of Carrier Aviation" and plans call for establishment of a major exhibit. Author's Collection & USS Gambier Bay Association

From top to bottom are the *Essex*-class carriers *Bon Homme Richard* (CV-31), *Hornet* (CV-12) and *Bennington* (CV-20) shown here in mothballs (1984) at Bremerton, Wash. Along with *Shangri-La*, mothballed at Philadelphia, these World War II veterans most likely will be scrapped when Lexington's tour as training carrier is terminated in the 1990s. None of the five just listed are strong candidates to join *Yorktown* and *Intrepid* as museum ships. Author's Collection

The *Essex* (CV-9) was a candidate for preservation at Bridgeport, Conn. Regrettably, the project did not succeed and CV-9 was scrapped; the leader of her class deserved a better fate. At *Essex* reunions a room is temporarily set up to display photos and memorabilia of the "oldest and the boldest." In the bottom picture, what appears to be the back of an automobile garage is actually parts of the *Essex* in storage at the Hampton Roads Naval Museum. There are tentative plans for a major exhibit to honor *Essex* there. Author's Collection

and/or models. The present building has been in use for only 10 years and as the beautifully appointed museum continues its rapid growth there will be even more exhibits recalling naval aviation in World War II.

In addition to carrier exhibits in the Naval Aviation Museum there is a Hall of Honor to recognize the great military and civilian contributors to the development of naval aviation in peace and war. An extensive art gallery includes numerous prints capturing World War II events; there is a special exhibit dedicated to the memory of naval aviation aces and a unique display honoring naval medal of honor recipients.

Although there is a section of this book concerning models it should be mentioned here that the Naval Aviation Museum, the Navy Memorial Museum in the Washington Navy Yard, the Smithsonian and the National Air and Space Museum are the most favored locations of the big (approximately 20 feet) Navy builder's models. Like other display items, these are rotated from time to time, but these are still the prime locations to see the most exact and exquisite models of World War II era carriers. The Naval Academy is also a favored location, but many of the models there are in buildings off limits to the tourist.

If a book on the subject of World War II Navy memories and memorials is written 10 years from now to survey what is left of the greatest fleet of all time, one would hope to find in those pages a narrative of the growth of World War II exhibits on the *Yorktown, Intrepid* and inside the Naval Aviation Museum. One would also hope to read about a major exhibit honoring the *Essex* at Hampton Roads Naval Museum or at one of the other sites just listed. Somewhere there needs to be a major exhibit for the *Franklin* and the *Bunker Hill*: the survivors of these two fighting ships should create some tangible remembrance for their shipmates lost during the war. Somewhere, too, there needs to be a memorial to *Yorktown* (CV-5), *Bogue* (CVE-9) and *Card* (CVE-11) in addition to the plaques in the "Arlington of Naval Aviation" aboard the *Yorktown*. To overlook the outstanding records, successes and sacrifices of deserving ships and crews is a negative precedent. And, time for creating memorials by those who served aboard is growing short.

Before leaving the discussion of carrier memorials, mention must be made of the carrier exhibit in the National Air and Space Museum in Washington, D.C., and the carrier exhibit within the San Diego Aerospace Museum. The major attraction in both exhibits is the aircraft. In the National Air and Space Museum an SBD Dauntless is suspended from the ceiling while a Wildcat fighter sits underneath. In the San Diego Aerospace Museum a Hellcat fighter rests beside a Japanese Zero. Both exhibits are generic, honoring World War II carrier aviation and not any one ship. This statement must be qualified to some degree as a very large mural of *Yorktown* (CV-10) serves as a backdrop for the San Diego exhibit while the first *Yorktown* (CV-5) and sister ships *Enterprise* and *Hornet* are featured in Washington for their participation in the Battle of Midway.

Just as the listing at the end of the previous chapter was incomplete, so too is the listing of artifacts from World War II carriers. The artifacts listed here are known to exist or to have existed in display status, and what is presented below is in addition to what has already been discussed. Again, it must be noted that the Navy holds tons of artifacts in storage.

CARRIER	ARTIFACT	LOCATION
Antietam CV-36	Bell Anchor	Sharpsburg, Md. (American Legion Post) Naval Aviation Museum, Pensacola, Fla.
Belleau Wood CVL-24	Brass wheel	Sarasota High School, Sarasota, Fla.
Bunker Hill CV-17	War record Flags	*USS Cassin Young*, Boston, Mass. Mass. Maritime Academy, Buzzards Bay, Mass.
Franklin CV-13	Barometer	U.S. Naval Academy, Annapolis, MD.
Hancock CV-19	Portholes Large model	Mass. Maritime Academy, Buzzards Bay, Mass. Bremerton, Wash.
Hornet CV-12	Scoreboard Commissioning plaque Plaques and helm	Naval Aviation Museum, Pensacola, Fla. Hampton Roads Naval Museum, Norfolk, Va. LeMoore NAS, Calif.
Langley CVL-27	Anchor	Naval Training Center, Orlando, Fla.
Monterey CVL-26	Bell	Allen Knight Maritime Museum, Monterey, Calif.
Ranger CV-4	Bell Builders model	Naval Aviation Museum, Pensacola, Fla. Navy Memorial Museum, Washington, D.C.
Ticonderoga CV-14	Bell	NAS, North Island, San Diego, Calif.
Wasp CV-18	Anchor	Peckville, Pa. (American Legion Post)

Because of considerable publicity announcing the establishment in Norfolk, Va., of a memorial incorporating a significant portion of the carrier Franklin's island, many have traveled to see it. It is not there. If "Big Ben" had been just another ship, the lost memorial would go unnoticed; instead, the country, the U.S. Navy, Norfolk and history all lost. Rendering by Joe Cason

U.S. NAVY COMBAT AIRCRAFT

Despite all the attention and emotions devoted to aircraft carriers, they nonetheless were a means to an end and not an end in themselves. As the prime target during air attacks during World War II, carriers developed some sharp-shooting anti-aircraft gunners. However, the major purpose for the carrier was to launch and recover its "main battery" of bombers, torpedo planes and fighters.

When the United States was thrust into World War II in December 1941, the U.S. Navy possessed 5,300 planes. In the course of the war the Navy lost 8,500 aircraft (combat and operational), but when hostilities ended in 1945 there were 41,000 planes available. Very few of these planes remain in 1985, but enough exist in museums–or on their grounds–to satisfy the curiosity of a generation that cannot remember a war 40 years past.

The best locations to find World War II Navy combat aircraft are the Naval Aviation Museum at Pensacola and the National Air and Space Museum in Washington, D.C. As all museums rotate aircraft displays, one's "best bet" to find the largest collection of World War II era combat aircraft is Pensacola. The 1985 collection at the Naval Aviation Museum is consistent with what has been on display for several years and will no doubt continue to be. A visit to this museum at any time of the year will enable one to see a Grumman F4F Wildcat, Grumman F6F Hellcat, and Vought F4U Corsair, the three major U.S.Navy fighters between 1941 and 1945. The Wildcat ended the war with a 7 to 1 kill ratio over the enemy while the Hellcat scored a 19 to 1 ratio and the Corsair registered an 11 to 1 ratio. Also at Pensacola is the most successful dive-bomber of the war, the Douglas SBD Dauntless, and her successor, the Curtiss SB2C Helldiver. A Grumman TBF Avenger torpedo bomber completes the World War II era combat aircraft display. Due to their historical significance, the six World War II combat planes are always displayed inside the museum. Outside, one can walk through the grounds and find a good number of other type aircraft from the 1941-1945 era that served in support and combat roles.

One major combat aircraft from World War II is not on display at Pensacola or any other location: the Douglas TBD "Devastator" is extinct. At the other end of the spectrum, there are more surviving Avengers than any other World War II combat aircraft. Several Corsairs exist, but many of these are post-World War II planes. Less than a dozen Wildcats and Dauntlesses survive and the once plentiful Hellcats now number approximately a dozen.

In October 1985 officials on the *Yorktown* dedicated a Hellcat and a Corsair to sit alongside an Avenger already on exhibit. The Corsair was raised from the bottom of Lake Washington and was restored to display condition. Such are the steps that museums and groups like the Yorktown Association must take to preserve history.

One of the few remaining Grumman Wildcat fighter planes still in existence is seen here at the Champlin Fighter Museum in Mesa, Ariz. Two other Wildcats are on display in the National Air and Space Museum in Washington, D.C., and at the Naval Aviation Museum in Pensacola. Until mid-1943 the Wildcat was the main U.S. Navy fighter. It served throughout the war and scored a 7 to 1 kill ratio over the enemy. Courtesy of Barrett Tillman

One of the most successful planes of World War II was the Douglas SBD Dauntless, seen here in formation. These dive bombers had their finest moments during the Battle of Midway when they sank four Japanese fleet carriers. In 1985 the number of surviving SBDs approximates the number seen in this wartime photo. USN

With a 19 to 1 kill ratio, the F6F Hellcat fighter was the most successful U.S. Navy fighter in World War II. This Hellcat was dedicated aboard the *Yorktown* (CV-10) on 13 October 1985. Author's Collection

A number of Corsairs exist, but few are strictly World War II veterans. The Navy's fastest fighter in World War II, Corsairs recorded an 11 to 1 kill ratio. The Corsair pictured here is in the Navy Memorial Museum. Claudia L. Pennington

The SBD Dauntless shown here is on display in the National Air and Space Museum in Washington, D.C. Sitting under the SBD is a Wildcat fighter. Author's Collection

The SB2C Helldiver, seen here within the Naval Aviation Museum in Pensacola, Fla., succeeded the Dauntless aboard carriers late in World War II. Like most other aircraft of the 1941-1945 period, very few Helldivers remain. Courtesy of Lawrence E. Seehafer

It is not possible to show a picture of the Douglas TBD Devastator in a museum as this torpedo bomber has been extinct since World War II. All that is left are memories, models and pictures from the late 1930s and early 1940s such as the one shown here. USN

There are more TBF or TBM Avengers still existing than any other combat plane from the World War II period. This Avenger is aboard the *Yorktown* (CV-10). During Yorktown Association reunions, another Avenger is used for a fly-by at the conclusion of memorial services. Note "Arlington of Naval Aviation" in background. Author's Collection

The OS2U Kingfisher was not a combat plane per se, but she flew from battleships and cruisers in the function of observation and scout. This Kingfisher is aboard the battleship *North Carolina* in Wilmington, N.C. A similar plane is aboard the battleship *Alabama* at Mobile, Ala. Author's Collection

One of the highlights of the San Diego Aerospace Museum is the Navy Carrier Exhibit which features a restored Japanese Zero and an F6F Hellcat (behind Zero). One of 10,445 Zero fighters produced in Japan, this fighter was brought to the United States in 1945, transferred to San Diego in 1981 on permanent loan from the Smithsonian Institution and placed on display in 1984. Courtesy of Margaret McGlasson

The remains of a Japanese Val dive bomber rest on the grounds of the Admiral Chester Nimitz State Historical Park in Fredericksburg, Texas. This plane was transferred to Texas from New Britain by Australian officials. In much better condition at the same museum is a Japanese float plane and an SBD Dauntless. Author's Collection

MODELS

USS *Missouri* (BB-63) builder's model (approximately 20') at the Smithsonian, Washington, D.C. (1985). Author's Collection

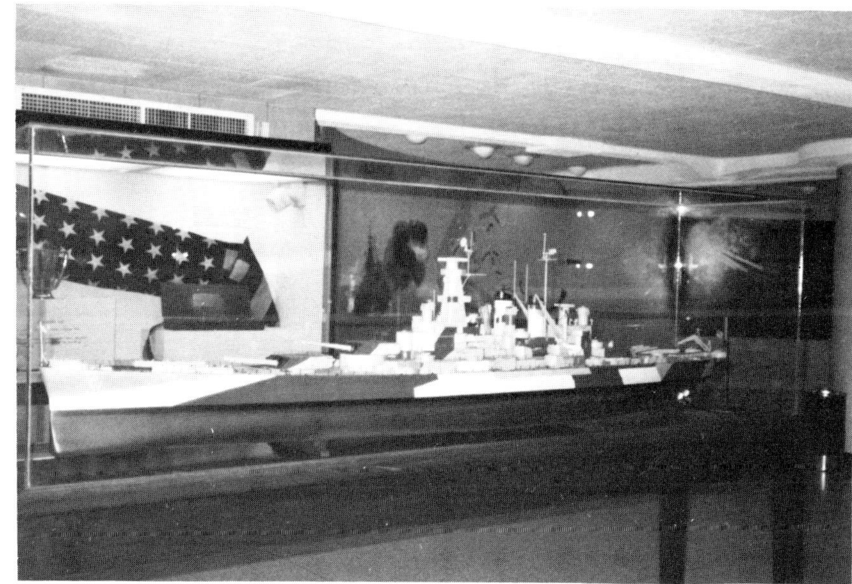

Seven-foot model of USS *North Carolina* on board BB-55 at Wilmington, N.C. (1985). Author's Collection

Waterline model (approximately 10') of USS *South Dakota* (BB-57) at "SoDak" memorial in Sioux Falls, S.D. (1985). Author's Collection

This 34-foot fiberglass model of USS *Arizona* (BB-39) was constructed by Cecil and Pat Gates of California. The model is six feet wide and has a draft of two feet. Author's Collection

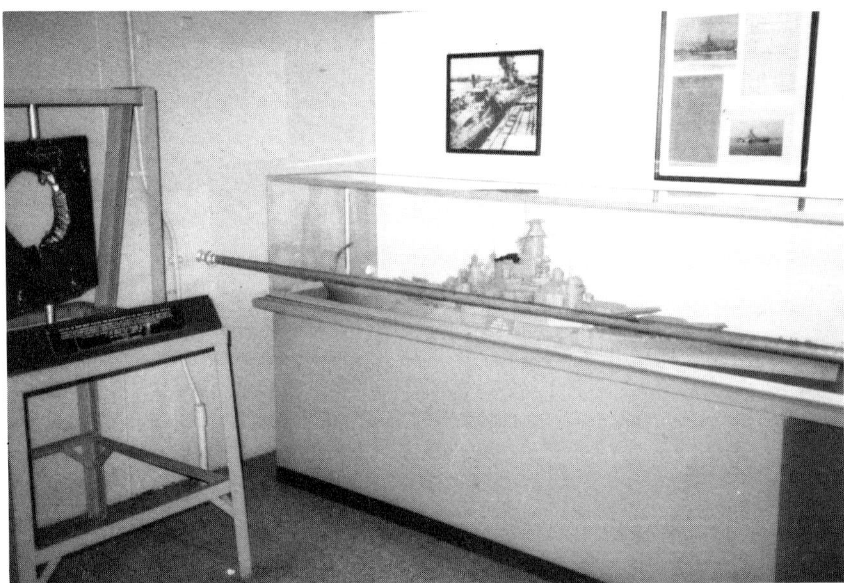

Six-foot model of USS *Massachusetts* on board BB-59 at Fall River, Mass. (1985). Author's Collection

Four-foot model of USS *Tennessee* (BB-43) inside Navy Memorial Museum, Washington, D.C., Navy Yard (1985). Author's Collection

Ten-foot builder's model of USS *Okalahoma* (BB-37) within the Kirkpatrick Center, Oklahoma City, Okla. (1985). Author's Collection

Close-up view of USS *California* builder's model (approximately 13') within the Navy-Marine Corps-Coast Guard Museum, San Francisco, Calif. (1985). Courtesy of Dean Schumacher

Builder's model of USS *Ranger* (CV-4) (about 17'), Navy Memorial Museum, Washington, D.C., Navy Yard (1985). Author's Collection

Four-foot, scratch-built model of USS *Essex* (CV-9), Buffalo & Erie County Naval & Servicemen's Park, Buffalo, N.Y. (1985). Author's Collection

Builder's model of USS *Yorktown* (CV-5) (approximately 18') at the Smithsonian, Washington, D.C. (1985). Author's Collection

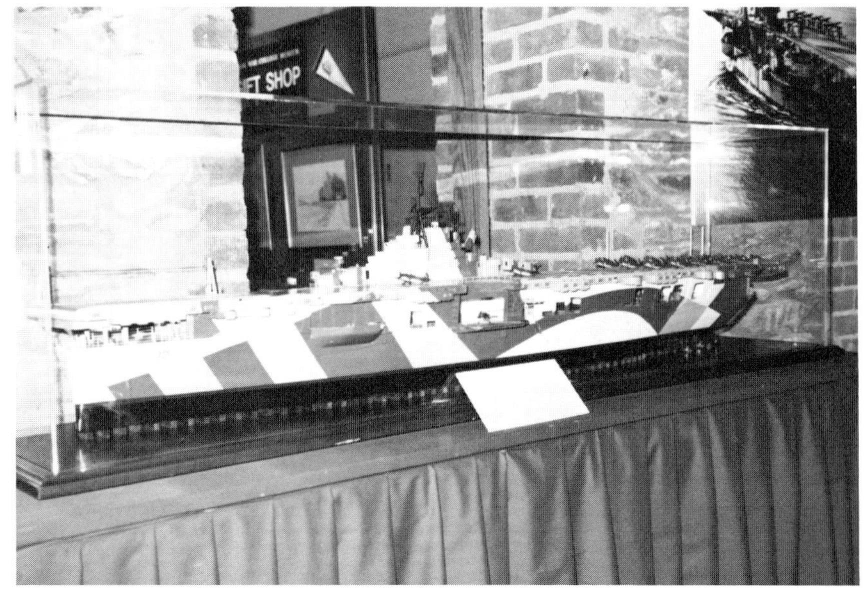

Five-foot, scratch-built model of USS *Yorktown* (CV-10) constructed by Albert Goodhue III within the Naval War College Museum, Newport, R.I. (1985). Author's Collection

Eleven-foot, scratch-built, radio-controlled model of USS *Enterprise* (CV-6). Navy veteran Hal Hague uses this model to assist Navy recruiters and for demonstrations to school children and veterans' groups. Courtesy of Hal Hague

Three-foot model of USS *Essex* (CV-9) at Hampton Roads Naval Museum, Norfolk, Va. (1985). Note other artifacts from *Essex* and *Indiana* (BB-58). Author's Collection

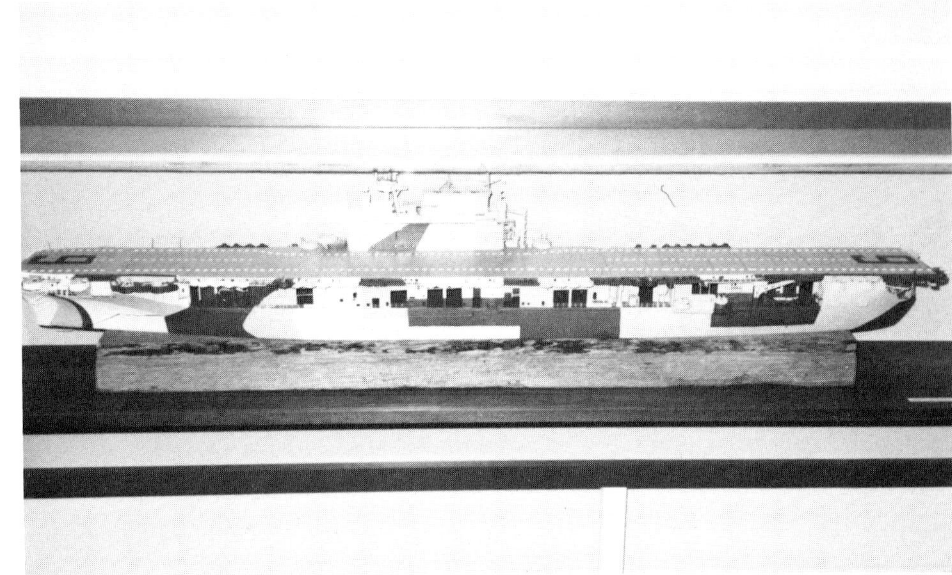

Four-foot, scratch-built model of USS *Enterprise* (CV-6) resting on a piece of the carrier's flight deck, Naval Aviation Museum, Pensacola, Fla. (1985). Author's Collection

Twelve-foot model of USS *Lexington* (CV-2) at the Mariner's Museum, Newport News, Va. (1985). Author's Collection

Five-foot model of USS *Columbia* (CL-56) in model dry dock, Navy Memorial Museum, Washington, D.C., Navy Yard (1985). Compare with photo in Chapter Three showing CL-56 entering dry dock in the Pacific. Author's Collection

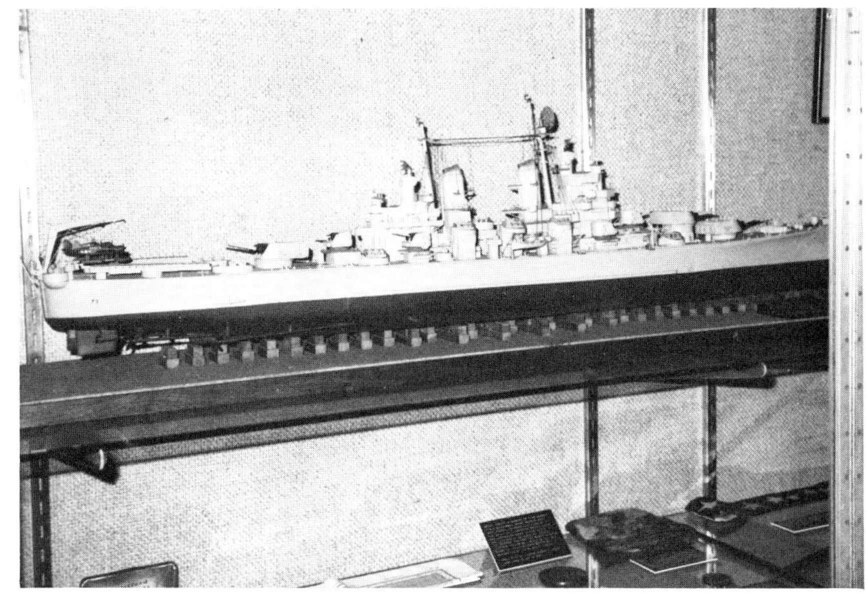

Four-foot model of USS *Pittsburgh* (CA-72) within the Naval Academy Museum, Annapolis, Md. (1985). Author's Collection

Six-foot model of USS *Augusta* (CA-31) at the Augusta-Richmond County Museum, Augusta, Ga. (1985). Built by Robert F. Sumrall, curator of ship models, U.S. Naval Academy Museum. Author's Collection

Builder's model (approximately 14') of the USS *Alaska* (CB-1), Navy Memorial Museum, Washington, D.C., Navy Yard (1985). Author's Collection

Close-up of USS *New Orleans* (CA-32) builder's model (approximately 10') on display at the Louisiana Maritime Museum, New Orleans, La. Courtesy of Louisiana Maritime Museum

Five-foot model of USS *Chicago* (CA-29), Navy Memorial Museum, Washington, D.C., Navy Yard (1985). Author's Collection

Four-foot model of USS *Brooklyn* (CL-40) at the Museum of Science and Industry, Chicago, Ill. (1985). Author's Collection

Five-foot model of USS *Pensacola* (CA-24), Naval Aviation Museum, Pensacola, Fla. (1985). Author's Collection

Four-foot model of USS *Atlanta* (CL-51), Navy Memorial museum, Washington, D.C., Navy Yard (1985). Author's Collection

Five-foot model of USS *Manley* (DD-74) – also APD-1, the Navy's first high speed transport to be converted from a destroyer – at the Navy Memorial Museum, Washington, D.C., Navy Yard (1985). Author's Collection

Three-foot model of USS *Cassin Young* (DD-793) at the Naval War College Museum, Newport, R.I. (1985). Author's Collection

Five-foot model of a PT boat with the USS *Massachusetts,* Fall River, Mass. (1985). This model was used in the 1965 movie *In Harm's Way.* Author's Collection

CHAPTER THREE CRUISERS

PRESIDENTIAL UNIT CITATION

USS Atlanta	CL-51
USS Houston	CA-30
USS San Francisco	CA-38

NAVY UNIT COMMENDATION

USS Birmingham	CL-62
USS Cleveland	CL-55
USS Columbia	CL-56
USS Denver	CL-58
USS Helena	CL-50
USS Honolulu	CL-48
USS Marblehead	CL-12
USS Montpelier	CL-57
USS Philadelphia	CL-41
USS Portland	CA-33
USS Salt Lake City	CA-25
USS Santa Fe	CL-60
USS St. Louis	CL-49

ULTIMATE SACRIFICE

USS Houston	CA-30....1942
USS Quincy	CA-39....1942
USS Vincennes	CA-44....1942
USS Astoria	CA-34....1942
USS Atlanta	CL-51....1942
USS Juneau	CL-52....1942
USS Northampton	CA-26....1942
USS Chicago	CA-29....1943
USS Helena	CL-50....1943
USS Indianapolis	CA-35....1945

BATTLE STARS

San Francisco	CA-38....17
Minneapolis	CA-36....17
New Orleans	CA-32....16
Portland	CA-33....16
San Diego	CL-53....15
San Juan	CL-54....13
Cleveland	CL-55....13
Montpelier	CL-57....13
Pensacola	CA-24....13
Louisville	CA-28....13
Wichita	CA-45....13
Santa Fe	CL-60....13
Salt Lake City	CA-25....11
St. Louis	CL-49....11
Chester	CA-27....11
Mobile	CL-63....11
Denver	CL-58....11
Boise	CL-47....10
Indianapolis	CA-35....10
Boston	CA-69....10
Columbia	CL-56....10
Nashville	CL-43....10
Biloxi	CL-80....9
Oakland	CL-95....9
Phoenix	CL-46....9
Baltimore	CA-68....9
Birmingham	CL-62....9
Honolulu	CL-48....8
Canberra	CA-70....7
Tuscaloosa	CA-37....7
Helena	CL-50....7
Northampton	CA-26....6
Detroit	CL-8....6
Miami	CL-89....6
Vincennes	CL-64....6
Pasadena	CL-65....5
Atlanta	CL-51....5
Philadelphia	CL-41....5
Astoria	CL-90....5
Wilkes-Barre	CL-103....4
Juneau	CL-52....4
Brooklyn	CL-40....4
Quincy	CA-71....4
Flint	CL-97....4
Reno	CL-96....3
Savannah	CL-42....3
Alaska	CB-1....3
Augusta	CA-31....3
Chicago	CA-29....3
Astoria	CA-34....3
Raleigh	CL-7....3
Houston	CL-81....3
Vicksburg	CL-86....2
Duluth	CL-87....2
Marblehead	CL-12....2
Houston	CA-30....2
Guam	CB-2....2
Vincennes	CA-44....2
Pittsburgh	CA-72....2
Topeka	CL-67....2
Springfield	CL-66....2
Richmond	CL-9....2
Atlanta	CL-104....2
Oklahoma City	CL-91....2
Omaha	CL-4....1
St. Paul	CA-73....1
Chicago	CA-136....1
Quincy	CA-39....1
Cincinnati	CL-6....1
Concord	CL-10....1
Amsterdam	CL-101....1
Trenton	CL-11....1
Tucson	CL-98....1
Dayton	CL-105....1

MEMORIES

The tendency to remember only the very best or worst of things may apply to the American public's memories of their U.S. Navy cruisers during World War II. After Pearl Harbor major American surface-action defeats primarily involved cruisers, and on no occasion did American cruisers score a clear-cut surface victory equal to their defeats at Savo Island in August 1942 or Tassafaronga in November 1942. Still, there was much for which American cruisers deserve to be remembered. When viewed in full, the history of these ships records success and triumph as much as sacrifice and frustration. From 7 December 1941 until 2 September 1945, 74 United States cruisers – two battlecruisers, 25 heavy cruisers and 47 light cruisers – fought in at least one battle against Germany, Japan or both and therefore received recognition by the award of a battle star. Cruisers participated in nearly all major surface battles and air-sea battles. Highly adaptable to unforeseen wartime needs, cruisers expanded their functions far beyond original expectations. Before the war was over cruisers had traded broadsides with enemy battleships, had practically steamed onto enemy-held islands to provide close gunfire support, and had even transformed nine of their sisters into aircraft carriers. (CVLs).

Heavy with awards and honors at the end of World War II, most of these cruisers rested in reserve for varying periods before being towed off to be broken up. Others, however, continued to serve through the Korean War era and even the Vietnam conflict before also being scrapped. Of the 74 cruisers to win one or more battle stars in World War II, only four cruisers and one light carrier that had been converted from a cruiser hull still exist in 1985. The carrier belongs to Spain (*Dedalo*, formerly the *Cabot*), two cruisers belong to Chile (*O'Higgins*, formerly the *Brooklyn*; and *Chacabuco*, previously *Capitan Prat* and *Nashville*), while neither of the two remaining cruisers (*Chicago* and *Oklahoma City*) is on active duty and neither resembles its World War II appearance. Unfortunately, no World War II era cruiser has been preserved in its original configuration and only the USS *Little Rock*, which was built during World War II but won no battle stars and has had her original appearance greatly altered, serves as a memorial. She is located at the Buffalo & Erie County Naval & Servicemen's Park in Buffalo, N.Y.

Cruisers were an important and integral part of the United States Navy long before World War II. From the beginning of the American Navy, there was a need for the functions eventually supplied by cruisers. Early sailing ships departed their home ports to scout and probe, to raid enemy commerce along well-established trade routes, and to close with and destroy enemy warships of relatively equal strength. To accomplish the several functions assigned to it, a cruiser had to be fast. It had to bring news of trouble before the trouble arrived, it had to overtake commercial vessels, and it had to possess sufficient speed to run away from larger, more heavily armed and armored ships which it could not outfight.

The coming of World War II did not diminish the early functions of the cruiser. Rather, new functions and expectations were added. But even with the new demands in World War II the basics of the cruiser changed little. Always the cruiser would be fast. It would for the most part be of medium tonnage, be capable of steaming long distances, possess a minimum of armor protection and carry armament that would allow it to join battle with any warship except a battlewagon. Too, the cruiser would provide an optimum return in terms of versatility and gunpower versus cost. When compared to the construction cost and extended operating expense of a battleship, the cruiser was an enticing bargain.

The terms "heavy cruiser" and "light cruiser" had expression during World War I and the distinction in the use of "heavy" or "light" depended primarily on whether a cruiser was scouting (light) or raiding shipping lanes (heavy). The more precise usage of the terms that would distinguish the two types of cruisers came into being soon after World War I when the Washington Naval Conference convened in November 1921 and the London Conference convened in January 1930. These conferences, inspired by a need for reducing government expenditures as well as a desire for peace, primarily addressed reduction in battleships. Even so, cruisers received meaningful attention.

By early 1922, when the governments of the United States, Great Britain, Japan, France and Italy approved the Washington Naval Treaty, the definition of a heavy cruiser was determined to be a warship not in excess of 10,000 tons with guns not capable of firing shells over 8 inches in diameter. A light cruiser would now be defined as a warship with gun calibers not exceeding 6 inches in diameter. The treaty set the same 5-5-3 ratio (United States, Great Britain and Japan, respectively) for heavy cruisers that was agreed upon for battleships but set no limits for the number of light cruisers that the signatories might possess. American delegates, who greatly favored the 8-inch gunned cruiser for potential use in the Pacific, championed the move for the limitation on heavy cruisers, while the British, who were quite sensitive to their need to protect widespread and extensive sea lanes, were the major proponents for an unlimited number of light cruisers.

With their definitions formalized by the Washington Conference, a class of 10 new American

USS *Salt Lake City* (CA-25) and her only sister ship *Pensacola* (CA-24) were the first two treaty cruisers. Navy Unit Commendation winner for her performance during the 26 March 1943 Battle of the Komandorski Islands, *Salt Lake City* is seen here in pre-war appearance. *Salt Lake City* received 11 battle stars in World War II; *Pensacola* had 13. USN

USS *Chester* (CA-27) and the other six members of the *Northampton*-class resembled the *Pensacola* and *Salt Lake City* (see previous photo). Instead of carrying four main 8-inch turrets, the *Northampton* class carried three. *Chester* was struck amidships on her starboard side by a submarine torpedo in October 1942 and was out of action for nearly a year, but still won 11 battle stars. USN

cruisers (*Omaha* class) authorized during World War I (1916) and completed after the war's end became "light" cruisers as their largest guns were 6-inch. Slow, armored cruisers that had been built around the turn of the century technically became heavy cruisers as they carried some 8-inch guns, but many of these cruisers would soon be scrapped in compliance with the treaty or due to obsolescence and none would fight in World War II. Many, however, would pass their names on to newer cruisers that would participate in the 1941-1945 conflict. Consequently, the first true "treaty" heavy cruisers were the two 8-inch gunned cruisers of the *Pensacola* class authorized in 1924.

The limitations agreed upon at Washington in 1922 along with later agreements at London in 1930-1931 resulted in some design constrictions with consequent performance disappointments. Newer construction techniques and design alterations would remedy early problems until the last pre-war heavy cruisers authorized in 1940 (*Baltimore* class) were freed from treaty limitations by the withdrawal of Japan in 1936 and the onset of the European war in September 1939. Still, from 1922 until 1939 American cruisers would conform to promises made at the Washington Conference.

The *Pensacola* and *Salt Lake City* were only two of

Authorized in 1916, the *Omaha*-class light cruisers were not completed until after that war but they proved their worth in World War II. *Detroit* (CL-8), shown here, led the *Omaha* class with six battle stars in World War II. USN

eight ships authorized in 1924. The original legislation called for eight cruisers, but the building of the last six was delayed due to appropriation problems, thanks in part to the conservative fiscal policies of President Calvin Coolidge. To some degree the delay was fortuitous. The *Pensacolas* were deficient in freeboard, rolled heavily at slow speeds and sacrificed a portion of their armor protection in order to carry ten 8-inch guns in four turrets. When the other six ships of the 1924 authorization were built – the *Northampton* class – changes were implemented. The most obvious change in the Northamptons was the arrangement of nine 8-inch guns in three turrets. Too, there was an improvement in armor, but until the end of treaty limitations and the design of the *Baltimore* class, all American cruisers were insufficiently armored.

In 1927 legislation was submitted to build 25 cruisers, but final authorization in 1929 called for 15, and when the London Treaty became operational in January 1931, the allowed number for heavy cruisers was reduced to 10. From this building program came the two heavy cruisers of the *Portland* class, the seven heavy cruisers of the *New Orleans* class and the one heavy cruiser of the *Wichita* class. The Northamptons, Portlands, New Orleans and *Wichita*-class cruisers were built between 1928 and 1939 and all were in commission before war broke out in Europe. Along with the earlier *Pensacola* class, each of these ships would see more than their fair share of the coming global conflict.

Although the provisions of the London Treaty went into effect on 1 January 1931, provisions concerning cruisers would soon prove to have little meaning. Limitations within the London Treaty even more precisely distinguished heavy cruisers from light cruisers: a light cruiser could displace a maximum of 10,000 tons, guns could not be more than 6.1 inches, and for the first time there would be aggregate tonnage limitations on light cruisers as well as the heavy cruisers. But before these provisions could meaningfully affect the U.S.Navy, political changes in Japan and Germany would inspire rearmament instead of disarmament. Beginning in 1931, military influence in Japanese political affairs would begin a long series of treaty violations. Of particular significance to naval interests was the appearance in the early 1930s of the Japanese *Mogami*-class cruisers. The Mogamis were supposedly light cruisers of 8,500 tons. Armed with fifteen 6-inch guns they would be a match for any 8-inch gunned heavy cruiser due to the more rapid rate of fire of their 6-inch guns. In fact, these ships would top out at 12,500 tons and by 1941 they had been modified to carry eight 8-inch guns to become heavy cruisers. Although the variance between the actual and announced figures on these cruisers was not known outside Japan, the U.S. Navy was sufficiently impressed with Japanese claims; a class of cruisers (*Brooklyn* class) was designed and built to meet the potential threat.

By the spring of 1933 Franklin D. Roosevelt had become president and the U.S. Navy could not have asked for a stronger friend in high places. Formerly assistant secretary of the Navy during President Wilson's tenure, Roosevelt quickly turned attention to the Navy he loved so dearly. Accomplishing several objectives with one action, he allotted $238 million to fight unemployment by providing work in American shipyards and to strengthen the Navy. Funds from Roosevelt's June 1933 grant, along with funds from the 1934 Vinson-Trammell Act, built the seven ships of the *Brooklyn* class. These gave the United States its answer to the Japanese Mogamis and they were the country's first modern light cruisers since the completion of the *Omaha* class in January 1925. The Vinson-Trammell Act also provided funding for the two light cruisers of the *Helena* class. The first two Atlantas

The *Portland* (CA-33), pictured here late in World War II, and sister ship *Indianapolis* (CA-35), were derivatives of the *Northampton* class. Note the location of the mast over the aft stack and the open bridge as these parts of the *Portland* still exist in a memorial to the cruiser in Fort Allen Park, Portland, Me. USN

The seven-member *Brooklyn* class plus *Helena* (CL-50) and *St. Louis* (CL-49) was a response of the U.S. Navy to the Japanese *Mogami* class. The *Brooklyn* and *Nashville* still exist in the navy of Chile with their overall configuration similar to their World War II configuration. Seen here is *Honolulu* not long after her 1938 commissioning date. The old *Phoenix* (CL-46), renamed *General Belgrano* by Argentina, looked essentially the same when she was sunk by a British submarine in 1982 during the Falklands War. USN

The seven members of the *New Orleans* class were also treaty cruisers, and as with other treaty cruisers and the Omahas they bore the brunt of action early in World War II. *Minneapolis* (CA-36) (pictured) tied another *New Orleans*-class cruiser, *San Francisco*, for most battle stars awarded to cruisers (17). Class leader *New Orleans* is credited with 16, but a 17th is presently under challenge. USN

Wichita (CA-45) was the last treaty heavy cruiser. The one-ship *Wichita* class was essentially a *Brooklyn*-class cruiser with 8-inch guns instead of 6-inch. *Wichita* served in both the Atlantic and Pacific and was awarded 13 battle stars. USN

were authorized in 1934, the second two in 1938 and last four in 1940.

By late 1939 and early 1940, problems in the Far East and Europe were such that Congress soon passed the Naval Expansion Act and the Two-Ocean Navy Bill. These pre-Pearl Harbor programs authorized the *Baltimore*-class heavy cruisers and the *Alaska*-class battlecruisers. Not all of the cruisers authorized in these last two classes would be complete in time to participate in World War II.

In general it can be stated that the later heavy cruisers were indeed heavier, better protected with armor, slightly faster and had a greater range. Most of the later light cruisers displaced the same tonnage as the heavy cruisers described in the treaty and mounted fewer main armament 6-inch guns. And as World War II progressed, all cruisers added medium and light anti-aircraft guns in every available topside location along with added gun directors and updated radar installations.

During World War II, cruisers were still utilized for raiding (mostly tracking German raiders), scouting (particularly with their planes), battling enemy surface forces and serving as flagships. Additionally, cruisers filled new and important roles in defending carriers from air attack and in supporting amphibious operations by providing fire support close inshore.

The 18 pre-war "treaty" cruisers repaid the taxpayer many times over in service to the country. All won battle stars, all suffered damage and casualties, and seven of the 18 (39 percent) were lost as a reslut of battle damage. The *Baltimore*-class heavy cruisers were not available until after the Pacific war began, but seven of the class won battle stars and proved especially useful in the final stages of the war when the Navy closed on the shores of Japanese island possessions as well as on the home islands themselves. None of the Baltimores was lost and the damage they incurred was relatively light. As fate would have it, only the pre-war "treaty" heavy cruisers would engage in the surface battles of 1942 and 1943. The Baltimores arrived after the character of the war had changed and fleet battles had become almost exclusively air-sea battles.

In the first year of the war American heavy cruisers assumed a primary role that in pre-war thinking would have been served by battleships. After Pearl Harbor, heavy cruisers–and light cruisers, for that matter–found themselves in the first line of surface defense even when it meant facing Japanese battleships. This did not occur often, and at war's end the American heavy cruisers' biggest problem had proved to be fast-running, long-lance torpedoes launched by Japanese destroyers. Throughout the war, however, the heavy cruisers fulfilled all the functions mentioned earlier and were invaluable in both the Pacific and Atlantic theaters.

The congressional legislation of 1940 authorized warships of many classes, but probably none of the authorizations was as unique as the six-ship class of large cruisers (official designation), more often referred to as "battlecruisers." By 1940 several fast German pocket battleships carrying 11-inch guns had caused alarm in Allied navies, and there was a concern that a similar class was being constructed by Japan. Although the Japanese were not building such a class, the United States Navy felt a need to respond to the potential threat in the Pacific and known threat in the Atlantic.

Response to the Axis threat was the *Alaska*-class

authorization in July 1940 of six ships (picture of *Alaska* model in Model section). *Alaska* and *Guam* would be commissioned in time to serve and earn three and two battle stars respectively. Although the recipients of adverse reviews by some naval authorities and historians, the Alaskas did fill the void between the slow, pre-1940s, big-gun battleships and fast, small-gunned cruisers. In theory the Alaskas could defeat any other cruiser thanks to their heavier armor and larger guns and could race away from slower battleships that could outgun them. By the time the two Alaskas that did see combat were commissioned, the character of the Pacific war was such that the functions of the ships were limited to air defense for carriers and shore bombardment. In these roles the ships were superb but not unique. History might have recorded a more glowing report of these ships if they had been available in time to protect the few American carriers struggling to defend Guadalcanal or meet the "Tokyo Express" in 1942-1943.

Light cruisers were not built to absorb severe damage; their functions reflected this characteristic. A light cruiser first and foremost was a fast ship assigned duties as a raider, a scout for the battle fleet, and a destroyer flotilla leader. Relatively inexpensive ships, their functions expanded in the 1930s when carrier planes and cruiser-borne float planes assumed the function of scouting. By 1941 light cruisers were serving as anti-aircraft platforms, shore bombardment vessels, and convoy escorts. In surface combat it was expected that the U.S. Navy's pre-war light cruisers would counter enemy destroyers and light cruisers, but on several memorable occasions they had to fire their 6-inch and 5-inch shells at battleships and heavy cruisers. Though never a match for battleships, the later classes of American light cruisers with their improved armor and rapid-fire 6-inch guns were felt to be the equal of enemy heavy cruisers.

During the course of World War II, 47 American light cruisers earned one or more battle stars. Of these 17 were in commission on 7 December 1941. When the war ended only three (*Atlanta* CL-51, *Juneau* CL-52 and *Helena* CL-50) had been lost to enemy action with the major factor in the sinkings being the torpedo. Of the seven heavy cruisers and three light cruisers lost by the United States Navy in World War II, nine were hit by torpedoes. Aerial torpedoes killed *Chicago*, submarine torpedoes killed *Indianapolis* and *Juneau* while destroyer-launched torpedoes killed six others.

Forty years after World War II the cruiser still commands a major position in the U.S. Navy. Though the 8-inch and 6-inch guns are gone, missiles and rapid-fire smaller caliber weapons give the present-day cruiser a punch her World War II ancestors would envy.

San Diego (CL-53) is shown here in the role for which she and her sister ships were intended. The *Atlanta*-class light cruisers were designed, in part, to provide anti-aircraft protection and they performed well in protecting carriers. The only two cruisers of the class to engage in a surface action (*Atlanta* and *Juneau*) were mortally damaged. USN

St. Paul (CA-73) was the last of the non-treaty *Baltimore*-class heavy cruisers to serve in the U.S. Navy. Seven members of the class won battle stars with long-serving *St. Paul*–pictured here in the early 1970s–recording only one in World War II but eight for Korea and eight for Vietnam. USN

Columbia (CL-56) was one of 22 *Cleveland*-class cruisers to win battle stars. The Clevelands were highly successful and even had nine hulls converted into light aircraft carriers (CVLs). *Columbia* is seen here in a forward Pacific dry dock late in the war. In the Model section of this book is a picture showing a model of both *Columbia* and the dry dock. USN

This painting by Joe T. Fleischman depicts the final moments of the *Houston* (CA-30), March 1942. Legend has it that Australian sailors during the war would stand at the mention of Houston's name for engaging overwhelming odds and fighting to the finish. For this action *Houston* received a Presidential Unit Citation after the war when the details of her battle and loss became known. USN

MEMORIES OF SACRIFICE

As mentioned above, seven heavy cruisers and three light cruisers were sunk by enemy action during World War II. All 10 cruisers were lost to Japanese forces and enemy torpedoes were primarily responsible for the damage that caused the sinkings. *Astoria* (CA-34) was the only cruiser to be lost as a result of gunfire alone.

When considering sacrifice among heavy cruisers, perhaps the most often recalled memory is that of the *Indianapolis*. The war was all but over in late July 1945 when CA-35 was hit by two torpedoes soon after the cruiser had delivered parts of the Hiroshima atomic bomb to Tinian. *Indianapolis* went down quickly and the plight of her survivors was not known until a plane *not* looking for the ship discovered debris and her men in the water. Only 316 of 1,196 officers and men survived the attack and 107 hours in the water; the majority of *Indianapolis'* men died in the water. The loss of the *Houston* (CA-30) was similar to that of the *Indianapolis* in that the men who died did not expire quickly. Fighting against overwhelming odds, *Houston* went down during the very early hours of 1 March 1942 in Sunda Strait. Less than 300 of the cruiser's crew eventually survived over three years in Japanese prison camps. The full story of the *Houston* was not known until after the war and, therefore, received relatively less publicity.

Over 900 cruiser men were lost on the night of 8-9 August 1942 during the Battle of Savo Island. Along with the Australian cruiser *Canberra*, the U.S. Navy lost three *New Orleans*-class heavy cruisers: *Astoria* (216 officers and men), *Quincy* (370 officers and men) and *Vincennes* (332 officers and men). Caught totally unprepared for action, the only favorable comment about the battle is that the Japanese force of seven cruisers and one destroyer did not continue on to attack the transports which were still unloading men and supplies in the early hours of the Guadalcanal invasion.

Just as the *New Orleans class lost three of her*

members, so too did the Northampton class. Already-mentioned *Houston* was the first to be lost and she was followed on 30 November 1942 by class leader *Northampton* (CA-26) and on 30 January 1943 *Chicago* (CA-29) went under. *Northampton* took two destroyer-launched torpedoes off Tassafaronga Point while *Chicago* took six aerial torpedoes off Rennell Island. Nearly 150 men were killed or missing when *Chicago* sank, but only 49 were lost with *Northampton*. As with other ships that were lost, many survivors reported to newer ships to continue the war. A considerable number of *Northampton* sailors went on to serve on the battleship *Iowa* and *Baltimore*-class heavy cruiser *Boston*.

In pure percentages, no cruiser loss was more sacrificial than *Juneau* (CL-52). After participating in the 13 November 1942 night action off Guadalcanal in which she was hit by gunfire and a destroyer-launched torpedo, *Juneau* was slowly steaming away from Guadalcanal in company with several other survivors of the battle when she was hit by a submarine-launched torpedo. Only 10 of 700 survived the cataclysmic explosion. Lost with *Juneau* were the five Sullivan brothers. A new cruiser inherited the name of the lost CL-52 and a new destroyer was named *The Sullivans* (DD-537), but the Navy therefter discouraged members of the same family from serving on the same ship.

Juneau was an *Atlanta*-class cruiser mounting 5-inch guns as main armament. The members of this class were designed as destroyer flotilla leaders and to provide anti-aircraft protection and they were not expected to engage in surface battles with larger ships. Only two did fight in a surface engagement and both were lost. Class leader *Atlanta* fought in the same 13 November night action as her sister ship and was crippled by gunfire and a torpedo. Had she not been so close to enemy-held territory, she might have been towed to safety. Instead, she was scuttled by her surviving crew and she carried 172 men with her to the bottom of "Ironbottom Bay."

Helena (CL-50), unlike *Atlanta* and *Juneau*, was designed and built to fight surface battles against large warships, but few ships of any design were able to

Less than a month after this picture was taken, three of the four cruisers closest to the camera would be lost in the August 1942 Battle of Savo Island. Those to die were *Astoria* (bottom), *Vincennes* (second from the bottom) and *Quincy* (third from bottom). Fourth from the bottom is the cruiser *New Orleans*. NA

Atlanta (CL-51) lived less than a year, but she was very active winning five battle stars and a Presidential Unit Citation for her heroic last fight in the Naval Battle of Guadalcanal. Regrettably, this fighting ship does not have a significant memorial. USN

withstand two torpedoes nearly side-by-side amidships. *Helena* had taken one torpedo on her starboard side during the attck on Pearl Harbor and was quickly repaired. During the 6 July 1943 Battle of Kula Gulf, however, *Helena* lost her bow to one torpedo hit on the port side and then took two destroyer-launched torpedoes that struck on the same side within a few feet of each other amidships. A total of 168 men were lost during the attack and in the 11 days following. Many survivors suffered through an unwanted adventure by swimming to a nearby island and then hiding from the enemy until rescued. Even then harrowing days were not over for all as many veterans of *Helena* went on to the new light cruiser *Houston* (CL-81), and they would experience again the devastation of Japanese torpedoes.

In most instances there was a correlation between the loss of a cruiser and the number of men killed in the fatal attack. There were, however, a few exceptions. *Northampton* lost only 49 men (too many, of course) when she went down while *Birmingham* lost 237 when the carrier *Princeton* blew-up beside her on 24 October 1944. *Savannah* lost 197 men (approximately 20 percent of her complement) to a German radio-controlled bomb near Salerno on 11 September 1943, but steamed away on her own for repairs and returned to service. Despite her terrible human toll, *Birmingham* was not in danger of sinking, but *Savannah* was seriously damaged – down by the bow 11 feet – and was saved only by outstanding damage control.

Pearl Harbor and Savo Island (7-8 August 1942) were the two worst defeats the U.S. Navy suffered in World War II, but the 30 November 1942 Battle of Tassafaronga was almost as bad as Savo Island. As noted, only *Northampton* sank, but *New Orleans* lost her bow back to the number two 8-inch turret, *Minneapolis* lost her bow back to number one turret and *Pensacola* took a torpedo aft. All three cruisers were lost for months; *Pensacola* suffered 125 men lost, 178 died aboard *New Orleans* while the losses on *Minneapolis* are nearly always described as "fearsome." *Minneapolis* and *New Orleans* returned to combat in late 1943 and fought through the remainder of the war without serious losses, but *Pensacola* – which also returned in late 1943 to fight to war's end – suffered again off Iwo Jima with 17 lost to six hits by enemy shore batteries.

San Francisco, Portland, Boise, St. Louis, Honolulu and *Salt Lake City* were also damaged in surface battles with the Japanese. *San Francisco* took 45 hits and lost 81 men during the night action of 13 November 1942 after having been crashed the previous afternoon by an enemy plane that killed 50 and destroyed the aft control station. The loss of the aft control station was particularly felt late that night when the force flag officer, commanding officer and most of his staff were killed by large-caliber hits on the bridge. *Portland* fought alongside *San Francisco* and suffered considerable damage in the same 13 November night action

Whereas only 49 men died when *Northampton* sank after the battle off Tassafaronga, *Birmingham*–which was not sunk–lost 237 when carrier *Princeton* blew up beside her 24 October 1944. On 4 May 1945 *Birmingham* lost 51 when hit by a kamikaze. *Princeton* survivors presented a plaque to the *Birmingham* after their mutual day of sorrow and their respective reunion associations still retain close ties. USN

Crewmen fight fires resulting from a German radio-controlled glide bomb. The bomb hit Savannah's number three turret, passed through three decks, blew holes in the bottom and side of the cruiser and killed 197 men. Note wounded and dead on deck. Not apparent in this picture is the flooding below decks that would have caused the loss of the cruiser except for outstanding damage control. NA

New Orleans (CA-32) lost 120 feet of her bow and the number one 8-inch turret to a Japanese torpedo during the November 1942 Battle of Tassafaronga. She is seen here with a temporary bow in December 1942. With a new bow and replacements for the 178 men lost at Tassafaronga, *New Orleans* returned to service and fought on to the end of the war. NA

against a superior Japanese force that included the battleship *Hiei*. Before morning, *Portland* had taken a torpedo hit from a destroyer that left her able to steam only in circles. *Boise* took at least six major-caliber shells and dozens of smaller caliber hits and came very close to blowing up during the 11-12 October 1942 Battle of Cape Esperance. Fortunately, enemy shells opened the hull, which flooded forward magazines just as it appeared fires would detonate them. With 107 dead *Boise* limped away from the battle still burning and at the same time taking on water. Six months later, however, she was back in service.

St. Louis, Honolulu and *Salt Lake City* – like the three cruisers just discussed – were constantly in battle and the law of averages would seem to dictate that sooner or later they would incur damage and lose officers and men. *St. Louis* was quite active during the Solomons campaign, often alongside her sister ship *Helena*, and she was fortunate not to take a serious blow until the 13 July 1943 Battle of Kolombangara in which she lost a chunk of her bow to a destroyer torpedo. *Honolulu*, a survivor of the battles of Tassafaronga and Kula Gulf, took a destroyer torpedo at Kolombangara that dropped her bow in a manner similar to that of *Minneapolis* at Tassafaronga; incredibly, no lives were lost aboard *Honolulu*. *Salt Lake City*, a veteran of the Battle of Cape Esperance, was part of a small force that fought a three-hour battle off the Komandorski Islands 26 March 1943. There, she was hit several times and lost power, but a determined attack by escorting destroyers and her big guns helped convince the enemy to break off the action. The major target during the long battle, *Salt Lake City* suffered few casualties and was quickly repaired.

American cruisers suffered as much damage from enemy planes during World War II as they did in surface actions. Aerial torpedoes struck *Raleigh, Denver, Honolulu, Canberra, Houston* (CL-81) and *Birmingham*. *Raleigh* was struck at Pearl Harbor, listed heavily, but did not touch bottom (her veterans stress that fact). *Denver* suffered 20 dead in a late November 1943 attack in the Solomons; *Honolulu* lost 60 sailors on 20 October 1944 off the Philippines; and *Canberra* lost 23 on 13 October 1944, the day before *Houston* (CL-81) took the first of her aerial torpedoes. On the 16th *Houston* took her second aerial torpedo which increased her casualty list to 55 killed as she and *Canberra* – "Bait Division One" – moved slowly away from Formosa.

Aerial bombs damaged *Savannah* (discussed above), *Birmingham, San Juan, St. Louis* and *Marblehead*. When one considers the hundreds of bombs aimed at U.S. Navy cruisers during World War II, the number of hits was amazingly low, testimonial in part to the seamanship of officers on the bridge and efficiency of ships' gunners. Often-wounded *Birmingham* suffered her first wounds to ship and personnel off Empress Augusta Bay on 9 November 1943 when she took an aerial torpedo and two bombs. Anti-aircraft cruiser *San Juan* took a bomb during the Battle of Santa Cruz that passed through the ship before exploding. *St. Louis* lost 23 men when a bomb hit her on 14 February 1944 near Bougainville and *Marblehead* took two bombs off Java in February which killed 12.

All classifications of American combat ships felt the pain inflicted by Japanese kamikaze pilots, and cruisers received their share. The plane that struck *San Francisco* in November 1942 was not an "official" kamikaze as this special suicide corps was not created until late 1944, but crashes such as the one against

Minneapolis (CA-36) was also a victim at Tassafaronga, losing her bow to a destroyer-launched torpedo. After repairs she returned to combat and was particularly effective in shore bombardment and call-fire. Off Guam she received considerable praise from Marines ashore in appreciation for her effective gunfire. USN & USN

CA-38 demonstrated the damage that could result from a human-guided bomb. This crash, and others by enemy pilots either wounded or over-zealous in giving their all for the Emperor, set a precedent for what would follow off the Philippines, Iwo Jima and Okinawa.

Birmingham took her last severe damage on 4 May 1945 off Okinawa from a kamikaze and added another 51 officers and men to her total casualty list of nearly 400 for the war. The kamikaze that hit *Indianapolis* on 31 March 1945 off Okinawa killed only nine, but it began the chain of events that eventuated in the cruiser's loss a few months later.

St. Louis, Louisville and *Columbia* were struck by two or more kamikazes. *St. Louis* took both of her's on the same day off the Philippines in November 1944 and lost 16. *Louisville* was also crashed off the Philippines in January 1945 by two kamikazes and suffered the loss of 32; on 5 June 1945 she was hit again, but suffered the loss of only one man. *Columbia* had 13 killed when hit 6 January 1945 off the Philippines, and added 24 to her list of dead and missing three days later when crashed again.

Because of their speed, cruisers were not often targets for submarine torpedoes, but *Indianapolis* and *Juneau* were lost to submarine torpedoes while *Chester* and *Reno* were damaged. *Chester* lost 11 killed on 20 October 1942 and *Reno* emerged from her travail with only two lost. *Chester* was able to steam away to safety and repairs under her own power, but *Reno* was nearly lost due to flooding.

Not all losses and severe damage to cruisers resulted from enemy action. *Pittsburgh* lost her bow in a typhoon on 5 June 1945 but did not lose any of her crew. *Nashville* and *Honolulu* were not as fortunate,

though, as *Nashville* lost 18 men in a turret explosion 12 May 1943 and *Honolulu* lost five men to "friendly gunfire" as she retired from the Philippines after being hit by an aerial torpedo 20 October 1944.

It is sometimes argued that the first American casualty of World War II was a cruiser sailor. There is support for this contention as an American sailor died aboard *Augusta* on 20 August 1937 when the ship was caught in Shanghai during fighting between the Japanese and Chinese. *Augusta* veterans are yet convinced that the shelling of their cruiser was no accident.

This close-up view of Presidential Unit Citation recipient *San Francisco* (CA-38) shows how the cruiser was peppered by enemy shells of varying size. The area circled in black shows the temporary patches covering entry holes made by the shells that took the lives of the officers commanding the ship during the Naval Battle of Guadalcanal. This section of the ship is presently part of a memorial to the cruiser and her men. USN

Despite victory in the 13 July 1943 Battle of Kolombangara, *St. Louis* lost a significant portion of her bow to an enemy destroyer-launched torpedo. Another ship behind the cruiser partially obscures the extent of damage to the Navy Unit Commendation winner. USN

Another Navy Unit Commendation recipient, *Honolulu* shows the effect of a Japanese destroyer-launched torpedo just after the 13 July 1943 Battle of Kolombangara. Incredibly, no lives were lost. However, an aerial torpedo hit on 20 October 1944 killed 60 and "friendly" gunfire accounted for five others. USN

On 5 June 1945 *Pittsburgh* lost her bow in a typhoon. Despite the damage, no lives were lost. Repaired after the war, CA-72 served in the Atlantic and Mediterranean during the Korean War. NA

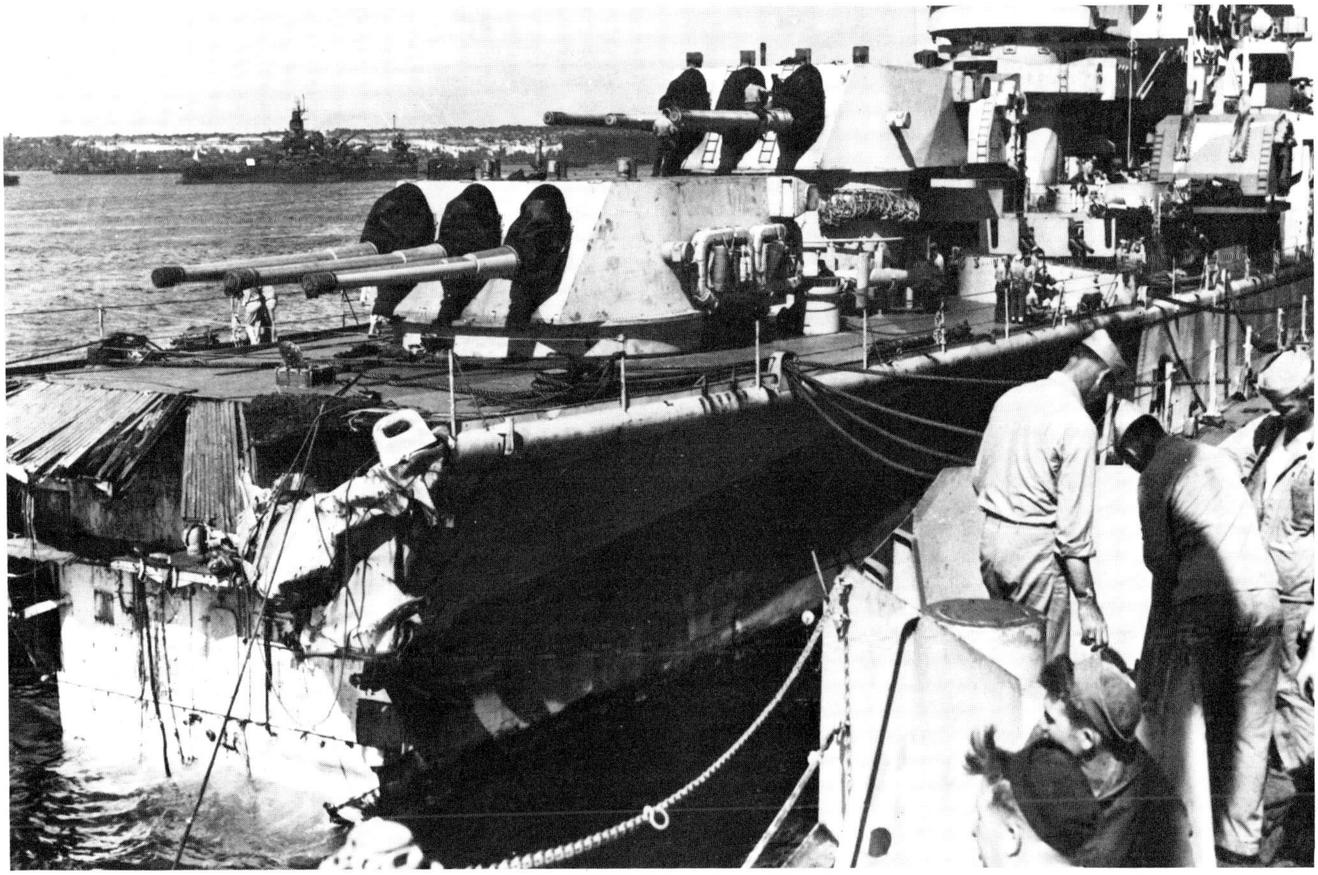

MEMORIES OF SUCCESS

If American cruisers in World War II had done nothing more than provide anti-aircraft protection for carriers, they would have been declared successful. However, their performance in supporting amphibious operations was particularly noteworthy and they received considerble praise from soldiers and Marines ashore. Although they did not achieve a tactical victory in surface battles equal to their losses at Savo Island and Tassafaronga, their performances in the battles of Cape Esperance, Kolombangara, Komandorski Islands, Empress Augusta Bay and the Naval Battle of Guadalcanal contributed considerably to eventual strategic victory.

One of the measures of success was the award of the Presidential Unit Citation. The highest award that can be bestowed upon a ship, the citation was presented to *San Francisco* for her successful fight off Cape Esperance and courageous attempt to turn back a more powerful enemy force during the 13 November 1942 night action portion of the Naval Battle of Guadalcanal. *Houston* (CA-30) was not awarded her Presidential Unit Citation until after the war when the account of her last hours became known. Perhaps the finest tribute to any cruiser is the story told by veterans of the southwest Pacific campaign concerning the *Houston*. During the war, Australian sailors would often rise from their seats at the mention of Houston's name. This demonstration of respect was based upon reports that the American cruiser had accepted battle against overwhelming odds and was still firing her guns when she finally slipped beneath the water.

Atlanta was only the third cruiser, and only light cruiser, to receive the prestigious award and her citation was for the same action off Guadalcanal for which *San Francisco* received her award. Ironically, there is evidence that salvos from *San Francisco* hit *Atlanta* that night. Rather than being interpreted as poor marksmanship, this occurrence is better understood when one considers how close the two opposing formations were to each other in this furious action. In the early morning hours of 13 November 1942 *Atlanta* was in a

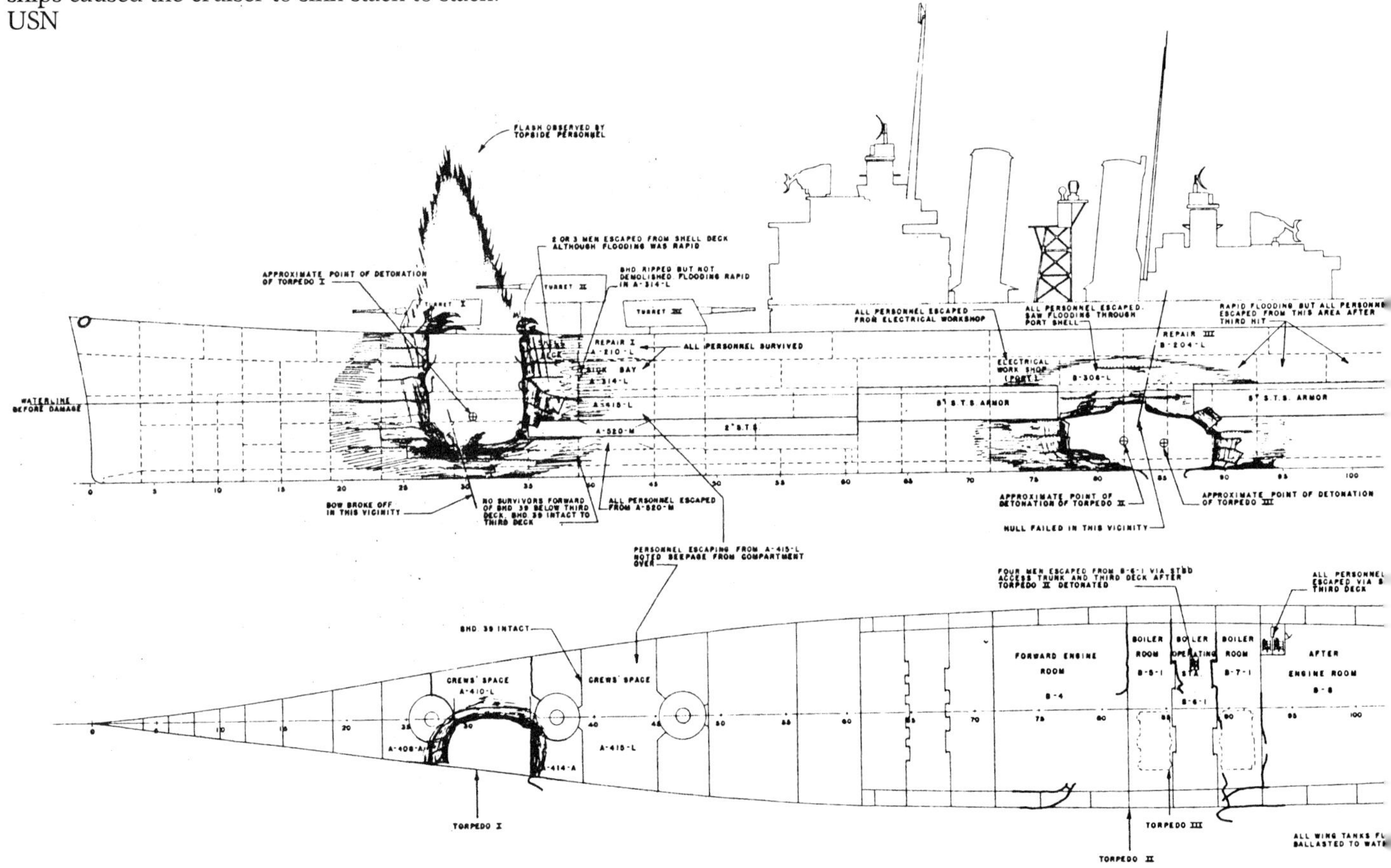

Always where the action was hottest, *Helena*–first cruiser to win the Navy Unit Commendation–was lost in the Battle Kula Gulf of 6 July 1943. Destroyer-launched torpedoes in this night action severed *Helena's* bow and the two hits side-by-side amidships caused the cruiser to sink stack-to-stack. USN

line of 13 American cruisers and destroyers which ran headlong into a Japanese formation of 14 warships that included two battleships. The night action of 13 November was the first of three major battles over a three-day period, but *Atlanta* lived only to fight in the battle of the 13th. Being the first cruiser in the American formation, *Atlanta* drew initial attention from the enemy and beams of light illuminated her. Atlanta's guns extinguished several enemy spotlights and blazed away at enemy ships on both sides of her. Within 10 minutes, however, the cruiser took at least one torpedo and approximately 50 major-caliber hits including several from battleship *Hiei*. Although *Atlanta* was lost as a result of this action, she hurt the enemy and displayed an inspiring fighting spirit.

A second major measure of success was the award of the Navy Unit Commendation. The first recipient of this award was *Helena* (CL-50), one of the greatest of all American warships. *Helena* was particularly known for being where the action was hottest, was known for the rapid fire of her 6-inch guns and was renowned for inflicting damage on the enemy in all her battles. When she was lost during the Battle of Kula Gulf, the Japanese thought she was firing 6-inch machine guns, and they were able to aim torpedoes at her as she was outlined by her own gunflashes. Flashless powder might have saved this fighting cruiser for additonal battles. When word of Helena's loss reached the *San Francisco*, beside whom she had fought at Pearl Harbor, off Cape Esperance and Guadalcanal, the following tribute was published in the "Frisco's" ship's newspaper:

Limping into port, worn and beaten, we flopped into our berth alongside a sister through fortune, a brother through battle, a twin through perserverance. On our cleaning stations we heard something, we bent our ears, our hearts jumped,life awakened, eyes opened, faces broke into smiles–life was worthwhile after all–the HELENA band was gathered on our well-deck playing music! A tribute to our dead, a shot-in-the-arm to our living.

The U.S.S. HELENA, who fought side by side with us, who gave and took as much as we, who stood mightily against the same odds, and who emerged as victorious as any, was proving herself a lady of magnanimity by giving us the credit she herself deserved as much as we.

The night of October 11, when the U.S.S. BOISE, was hit and afire from stem to stern, we were aware that the HELENA pulled up to protect her, and as she placed herself between this unfortunate sister of the seas and the enemy, her guns were blazing in tempo with every beat of her huge heart. The effects of her firepower were felt by the Jap Navy, even if not publicized by our own.

The morning of the 13th of November, as the FRISCO pulled away from the enemy battle-fleet, the HELENA seemed to know our Admiral was gone, our Captain, Executive Officer, and Navigator were lost, she seemed to feel our helplessness and waded in to lend a helping hand. With the care of a Guardian Angel she hovered about us directing and leading, literally hustling us into a port of safety.

Then with little thought for herself, she sent her men aboard to cheer us up, to brighten our lives, to tell us we had finished a job well-done–a job she herself had played more than her part to finish.

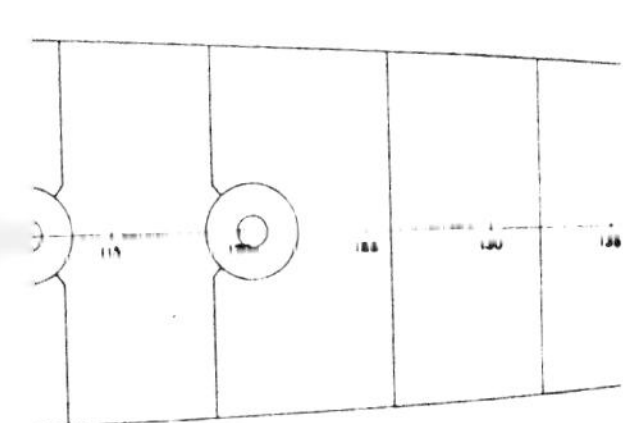

Pictured here are three of the U.S. Navy's most successful World War II cruisers. *Philadelphia* (CL-41) (foreground) won a Navy Unit Commendation for action in the Mediterranean; *Pensacola* (upper left) received 13 battle stars and *Salt Lake City* (behind *Pensacola*) was awarded the Navy Unit Commendation for her performance in the Battle of the Komandorski Islands. NA

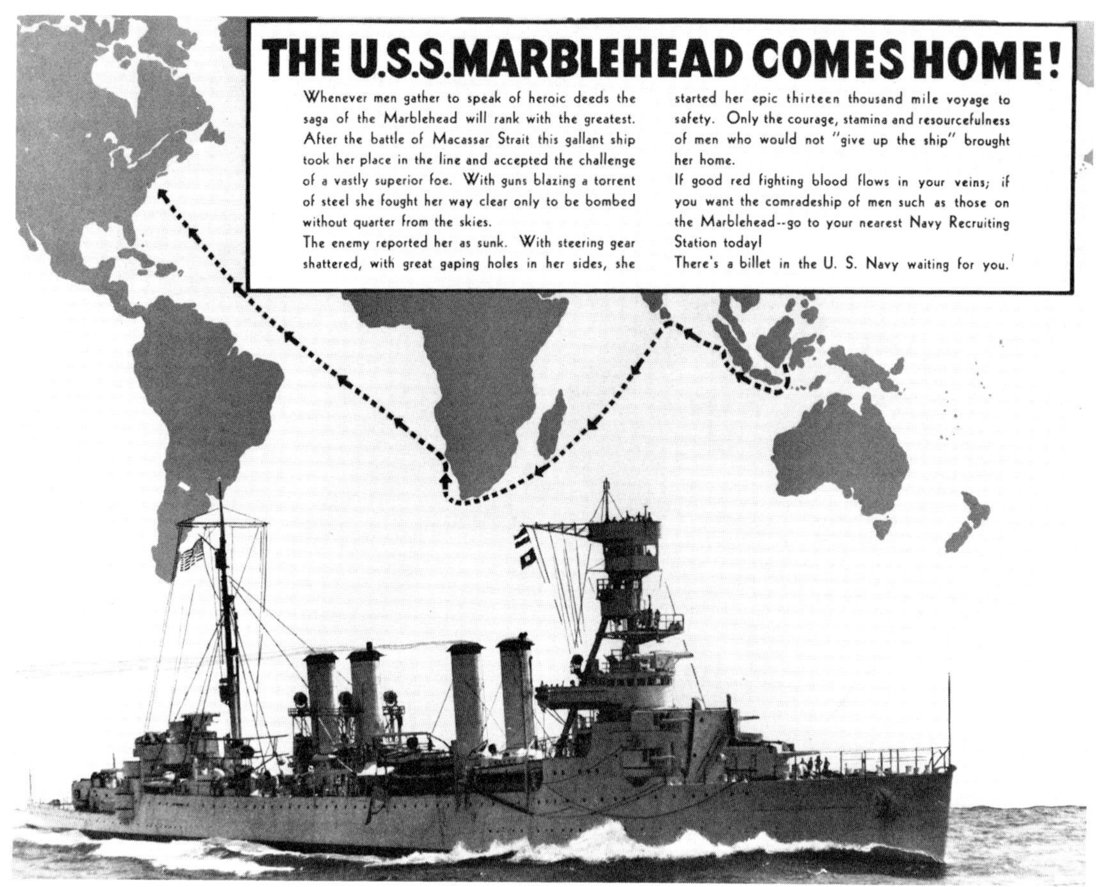

This wartime poster relates the story of the USS *Marblehead* (CL-12). Her's was one of the great stories of courage and resourcefulness to come out of World war II. Heavily damaged in the Java Sea alongside *Houston* (CA-30), the crew of *Marblehead* patched their ship and steamed nearly half way around the world to New York City for repairs. USN

While all her comrades pulled out and away to recuperate from all their wounds, the HELENA Princess merely shined her guns and greased her engines, and stayed on to fight, and stand her ground even until her end!

We know not the circumstances surrounding her death, but we do know the consequences thereof – Uncle Sam's Navy has lost another fighting lady, a lady with a heart of pure gold... Few men on few ships could appreciate the fighting ability and courageous spirit of *Helena* better than the men of another great fighting ship, the *San Francisco*.

Nine other cruisers were awarded the Navy Unit Commendation for a single action or for a series of commendable performances. *Cleveland, Columbia, Montpelier* and *Denver* won their award as units of highly successful Cruiser Division 12. Through the Central Solomons, the Bismarcks and the Philippines these *Cleveland*-class cruisers compiled an enviable combat record. As a team they shared in several favorable engagements against the Japanese with the Battle of Empress Augusta Bay their most significant victory. Here on 2 November 1943 the four cruisers and eight destroyers fought a Japanese force of two heavy cruisers, two light cruisers and six destroyers. No American ship was lost, but the Japanese lost light cruiser *Sendai* and destroyer *Hatsukaze*.

Salt Lake City acquitted herself well in the Battle of Cape Esperance, but her Navy Unit Commendation was awarded for her running battle off the Komandorski Islands where on 26 March 1943 she, *Richmond* (CL-9) and four destroyers turned back a Japanese force of two heavy cruisers, two light cruisers, five destroyers and several transports. *Portland* won her commendation for the 13 November 1942 night action off Guadalcanal when she traded broadsides with enemy battleship *Hiei* and put the final shells into destroyer *Yudachi*. Before her fighting days were over, *Portland* engaged in the action in Surigao Strait where she aimed her 8-inch guns at Japanese battleships, cruisers and destroyers in the last major surface action of the war. Honolulu's award included her actions at Tassafaronga, Kolombangara – where the Japanese lost cruiser *Jintsu* – Kula Gulf and the Philippines; while *St. Louis* won hers for Kula Gulf, Kolombangara, Leyte (Philippines) and Okinawa. *Honolulu* was one of the few members of the *Brooklyn*-class not to be sold to a South American country after World War II. *St. Louis* was sold to Brazil in 1951 where she served for nearly a quarter of a century. While under tow to a scrap yard in the early 1980s, *St. Louis* sank, an event that brings smiles to her veterans. Like *St. Louis, Philadelphia* was

For the damage control personnel of the *Houston* (CL-81), the enemy was not only the Japanese. Hit by aerial torpedoes on 14 October 1944 and again on 16 October, the men of the *Houston* battled the sea in a protracted but successful effort to save their ship. The burial service shown here occurred after the first attack; before the second attack, the damaged Kingfisher seaplane was jettisoned. USN

sold to Brazil in 1951, and she too won a Navy Unit Commendation. *Philadelphia* was the only cruiser to win this award for service in the Mediterranean. There, she distinguished herself by battling shore batteries, by supplying accurate gunfire around Palermo against German tanks and by providing anti-aircraft fire.

Santa Fe enjoyed a successful afternoon with *Biloxi, Mobile* and *Oakland* on 4 August 1944 when they and several destroyers caught a small enemy convoy and sank three enemy ships, but her Navy Unit Commendation was awarded for the three hours she spent alongside the burning carrier *Franklin* on 19 March 1945. Her firefighting and rescue efforts deserve praise as the *Birmingham-Princeton* tragedy had proved the risks and dangers of such actions. Often-damaged *Birmingham* suffered her worst experience in lives lost alongside the *Princeton* on 24 October 1944, but it was this action that brought her the Navy Unit Commendation. Despite her wounds *Birmingham* always came back, serving even for a short period in the Pacific on occupation duty after the war.

The story of the *Marblehead* was one of the first great stories of courage and resourcefulness to come out of the Pacific war. Heavily damaged in the Java Sea alongside *Houston*, the crew of *Marblehead* patched their ship and sailed her nearly half-way around the world to New York City for repairs. Only the heroic efforts of the second *Houston* (CL-81) and the carrier *Franklin* rank with the exploits of *Marblehead* in saving a severely damaged ship although the damage control teams aboard *Savannah, Reno, Minneapolis, New Orleans* and *Canberra* deserve plaudits.

Those cited above are all that won either the Presidential Unit Citation or Navy Unit Commendation among cruisers during World War II, but they are not all that deserve mention. Chief among the non-winners are *Minneapolis, New Orleans, Pensacola* and the second *Houston* (CL-81). *Minneapolis* and *San Francisco* each had 17 battle stars, tops among cruisers and second only to carrier *Enterprise* (20) for the war. *New Orleans* had 16 battle stars (a 17th star is presently under challenge) and *Pensacola* 13 as these cruisers fought from the beginning to the end of the war. The danger aboard *Houston* (CL-81) was commensurate with if not worse than that of *Marblehead* and the performance of the damage control team was excellent.

Numerous other cruisers lacked a singular notable moment or experience of significant magnitude necessary to win an award, but they still had long, effective combat careers and these cruisers should not be forgotten. In this category are *Chester* (especially as a participant in the early raids against the Marshalls); *Louisville* (particularly for her service in the Aleutians and Philippines); *Tuscaloosa* (for helping sink the Vichy French destroyer *Fougueux* off Casablanca); *Brooklyn* and *Augusta* (for putting the French destroyer *Boulonnais* out of action off Casablanca) *San Diego* (15 battle stars and never a serious wound); *San Juan* (13 battle stars and available early in the war when the need was critical); *Mobile* (an excellent combat record not well remembered due to the presence of other effective ships); *Detroit* (most battle stars for her class – six – while operating throughout the Pacific); *Wichita* (good shooting with *Mobile* off Cape Engano) and *Wilkes-Barre* (fire-fighting and rescue alongside the burning *Bunker Hill*). And, there were some cruisers that came along too late in the war to make much of a name for themselves in World War II, but did go on to outstanding careers off Korea and Vietnam. Chief among these were *St. Paul* (one battle star for World War II, but eight for Korea and eight for Vietnam); *Boston* (10 battle stars for World War II and a Navy Unit Commendation for service off Vietnam); *Canberra* (CA-70) and *Chicago* (CA-136) which distinguished themselves as missile cruisers off Vietnam.

Numerous cruisers lacked a singular experience of sufficient magnitude to win an official award but still provided long, effective combat service. *Louisville*, seen here before the war, was one such ship. Damaged twice by kamikazes, CA-28 was awarded 13 battle stars. USN

No World War II battle-star-winning cruiser has been preserved as a memorial. It would seem as though some agency would have wanted to preserve at least one of the combat veterans seen in this post-war photo of the Philadelphia Navy Yard reserve fleet. At the upper right are five *Baltimore*-class cruisers with the unfinished large cruiser *Hawaii* behind. Immediately to the left are *Cleveland*-class cruisers with *Montpelier* nearest the camera pointed toward *Wichita*. At the lower end of the photo are the survivors of the *Northampton* class (left) with three *New Orleans*-class cruisers at right. NA

CRUISER MEMORIALS

Fortunately for the person interested in World War II history there are battleships, destroyers, a destroyer-escort and submarines that have been memorialized that still retain configurations of the 1941-1945 era. Not so for carriers, as noted in the previous chapter, and not so for cruisers. Although there is now no possibility of preserving a carrier in World War II configuration, there is the possibility – albeit remote – that a World War II era cruiser could be preserved that still carries much of its original appearance. At the time of this writing (1985) the old *Brooklyn* (CL-40) and the *Nashville* (CL-43), another *Brooklyn*-class cruiser, are still afloat in the navy of Chile. Since 1951 *Brooklyn* has carried the name *O'Higgins* while *Nashville* has had two names – *Capitan Prat* from 1951 until 1982 and *Chacabuco* since that year.

The chances are not favorable of either cruiser making its way back to ownership by either the public or private sector in the United States. Veterans of the *Brooklyn* have contacted government officials, but the return of the cruiser even to the borough for which she was named is not likely because of the great expense involved. And, the recent experience of the *Intrepid*

After serving successfully in the U.S. Navy during World War II, *Brooklyn* and *Nashville* were sold in 1951 to Chile. *Brooklyn* (CL-40) (top) was renamed *O'Higgins*; *Nashville* was renamed *Capitan Prat* and later *Chacabuco*. Into 1985 the two cruisers still serve and are seen here operating under the Chilean flag. The only two surviving World War II cruisers in near-original configuration, *Brooklyn* or *Nashville* (bottom) would be unique memorials either in Chile or back in the United States. U.S. Naval Institute and U.S. Naval Institute

Although their World War II appearances have long since changed, two battle-star-winning cruisers still exist in mothballs at Bremerton, Wash. *Chicago* (top) and *Oklahoma City* (bottom) will most likely go to the scrap heap, but there is a remote chance that citizens of Chicago may be able to preserve CG-11, ex-CA-136. Author's Collection

has not strengthened arguments that the cruiser would have tourist appeal in New York City. If an interested party could bring the ship back to some southeastern port such as Charleston, S.C., or Tampa, Fla., one would think that New Yorkers and history buffs from all over the country would find reason to visit. Either the *Brooklyn* or the *Nashville* would have a singular claim to history – the last World War II combat cruiser in near-original appearance. Unquestionably, such a memorial would have unique appeal. One would even have to wager that the tourist trade of Chile would show an increase if either of the cruisers was memorialized there and enthusiastically marketed. The reader may be assured that this writer will have no objection to this page being photocopied and sent to the Chilean Embassy or officials in Charleston or Tampa.

There are two World War II era cruisers still afloat in the United States that won battle stars in that war, but the problem is that neither resembles its World War II configuration. Forty years after the end of World War II *Chicago* (CA-136, more recently CG-11) and *Oklahoma City* (CL-91, CLG-5) rest quietly at Bremerton, Wash., in mothballs. At present there is no major effort being made to preserve *Oklahoma City*, but the veterans of *Chicago* and other interested citizens of "the Windy City" have been trying for several years to bring *Chicago* to their city as a memorial. Of course, a sympathetic city government is critical to such an effort and this factor to date has not been totally supportive as Chicago, like most other cities, has many constituencies with many needs and wants. Lack of funds will most likely doom this project.

One cruiser that was built during World War II has been preserved as a memorial, but it did not win any battle stars for World War II participation and, like *Chicago* and *Oklahoma City*, it was converted to a guided missile light cruiser and consequently does not resemble her original *Cleveland*-class appearance. Still, a visit to *Little Rock* (CLG-4) at the Buffalo and Erie County Naval & Servicemen's Park in Buffalo, N.Y., is worthwhile. One can acquire the feel for the size of the World War II light cruiser by viewing the hull, and when standing near the bow one can easily see why so many cruisers lost all or major portions of their bow when hit by torpedoes. *Little Rock* retains her World War II era appearance only from the single 6-inch turret forward; all else topside is completely different. Moored immediately behind *Little Rock* is the memorialized destroyer *The Sullivans* (DD-537); the two ships plus a PT boat, museum building, tank and other artifacts make this Naval Park a "must" on the historian's itinerary.

In the absence of a memorialized World War II combat cruiser, emphasis here shifts to cruiser memorials featuring parts of ship. Cruisers fared well in this category inasmuch as most were named for ma-

Little Rock (CLG-4) was built as a *Cleveland*-class light cruiser during World War II but did not see action. Preserved as a memorial at the Buffalo & Erie County Naval & Servicemen's Park in Buffalo, N.Y., only the bow and number one 6-inch turret retain original configuration as the ship was rebuilt to serve as a missile cruiser. Author's Collection

Seemingly out of place is the social use of the stern of the *Little Rock*, but this practice is frequent on nearly all memorialized warships. Private parties, even weddings, are held aboard. As money is an ever present problem for maintcnancc of prc-served ships, social activities will continue to be welcome. Author's Collection

This close-up shows the shell-riddled bridge windscreens removed from *San Francisco* (CA-38) after the Naval Battle of Guadalcanal. A full view of the *San Francisco* memorial is presented on the back cover of this book. No World War II Navy memorial is more dramatic or captivating. Courtesy of Dean Schumacher

jor cities across the United States. Practically all the cruiser memorials were set up as a cooperative venture between cities and veterans groups with respective cities assuming responsibility for maintenance and perpetual care.

Five of the cruiser memorials are strictly outdoor displays and although each rests in a dignified setting, one captivates the historian more than the others – the USS *San Francisco* Memorial, which sits 200 feet above the Pacific on Point Lobos with the ocean to the west and Golden Gate to the north. This significant memorial almost suffered the fate of the planned *Franklin* (CV-13) memorial. When the damaged cruiser limped back into her namesake city after the Naval Battle of Guadalcanal, she was enthusiastically met by residents. Amid this outpouring of respect and emotion, the shell-riddled navigation bridge windscreens were removed and the Navy offered the sections of steel to the city to be used in a memorial to the ship and the men lost aboard in the critical November 1942 battle. After the war a city official proposed to sell the metal for scrap (valued at $360). When this proposal was publicized, other city officials and veterans groups moved quickly to save the bridge sections and on 12 November 1950 – exactly eight years after the battle – these were dedicated in an appropriate ceremony with a mast and bell from CA-38 and three large plaques.

In 1985 the shell-torn bridge sections and the plaques remain at Land's End, but the mast and bell have been removed due to deterioration and vandalism. A flagpole now rests atop the concrete pedestal that once supported the mast. The three plaques placed in 1950 show a little age, but they are still there. One plaque honors the 107 dead, including the seven Marines lost on the night of 12-13 November 1942; a second honors the officers, men and San Francisco native Rear Adm. Daniel J. Callaghan who commanded U.S. Naval forces on that fateful night and lost his life to one of the enemy shells that passed through the still-extant bridge screen (see back cover and photo in this chapter); and the third plaque is another salute to Rear Admiral Callaghan, officers and men with tribute from President Roosevelt. Several of the comments on this plaque stated by the president are incorrect in recounting the details of the battle,[1] (a not uncommon occurrence during the war when only "our-side" information was available) but the essence of his remarks was valid and there is no question concerning his pain over the loss of his former aide (Callaghan) or his evaluation of the valor of CA-38's crew. At the base of the pedestal is a compass oriented on a great circle course to Guadalcanal. If properly maintained, this memorial will continue to be one of the great World War II shrines honoring a great ship. At present it still has great meaning to someone as it is not unusual to find an impressive wreath of fresh flowers at the base of the pedestal.

Although the memorial to the *Portland* (CA-33) does not show battle scars received when she too fought in the 12-13 November 1942 Naval Battle of Guadalcanal, it nonetheless shows other similarities to the *San Francisco* memorial. The *San Francisco* memorial is unmatched for conveying the stark reality of historical moments, but the *Portland* memorial is its equal in solitude and ambience. The idea and decision

1. *Atlanta* led the formation, not *San Francisco*; the enemy battleship *Hiei* was hurt but not "silenced;" and it is not known exactly which ship to credit for the two Japanese destroyers sunk that night although it is known that *Portland* "finished off" *Yudachi*.

to place the CA-33 memorial on a hillside in Fort Allen Park overlooking Casco Bay in Portland, Me., was inspired. At Land's End in San Francisco and Fort Allen Park in Portland, visitors find not only a spectacular view but also a peace that stimulates the spirit. A quiet afternoon at either location watching sailboats on the distant blue induces a thankfulness for life and its finest moments. What better settings for remembrances of men who paid the price to allow future generations occasions to enjoy the blessings of peace.

As can be seen in this chapter and the Color section, the *Portland* memorial consists of a large tripod mast that supports the ship's bell, a large section of the open bridge and a large monument with two plaques. One plaque reads "This monument dedicated to the memory of those men who served on board USS *Portland*." The plaque facing the mast lists the cruiser's battle record. Leaning against the former bridge section, one notes the voice tube attached thereto. This, with the view of the sea and hovering presence of the mast, gives one the feel for the ship as if she was once again underway.

The *Portland* (CA-33) memorial does not show battle scars but does rest in an environment similar to that of the *San Francisco* memorial. Severely damaged in the same night battle as *San Francisco*, the *Portland* is memorialized at Fort Allen Park, Portland, Me. The memorial consists of CA-33's mast, bell, open bridge, monument and plaques. Author's Collection

The mast of the *Biloxi* (CL-80) rests within sight of the Gulf of Mexico at Biloxi, Miss. (see picture in this chapter and in Color section). Whereas the *San Francisco* and *Portland* memorials are set in relatively quiet, reflective environments, the *Biloxi* memorial is set in a more lively environment. Only a few feet from the mast is a large marina and several restaurants. Natives of Biloxi prefer to spend their reflective moments on the water and prefer to view the mast from the water instead of the grounds on which it rests. Less than a mile west on the same highway (U.S. 90) where one will find the mast of CL-80, a 40mm gun mount from the cruiser has been placed. The mount faces the gulf and technically is on loan to the local VFW whose building sits well back from the road. No plaque exists on the mount (several residents expressed surprise that anyone other than themselves would be interested in the mount or the memory of their cruiser). At City Hall the bell of the *Biloxi* is on display and other mementoes are stored in the old City Library.

Surprisingly little information about CL-80 is available in its namesake city, although this is the norm for most World War II cruisers. Even the plaque at the base of the *Biloxi* mast commemorates citizens of the city lost in the August 1969 hurricane (Camille). A few feet from the mast toward the highway is a large, impressive monument placed by the Guice family in memory of one of their own (William Lee Guice, Jr., Lt. USN) who was lost in the 13 November 1942 Naval Battle of Guadalcanal.

Not far from another body of water, the Pacific Ocean, stands the mast of the cruiser *Oakland*. The care of this memorial is accentuated by a bed of flowers surrounding the base; a close-up photo of the base is included in the Color section of this book in an effort to capture and convey its beauty. In addition to the mast, the cruiser's nameplate is bonded to the foundation supporting the mast. It is surprising that the practice of including a ship's nameplate in memorials has not found more expression. With all that was removed from the battleship *South Dakota*, it is particularly surprising that the nameplate was not preserved. Dedicated 11 November 1965, the *Oakland* mast and nameplate were presented by the Navy to the people of Oakland and was placed by the Oakland Board of Port Commissioners.

Still near the water is the mast of the *Biloxi* (CL-80) and a 40mm mount. The mast from the cruiser and the gun mount face the Gulf of Mexico in the coastal Mississippi city. The cruiser's bell rests inside City Hall. Author's Collection

Located on the grounds of the Last Chance Gulch Mall in Helena, Mont., the *Helena* memorial consists of a propeller, anchor, chain and bell from *Helena* (CA-75) and is intended to honor the famous light cruiser CL-50 of World War II fame and the heavy cruiser that inherited her name. Stan Cohen

Not far from the Pacific Ocean in Oakland, Calif., stands the mast and nameplate of the *Oakland* (CL-95). The memorial is accentuated by a bed of flowers (see Color section). Courtesy of Dean Schumacher

The memorial to the two cruisers that carried the name *Helena* in World War II is far removed from any water. Located on the grounds of the Last Chance Gulch Mall in Helena, Mont., the memorial consists of a propeller, anchor, anchor chain and bell from *Helena* (CA-75) and is intended to honor the famous light cruiser CL-50 of World War II fame and the heavy cruiser that inherited her name. The second *Helena* had a distinguished career off Korea and was present for the Navy Day ceremonies in New York City in October 1945, but did not see combat in World War II. As the first cruiser *Helena* was sunk in 1943 it was not possible to include any artifacts from her in the memorial, but citizens of her namesake city know well the history of CL-50. At the 10 September 1977 dedication, emphasis was indeed placed on the first *Helena*; and veterans of the cruiser, who earned a great fighting reputation before their ship was sunk, were on hand to participate in the ceremonies. The memorial in Helena was by no means just "placed"; an architect designed the project, numerous businesses and individuals contributed expertise, and the local Naval Reserve Unit was responsible for the construction. The success of their collective efforts is evident in the picture contained here.

Most of the remaining World War II cruiser memorials and/or artifacts are located indoors, except for the bell of the *Pensacola*, which sits in a lonely corner outside the former City Hall building, the bell of the *Oklahoma City*, located immediately outside an entrance to the Kirkpatrick Center in Oklahoma City, and the bow section of the *Fall River* (*Fall River* was built during World War II but did not see action) at Battleship Cove in Fall River, Mass. And, the norm is that not all that is left of a cruiser is found in one location. The memory of the *Reno* (CL-96) has been honored by the placement of a six-foot model built by a former crewmember and the ship's bell near the mayor's office in Reno, Nev., but the largest surviving segment of the cruiser is a pair of 5-inch guns in the Navy Memorial Museum in the Washington Navy Yard. The mount's housing has been removed to facilitate viewing, and a display panel (visible in photo) carries a picture of the cruiser and two plaques.

The bell of the first treaty cruiser, *Pensacola* (CA-24), survived 13 battles and two atomic bomb blasts at Bikini. In 1985 the bell sits in a lonely corner outside the former City Hall building. Author's Collection

The *Fall River* was built during World War II, but did not commission in time to fight. The bow of the cruiser is on display at Battleship Cove in Fall River, Mass. Author's Collection

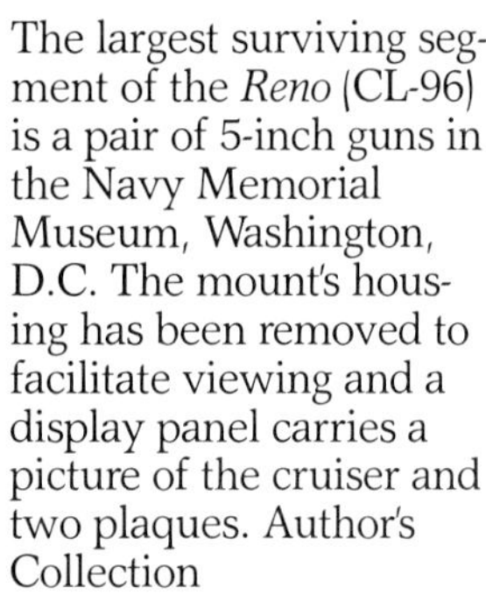

The largest surviving segment of the *Reno* (CL-96) is a pair of 5-inch guns in the Navy Memorial Museum, Washington, D.C. The mount's housing has been removed to facilitate viewing and a display panel carries a picture of the cruiser and two plaques. Author's Collection

One seeking to touch the history of the *Mobile* (CL-63) will also have to make more than one stop. First stop would be the *Mobile* Room on the battleship *Alabama.* Several items of interest are on display including the 1943 builder's plaque from Newport News, throttle wheels, 60-inch tompion, ship's bell, model and the usual photographs and newpaper clippings found in most exhibits. The most unusual artifact in the *Mobile* Room is a radio taken after the war from the Japanese battleship *Nagato.* Unquestionably, the most interesting World War II exhibit would be all the artifacts never placed in museums but "appropriated" by historically inclined sailors who have assumed the responsibility of safeguarding the objects in their personal archives or on their mantels. While touching on this subject, one would be interested to know *how* portions of the USS Mobile's wooden deck ended up as paneling in the "Candlis Room," a banquet room in the famous San Francisco Fairmont Hotel. Additional tompions from the *Mobile* are at the Hampton Roads Naval Museum in Virginia while the ship's annunciator pedestal is on loan to the Kirkpatrick Center in Oklahoma City. The ship's beautiful silver service is displayed in the Mobile City Museum, which is less than a mile from the battleship *Alabama.*

At Nimitz Junior High School in Huntington Park,

Calif., is some deck planking from *Augusta* (CA-31) and at the Hampton Roads Naval Museum one will find a small model and the aft steering wheel from the cruiser. As *Augusta* was built at Newport News, it is only natural to find some mention of her in this relatively new museum. However, the major display honoring the cruiser that housed world leaders for major conferences before and during World War II is located in the Augusta-Richmond County Museum in Augusta, Ga. If one is interested in a location that is reminiscent of the old South, it may be found near this museum where magnolia trees abound and squirrels unabashedly run across your feet. Inside the museum a good-sized room has been devoted to the cruiser and its special place in history. Pictures document the cruiser's combat experiences off North Africa and Normandy and document the conferences held within her. A dinner menu bearing signatures of President Roosevelt, Prime Minister Winston Churchill, General George Marshall, Adm. Ernest King and other notables of the era is on display along with several paintings and drawings, the cruiser's silver service, engine order telegraph, commissioning pennant and annunciator. A three-foot model rests under a large map while a specially built six-foot model dominates the attractive exhibit.

The *Mobile* Room aboard the battleship *Alabama* houses CL-63's builder's plaque, throttle wheels, 6-inch tompion, ship's bell, model, photographs and clippings. The cruiser's silver service is located approximately one mile away in the Mobile City Museum. Author's Collection

The major display honoring the USS *Augusta* (CA-31) is located in the Augusta-Richmond County Museum in Augusta, Ga. A six-foot custom-built model is on display along with the cruiser's annunciator, engine order telegraph, silver service, photos and historical documents. Author's Collection

Driving in downtown New Orleans is a lot easier than driving in New York City, but that is not to say that driving in "the city of dreams" is a joy. And when you are looking for the Louisiana Maritime Museum, which has a propensity to change its address, and you finally locate it only to find it closed (the *Intrepid* in New York City also has had the habit of closing on certain weekdays), one's mind conjures up a new, creative vocabulary that would surpass even the most eloquent utterances of a boiler-room sailor. Still, the contents of this museum are such that another special trip is justified. Across the country are many excellent ship models built by employees of the Navy, shipyards and private model enthusiasts. Several are the equal of the model of *New Orleans* (CA-32), but none are superior. Attention to detail, including paint, is first-class. Attention, too, has been given to the case, a factor greatly overlooked in the display of some of the outstanding models: the full length of the model is unobstructed.

Just as the 10-foot model of the *New Orleans* is unsurpassed in quality, so too is the bell removed from the cruiser and now displayed next to the model (see Bell section for picture). Unlike most ship's bells, which carry only the vessel's name and date of completion, the bell of the *New Orleans* is uniquely ornate from top to bottom. Originally presented to an earlier cruiser of the same name in 1898, the bell has the following engraved on it: "Presented to the USS *New*

Orleans by the people of New Orleans, La., as a token of their appreciation of the honor of having a vessel of the U.S. Navy named for their city." A plaque above the bell relates how the local Navy League chapter brought the bell "home" after CA-32 was decommissioned. A battle flag flown during the Battle of Tassafaronga, silver service, trophy, pictures and mementoes complement the model and bell and provide a great memorial display for an outstanding ship.

When the battle-damaged USS *Juneau* (CL-52) was caught limping away from Guadalcanal and sunk by a submarine torpedo on the afternoon of 13 November 1942, five brothers perished with the cruiser. The destroyer *The Sullivans* (DD-537) was named to honor Joseph, Francis, Albert, Madison and George Sullivan, and today there is a special exhibit aboard the memorialized destroyer honoring the *Juneau* and the five forever-young sailors. The wardroom exhibit contains pictures of the cruiser, the five brothers and several lengthy, well-written narratives covering the history of the cruiser, the Naval Battle of Guadalcanal where the cruiser received her initial damage, the torpedo attack and the loss of the Sullivan brothers and 99 percent of the ship's crew.

In some instances, plaques are all that remain on display in 1985 to jog the memory of fighting ships. When *St. Louis* sank while under tow to be scrapped after serving a quarter century in the navy of Brazil,

The Louisiana Maritime Museum is home for an elaborate 10-foot model of the cruiser *New Orleans* (CA-32) and its ornate bell. Other artifacts from the ship and mementoes donated by veterans make this an outstanding memorial. Courtesy of the Louisiana Maritime Museum

A compartment aboard the memorialized destroyer *The Sullivans* (DD-537) has been designed to call to remembrance the cruiser *Juneau* (CL-52) and the five Sullivan brothers who died with her in November 1942. Maps, narratives and pictures fill the compartment. Author's Collection

the possibility of removing meaningful artifacts from her also disapperaed. A few parts from the long-serving World War II fighter would have looked especially good to veterans of the ship if they could have been placed on the USS *Inaugural* a memorialized World War II minesweeper, open to the public on the Mississippi River under the arch in St. Louis. As it is, only the builder's plaque from the *St. Louis* is on display in the Hampton Roads Naval Museum. A few feet from the builder's plaque of the *St. Louis*, the builder's plaque of the second *Houston* (CL-81) is mounted just under tompions from the *Biloxi* and *Mobile*. On board the battleship *Texas* a compartment has been set up as a *Houston* Room to honor both CA-30 and CL-81. When this writer visited the *Texas*, the *Houston* Room was undergoing renovation and was therefore not available

The builder's plaques of the *St. Louis* (CL-49) and *Houston* (CL-81) (at left) are on display inside the Hampton Roads Naval Museum, Norfolk, Va. A small model and aft steering wheel (not shown here) from *Augusta* (CA-31) honors the memory of the cruiser that hosted important conferences before and after the war. Author's Collection

for visitation. A few miles south of the *Texas* in Corpus Christi, one will find the bell of *Houston* (CL-81); a porthole is on loan to the Navy Club in Fort Wayne, Ind., while another porthole is on display at the University of Illinois. Although veterans of the *Minneapolis* (CA-36) know that navigation and running lights from their cruiser are at the Naval Reserve Facility in Bloomington, Ind., and that a 24-inch steering wheel and 48-star battle flag is at the American Legion Post 472 in Minneapolis, a plaque that was never on their ship holds particular significance to them. A large crowd filled the Naval Station Chapel at Philadelphia on 19 May 1984 to dedicate a plaque that reads as follows:

> IN GRATEFUL MEMORY OF THE OFFICERS AND MEN WHO SERVED IN THE USS MINNEAPOLIS CA-36 COMMISSIONED 1934 PHILADELPHIA NAVY YARD WORLD WAR II 17 BATTLE STARS DECOMMISIONED 1946 PHILADELPHIA NAVY YARD MAY 19, 1984 THE 50th ANNIVERSARY OF HER COMMISSIONING PRESENTED BY THE CITY OF MINNEAPOLIS

Veterans of the two cruisers that carried the name *Quincy* have contributed pictures and memorabilia for an exhibit in the Quincy, Mass., City Hall Building while veterans of the *Columbia* (CL-56) have elected to direct their major efforts toward a Naval ROTC scholarship at the University of South Carolina. Veterans of these ships, like many others, will occasionally find pictures, paintings, clippings and other remembrances in naval and maritime museums, an example being the model of the *Columbia* sitting in a model dry dock. The reader will want to compare the two pictures in this book of *Columbia* actually in dry dock during the war and the photo of the model of CL-56 set in a model dry dock (see Model section) within the Navy Memorial Museum in Washington, D.C.

Pictures of several cruiser models appear in the Model section of this book and comments are offered there about them. Likewise, pictures of several cruiser bells appear in the Bell section with comments on bells from three cruisers lost during the war: *Northampton, Indianapolis* and *Chicago*. Beyond what has already been said, little else remains to be said concerning memorials to World War II cruisers. There has been no pattern of honoring World War II cruisers by passing their names on to other cruisers although a recently completed cruiser does carry the name *Vincennes*. It is a member of the *Ticonderoga* class and another of its sister ships carries the name *Yorktown*, names inherited from famous carriers. Somewhat surprisingly, it is more likely to find names like *Pittsburgh, Louisville* and *Augusta* on new submarines.

Below is a brief and incomplete list of parts of World War II cruisers not already mentioned that have been placed on display throughout the country. It would not be correct to state that these individual parts constitute a memorial per se, but in the interest of providing an example of what remains, the list is presented. One should keep in mind the comments made in the Introduction to this book concerning museums' policies of rotating exhibits, and remember that the Navy has thousands of artifacts in storage that may be taken from storage and placed on loan at some future date.

The names of some World War II cruisers have been passed to newer vessels including submarines. Few newer cruisers have inherited names from World War II cruisers, but one exception is the new *Ticonderoga*-class cruiser *Vincennes* seen here in 1984 while under construction at Ingalls Shipbuilding Corporation in Pascagoula, Miss. Author's Collection

CRUISER	ARTIFACT	LOCATION
Alaska CB-1	Binnacle, draft gauge Steering Wheel, Tompion	Kirkpatrick Center, Oklahoma City, Okla. University of Alaska
Baltimore CA-68	Bell War record plaque	University of Baltimore Baltimore, Md.
Birmingham CL-62	War record plaque Side lights Bell	Hampton Roads Naval Museum, Va. Philadelphia Navy Yard Naval Reserve Armory, Birmingham, Ala.
Chester CA-27	Running lights Bell 24″ steering wheel	Naval Reserve Training Center, Adelphia, Md. Bethel Township, Boothwyn, Pa. Penn State University
Canberra CA-70	Plot board	Senaca Valley High School Germantown, Md.
Columbia CL-56	Pelorus	Battleship Cove Falls River, Mass.
Louisville CA-28	Annunciator pedestal	V.F.W. Post Collinswood, N.J.
Miami CL-89	Porthole Porthole Wind & course indicator	Navy Club, Fort Wayne, Ind. Kirkpatrick Center, Oklahoma City, Okla. Harry Lundeberg Museum, Piney Point, Md.
New Orleans CA-32	Helm Wheel Annunciator Tompion	Battleship Cove Fall River, Mass.
Pittsburgh CA-72	Pelorus stand Anchor, chain, propellor Clock	W.R. Boone High School, Orlando, Fla. Springfield, Ore. Pt. Loma High School, San Diego, Calif.
San Diego CL-53	Gauge	Naval Hospital Bethesda, Md.
San Francisco CA-38	48″ capstan cover	Surface Warfare Officers School Newport, R.I.
St. Paul CA-73	Barometer Signal Lamp After steering wheel, plaque	University of Washington, Seattle Nimitz Museum, Fredricksburg, Texas Pipestone, Minn.
Tuscaloosa CA-37	Steering stand	Naval Reserve Facility Bloomington, Ind.
Wichita CA-45	Annunciator binnacle	Florida A&M University Tallahassee, Fla.
Alaska, Montpelier Cleveland, Birmingham Mobile, Santa Fe Savannah, Tuscaloosa Guam, Wichita Honolulu, Houston Miami, Denver Duluth	Deck planking (Altar of Naval Academy Chapel)	U.S. Naval Academy, Annapolis, Md.

CHAPTER FOUR
DESTROYERS AND DESTROYER ESCORTS

PRESIDENTIAL UNIT CITATION

Destroyers

*Aaron Ward	DD-773, DM-34
*Alexander Dallas	DD-199
Barry	DD-248, APD-29
Belknap	DD-251, APD-34
*Bennion	DD-662
*Bernadou	DD-153
Borie	DD-215
*Buchanan	DD-484
Charles Ausburne	DD-570
Claxton	DD-571
Clemson	DD-186, APD-31
*Cole	DD-155
Converse	DD-509
*Cowell	DD-547
Dupont	DD-152
Dyson	DD-572
*Evans	DD-552
George E. Badger	DD-196, APD-33
Goff	DD-247
Greene	DD-266, APD-36
*Harry F. Bauer	DD-738, DM-26
Heerman	DD-532
*Henry A. Wiley	DD-749, DM-29
Hobson	DD-464, DMC-26
Hoel	DD-533
*Hugh W. Hadley	DD-774
*John D. Ford	DD-228
Johnston	DD-557
*Laffey	DD-459
*Laffey	DD-724
Lea	DD-118
*Maury	DD-401
*McFarland	DD-237, AVD-14
*Nicholas	DD-449
*O'Bannon	DD-450
Osmond Ingram	DD-255, APD-35
*Pope	DD-225
*Radford	DD-446
*Smith	DD-378
Spence	DD-512
Stanly	DD-478
*Sterett	DD-407
*Wadsworth	DD-516

Destroyer Escorts

*Bronstein	DE-189
Chatelain	DE-149
Dennis	DE-405
*England	DE-635
Flaherty	DE-135
Francis M. Robinson	DE-220
*Frost	DE-144
Haverfield	DE-393
Janssen	DE-396
Jenks	DE-665
John C. Butler	DE-339
Pillsbury	DE-133
Pope	DE-134
Raymond	DE-341
Samuel B. Roberts	DE-413
Swenning	DE-394
Wilhoite	DE-397
Willis	DE-395

*Individual award as opposed to unit award.

NAVY UNIT COMMENDATION

Destroyers

Adams	DD-739, DM-27
Albert W. Grant	DD-649
Ammen	DD-527
Anthony	DD-515
Bailey	DD-492
Barton	DD-722
Bennett	DD-473
Blue	DD-744
Bradford	DD-545
Brooks	DD-232, APD-10
Brown	DD-546
Bryant	DD-665
Butler	DD-636, DMS-29
Cassin Young	DD-793
Crosby	DD-164, APD-17
Emmons	DD-457, DMS-22
Gainard	DD-706
Gwin	DD-772, DM-23
Hamilton	DD-141, DMS-18
Heywood L. Edwards	DD-663
Hickox	DD-673
Hilary P. Jones	DD-427
Hopkins	DD-249, DMS-13
Hovey	DD-208, DMS-11
Hudson	DD-475
Ingraham	DD-694
Irwin	DD-794
J. William Ditter	DD-751, DM-31
Kilty	DD-137, APD-15
Long	DD-209, DMS-12
Macomb	DD-458, DMS-23
Manley	DD-74, APD-1
McKean	DD-90, APD-5
Miller	DD-535
Montgomery	DD-121, DM-17
Morrison	DD-560 (2 awards)
Newcomb	DD-586
Plunkett	DD-431
Prichett	DD-561
Purdy	DD-734
Robert H. Smith	DD-735, DM-23
Rodman	DD-456, DMS-21
Sands	DD-243, APD-13
Shea	DD-750, DM-30
Southard	DD-207, DMS-10
Stringham	DD-83, APD-6

Trever	DD-339, DMS-16
Taylor	DD-468
VanValkenburgh	DD-656
Ward	DD-139, APD-16
Wickes	DD-578
Woolsey	DD-437
Zane	DD-337, DMS-14

Destroyer Escorts

Buckley	DE-51
Frederick C. Davis	DE-136
Herbert C. Jones	DE-137
Horace A. Bass	DE-691, APD-124
John C. Butler	DE-339
Johnnie Hutchins	DE-360
Loy	DE-160, APD-56
Richard W. Suesens	DE-342
Tabberer	DE-418

ULTIMATE SACRIFICE

Aaron Ward	DD-483....1943
Abner Read	DD-526....1944
Barry	DD-248, APD-29....1945
Barton	DD-599....1942
Beatty	DD-640....1943
Benham	DD-397....1942
Blue	DD-387....1943
Borie	DD-215....1943
Bristol	DD-453....1943
Brownson	DD-518....1943
Buck	DD-420....1943
Bush	DD-529....1945
Callaghan	DD-792....1945
Chevalier	DD-451....1943
Calhoun	DD-801....1945
Colhoun	DD-85, APD-2....1942
Cooper	DD-695....1944
Corry	DD-463....1944
Cushing	DD-376....1942
De Haven	DD-469....1943
Dickerson	DD-157, APD-21....1945
Drexler	DD-741....1945
Duncan	DD-485....1942
Edsall	DD-219....1942
Emmons	DD-457, DMS-22....1945
Gamble	DD-123, DM-15....1945
Glennon	DD-620....1944
Gregory	DD-82, APD-3....1942
Gwin	DD-433....1943
Halligan	DD-584....1945
Hammann	DD-412....1942
Henley	DD-391....1943
Hoel	DD-533....1944
Hovey	DD-208, DMS-11....1945
Hull	DD-350....1944
Ingraham	DD-444....1942
Jacob Jones	DD-130....1942
Jarvis	DD-393....1942
Johnston	DD-557....1944
Laffey	DD-459....1942
Landsdale	DD-426....1944
Leary	DD-158....1943
Little	DD-79, APD-4....1943
Little	DD-803....1945
Long	DD-209, DMS-12....1945
Longshaw	DD-559....1945
Luce	DD-552....1945
Maddox	DD-622....1943
Mahan	DD-364....1944
Manneri L. Abele	DD-733....1945
McKean	DD-90, APD-5....1943
Meredith	DD-434....1942
Meredith	DD-726....1944
Monaghan	DD-354....1944
Monssen	DD-436....1942
Montgomery	DD-121, DM-17....1944
Morrison	DD-560....1945
Noa	DD-343, APD-24....1944
O'Brien	DD-415....1942
Palmer	DD-161, DMS-5....1945
Parrott	DD-218....1944
Peary	DD-226....1942
Perkins	DD-377....1943
Perry	DD-340, DMS-17....1944
Pillsbury	DD-227....1942
Pope	DD-225....1942
Porter	DD-356....1942
Preston	DD-379....1942
Pringle	DD-477....1945
Reid	DD-369....1944
Reuben James	DD-245....1941
Rowan	DD-405....1943
Sims	DD-409....1942
Spence	DD-512....1944
Stewart	DD-224....1942
Strong	DD-467....1943
Sturtevani	DD-240....1942
Thornton	DD-270, AVD-11....1945
Truxiun	DD-229....1942
Tucker	DD-374....1942
Turner	DD-648....1944
Twiggs	DD-591....1945
Walke	DD-416....1942
Ward	DD-139, APD-16....1944
Warrington	DD-383....1944
Wasmuth	DD-338, DMS-15....1942
William D. Porter	DD-579....1945
Worden	DD 352....1943

Destroyer Escorts

Bates	DE-68, APD-47....1945
Eversole	DE-404....1944
Fechteler	DE-157....1944
Fiske	DE-143....1944
Frederick C. Davis	DE-136....1945
Holder	DE-401....1944

Leopold	DE-319....1944
Oberrender	DE-344....1945
Rich	DE-695....1944
Samuel B. Roberts	DE-413....1944
Shelton	DE-407....1944
Underhill	DE-682....1945

BATTLE STAR LEADERS

Destroyers

O'Bannon	DD-450....17
Maury	DD-401....16
Russell	DD-414....16
Saufley	DD-465....16
Nicholas	DD-449....16
Morris	DD-417....15
Buchanan	DD-484....15
Taylor	DD-468....15
Fletcher	DD-445....15
Farragut	DD-348....14
Conyngham	DD-371....14
Hughes	DD-410....14
Edwards	DD-619....14
Jenkins	DD-447....14
Dewey	DD-349....13
MacDonough	DD-351....13
Aylwin	DD-355....13
Patterson	DD-392....13
Mustin	DD-413....13
Grayson	DD-435....13
Brown	DD-546....13
Halford	DD-480....13
Dale	DD-353....12
Monaghan	DD-354....12
Phelps	DD-360....12
Bagley	DD-386....12
Ralph Talbot	DD-390....12
Stack	DD-406....12
Sterrett	DD-407....12
Frazier	DD-607....12
Lansdowne	DD-486....12
Bradford	DD-545....12
Thatcher	DD-514....12
Waller	DD-466....12
Radford	DD-446....12
Shaw	DD-373....11
Drayton	DD-366....11
Helm	DD-388....11
Lang	DD-399....11
Wilson	DD-408....11
Schley	DD-103....11
Farenholt	DD-491....11
Cowell	DD-547....11
Boyd	DD-544....11
Cony	DD-508....11
Converse	DD-509....11
Eaton	DD-510....11
Hull	DD-350....10
Gridley	DD-380....10
Anderson	DD-411....10
Ellet	DD-398....10
Kilty	DD-137....10
Caperton	DD-650....10
McDermut	DD-677....10
Dashiell	DD-659....10
Melvin	DD-680....10
Porterfield	DD-682....10
Remey	DD-688....10
Mertz	DD-691....10
Hobby	DD-610....10
McCalla	DD-488....10
Lardner	DD-487....10
Wilkes	DD-441....10
Nicholson	DD-442....10
Pringle	DD-477....10
Stephen Potter	DD-538....10
Hazelwood	DD-531....10
Sigsbee	DD-502....10
Ringold	DD-500....10
Schroeder	DD-501....10
Lavallette	DD-448....10

Destroyers Escorts

Riddle	DE-185....12
Bangust	DE-739....11
England	DE-635....10
Swearer	DE-186....9
Lamons	DE-743....9
Mitchell	DE-43....9
Weaver	DE-741....9
Waterman	DE-740....8
Reynolds	DE-42....8
Hilbert	DE-742....8
Samuel S. Miles	DE-183....8

Over 60 destroyers and destroyer escorts were awarded the Presidential Unit Citation for World War II service. Over 60 won the Navy Unit Commendation. And, 100 were lost.

There is a temptation to close the chapter on destroyers and destroyer escorts at this place and let these significant statistics speak for themselves. But that, of course, would not be fair to the memory of the ships that fought successfully and sacrificially against all comers in all major battles in all places where American and Axis naval forces met. No other combat ship was as versatile as the destroyer, no other major combatant was as fast, and no other major combatant was any more taken for granted.

One reason for taking the destroyer for granted was the fact that there were so many of them. Over 350 destroyers were built during the war to serve with 173 already in commission when the war began. An additional 46 "flush-deckers" were in commission as fast minelayers (8 DMS), fast minesweepers (18 DMS), high-speed transports (4 APD), seaplane tenders (14 AVD) and other auxiliary types (2). Nearly 500 destroyer escorts were built during the war with many transferred to Allied nations and/or converted to transports.

Together destroyers and destroyer escorts totaled approximately 900 in wartime service with the U.S. Navy. With these figures in mind, it is perhaps not surprising to see so many awards for destroyers, not surprising to note that so many were lost, and consequently not surprising that these ships were so often taken for granted.

That destroyers were taken for granted is partially understandable due not only to their large numbers but also their small size. For purposes of historical remembrance the analogy can be made with the journalistic interest in heavyweight boxers as opposed to lightweights; likewise, there is continuing interest in the "glamorous" battleships or carriers as opposed to the destroyer. Despite this preoccupation with size and attendant glamour in historical remembrance, the World War II destroyer was not taken for granted by the armed services that fought the war. They knew the many functions of the destroyer and depended upon them for protection from submarines, for anti-aircraft protection, for gunfire support, for fast transportation to battle sites and a host of other functions. Often enough, enemy submarines and planes broke through defenses, and then the prevailing opinion was that there were not enough destroyers – especially if rescue operations were necessary. The bottom line is that destroyer veterans have reason to hold their heads as high as veterans of any type ship, and if history does not record or remember their salient contributions in proper perspective, then history is the loser.

Although the Army was unable to use much left from World War I, the World War II U.S. Navy inherited a wealth of battleships and destroyers. The German submarine campaign of World War I inspired the building of 267 "flush-deck" destroyers (completed 1918-1921), and even though they were overage (16 years was declared to be the life of a destroyer) and rusty in December 1941, they were immediately ready for service. Fifty were transferred to Great Britain in 1940 in the "ships for bases" transaction, and one of these, *Campbeltown* – formerly USS *Buchanan* (DD-131) – garnered fame as a "suicide ship" when in March 1942 she smashed into the outer gate of the Normandie Dock at St. Nazaire on the French Atlantic coast loaded with commandos and explosives. *Ward* (DD-139), a sister ship of the *Campbeltown* but serving with the U.S. Navy, fired the first shots of the war on the morning of the Japanese attack at Pearl Harbor and sank an enemy midget submarine. Many other flush-deckers, also referred to as "four pipers" or "four stackers," served with distinction throughout the war. Like later sisters, they also suffered. The *Reuben James* (DD-245) was lost to a German submarine torpedo in the Atlantic on 31 October 1941, five weeks before war was declared. Later in the war, *Ward*, serving in 1944 as a high-speed transport (APD), was sunk. Others joined these two under the waves, but on balance the old World War I vintage flush-deckers and the even older *Allen* were definitely in the credit column at war's end.

The first of the post-World War I destroyers were members of the *Farragut* class. These ships, completed in 1934-1935, were the first destroyers to emphasize anti-aircraft protection, and main armament was the 5-inch gun instead of the 3-inch or 4-inch guns of the flush-deckers. Seven members of this class won 10 or more battle stars and had *Worden* (DD-352) not been sunk in January 1943, probably the entire class would have achieved this distinction. After the *Farraguts* came the *Mahans* and the *Porters* (completed 1936-1937), the *Somers* and *Gridleys* (1937-1938), the *Benhams* and *Sims* (1939-1940), the *Bensons* – including the *Gleaves*, *Livermores* and *Bristols* (1940-1943), the *Fletchers* (1942-1944), the *Sumners* (1943-1945), and finally, the *Gearings* (1944-1946). All these classes recorded battle stars with five *Fletcher*-class destroyers ranking among the top nine for all destroyers. Although a number of *Sumners* and *Gearings* commissioned in time to win battle stars, the earlier classes carried most of the World War II combat load.

That so many World War I vintage flush-deckers would serve in World War II with distinction is indicative of the clear vision naval leaders had for many years concerning the functions of destroyers. Destroyers built during the 1930s and into the war years of the 1940s were larger, especially in standard displacement and beam measurements, but overall armament and speed changed relatively little. During the war, changes were made to meet obvious needs

Over five weeks before the Japanese attacked Pearl Harbor, the USS *Reuben James* (DD-245) was sunk in the Atlantic by a German submarine. The destroyer *Greer* was attacked in September 1941, but not hit and the destroyer *Kearny* (DD-432) was torpedoed and damaged 17 October 1941. The World War I vintage "four piper" *Reuben James*, "first to die," sank quickly with the loss of 115 officers and men. USN

The *Ward* (DD-139) made history during her 1917 construction as she was built in less than a month. Considerable fanfare attended the launch of the destroyer after her record-setting construction, and she went on to set another record in another war. In the early morning hours of 7 December 1941, *Ward* fired upon and sank one of the Japanese midget submarines attempting to enter Pearl Harbor. The number three 4-inch gun that fired the telling round into the sub has been preserved as a memorial in St. Paul, Minn. USN

Borie (DD-215), a four-piper sister of *Reuben James* and *Ward*, experienced an eventful combat career in the Atlantic during World War II before she fatally damaged herself by ramming and sinking a German submarine on 1 November 1943. Before her loss, this famous destroyer won the Presidential Unit Citation and three battle stars. USN

One of the more memorable photographs of the war is this one showing the destroyer *Shaw* (DD-373) exploding in dry dock during the attack on Pearl Harbor. The bow of the *Shaw* was completely blown off when the ship's forward magazine exploded, and the dry dock was sunk. However, *Shaw* was fitted with a new bow, refurbished and sent back into the war where she earned 11 battle stars. USN

such as the removal of torpedo tubes in favor of more anti-aircraft weapons in the last months of 1944 and 1945. This, of course, was a response to the absence of surface targets and the increased threat from the air as the U.S. Navy neared the shores of Japan. Japanese submarines and suicide boats were a threat even in the closing days of the war; consequently, depth charge tracks and projectors were not removed.

The chart below provides a comparison of basic destroyer characteristics for the oldest class of destroyers to serve in the war (flush-deckers), as well as the first "new" destroyer class (*Farraguts*) completed in 1934-1935, the largest class to serve and the one class wherein all units were completed during the war (*Fletchers*), and the last class to commission in time to earn battle stars (*Gearings*).

TYPICAL WARTIME CHARACTERISTICS

	Standard Displacement	Length	Beam	Wartime Armament	Complement	Speed	Cruising Radius at 15 Knots
"Flushdeckers"	1,190	314′	31′	6 3-inch or 4 4-inch 4-6 20mm 2 DC tracks 4-6 DC projectors 2 21″ TT (triple)	160	33	2,500
Farragut Class	1,365	341′	34′	4 5-inch 2 40mm twins 5 20mm 2 DC tracks 4 DC projectors 2 21″ TT quads	300	37	5,200
Fletcher Class	2,050	376′	40′	5 5-inch 4-5 40mm twins 6-11 20mm 2 DC tracks 6 DC projectors 2 21″ TT quints	335	37	4,400
Gearing Class	2,425	390′	41′	6 5-inch 2 40mm quads 2 40mm twins 11 20mm 2 DC tracks 6 DC projectors 2 21″ TT quints	345	34	4,600

Before leaving the subject of destroyer characteristics, comment must be made concerning destroyers' ability to sustain damage. No ship is made without some attention given to survivability, but given the beam of a destroyer—whether the 41-foot beam of a *Gearing*, the 40-foot beam of a *Fletcher* or the

The *Bristol*(DD-454) (shown here) was one of the *Benson*-class derivatives that comprised the last class of destroyers to enter service before the United States officially entered World War II. The *Benson* class included the Gleaves, Livermores and Bristols – all very similar but with a few distinguishing differences. *Bristol* won three battle stars before being lost. USN

The *Fletcher* (DD-445) was the class leader of 175 units that were commissioned during the war. The Fletchers are generally acclaimed as the most successful destroyer type to fight in World War II, and recognized as being one of the most successful designs. The class leader won 15 battle stars, and five of the nine leading battle star winners among destroyers were members of the *Fletcher* class. USN

31-foot beam of a flush-decker – and the relative paucity of armor, there was not much that could be done to protect a destroyer from the kind of damage a torpedo or heavy bomb could inflict. In reading the damage reports of destroyers, especially those that were sunk, it is not unusual to learn that some destroyers disappeared in seconds: *Rowan* (DD-405), hit by a torpedo off Salerno on 10 September 1942, sank in 40 seconds with only 72 survivors, while *Maddox* (DD-622), hit by a bomb off Sicily on 10 July 1943, went under in less than two minutes. Seventy-four survived. There are instances of heavily damaged destroyers such as *Evans* (DD-552), *Hugh W. Hadley* (DD-774) and *Laffey* (DD-724) taking multiple hits and surviving, but when one stands on the deck of one of the memorialized *Fletcher*-class destroyers – which had a beam wider than all destroyer escorts and all earlier destroyer classes – it is readily apparent that any destroyer that ever survived a bomb or torpedo was indeed most fortunate. When comparing the thickness of armor on battleships and some cruisers to that of destroyers, the "armor" on destroyers was hardly worthy of the name. When visiting the memorialized *Kidd* (DD-661) in Baton Rouge, one should remember that the kamikaze crashed on the starboard side of the ship, but damage was very severe to the port side as the bomb passed *through* the ship before exploding. A destroyer was no place for the timid.

Most of the 498 destroyer escorts built during World War II did serve with the U.S. Navy and did serve as escort vessels. The United Kingdom received most of the 92 DEs that were transferred, or leased, to Allied powers with Brazil and France receiving the others. Like their larger "big sister" destroyers, some destroyer escorts were also converted to fast transports. In terms of overall characteristics as compared to destroyers, destroyer escorts were lighter in standard displacement (1,400 tons), shorter (306 feet), carried a smaller complement (approximately 210), and slower (23-24 knots). However, the mass-produced destroyer escort was more maneuverable and less expensive than a destroyer. The attribute of maneuverability was particularly favorable as the primary function of the destroyer escort was to track, pursue and attack submarines. Although the destroyer escort did not carry armament to greatly challenge surface vessels (main armament was either two 5-inch guns or three 3-inch), they did carry a full complement of anti-submarine weapons (usually two depth charge tracks, eight single DC projectors and one multiple projector). Toward the end of the war, some destroyer escorts lost their single 21-inch, triple torpedo tubes in favor of more anti-aircraft guns. Typical original anti-aircraft weaponry consisted of one 40mm twin, four 40mm singles and ten 20mm.

In their role as part of the carrier-destroyer escort "hunter-killer" team, the destroyer escorts' contribution cannot be overstated. These teams proved to be the weapon that enemy submarines could not defeat, and the formerly offense-minded submarine became prey instead of pursuer from early 1943 to war's end. Although smaller and slower, several destroyer escorts established war records as memorable as any battleship, carrier, cruiser, destroyer or submarine.

This close-up of the *Patterson* (DD-392), a *Bagley*-class destroyer, gives evidence of the design effort to save superstructure weight. Also, note the narrow beam. In this photo, the *Patterson* is returning a pilot to his carrier. Events such as this usually meant a list of several degrees on both destroyer and carrier as crews joyfully welcomed a man earlier considered lost. USN

The functions of the destroyer ranged from surface combat to anti-submarine and anti-aircraft roles. When not directly confronting the enemy, the versatile destroyer still was a busy ship. A destroyer is shown here approaching a carrier to deliver mail. Destroyers were always near carriers serving as plane guards, rescuing pilots and guarding against submarine attack. USN

MEMORIES OF SUCCESS

Memories of the many successes of destroyers and destroyer escorts would fill a number of large volumes, but attention in this book is centered only on several of the more highly visible battles and individual exploits. From time to time classic stories appear and reappear, and the endeavor herein is to highlight the events that destroyer men will continue to tell as long as there is a U.S.Navy.

In modern times the destroyer developed as a small, fast vessel that could launch torpedoes at larger ships. To defend capital ships against this threat, it was necessary to develop "torpedo boat destroyers." Consequently, the best defense against the new offensive weapon was the same vessel. About the same time that the destroyer entered the fleet, early functional submarines carried the ability to launch torpedoes under the surface. The ship best able to meet this new threat was already available as destroyers added depth charges and developed underwater listening devices. That the destroyer, and later the destroyer escort, was more than equal to the submarine threat is perhaps best illustrated by the extraordinary success of the USS *England* (DE-635) in May 1944. If an analogy could be made between a major league baseball hitter and the exploits of the *England,* it would go something like this: a destroyer or destroyer escort that sank one submarine would be a .300 hitter; to sink two enemy submarines would raise the average to .380; and to sink three enemy submarines would bring the rare distinction of a .400 batting average. *England* sank six Japanese submarines in two weeks. A major league baseball player would have to average about .500 to equal England's incredible performance.

What *England* did in May 1944 was to sink what later records would reveal as a scouting line placed to alert the Japanese command of the U.S. Navy's direction of attack. In June 1944 the attack on the Marianas began, and thanks to *England* the enemy was without full information as to American fleet movements. *England* was not alone in the last two weeks of May. Like most destroyer escorts she was in company with other units of an anti-submarine division, but the depth charges that sank the six enemy submarines were "ashcans" or "hedgehogs" from *England.* One of only three destroyer escorts to win the Presidential Unit Citation for individual actions (as opposed to being part of a successful and/or particularly effective unit), England's name is imperishably written in the history of naval warfare.

Due to the uniqueness of the event and the fact that the captured enemy submarine still exists and is on display at the Chicago Museum of Science and Industry, history will long remember the success of the destroyer escorts *Chatelain* (DE-149), *Jenks* (DE-665), *Pillsbury* (DE-133) and the escort carrier *Guadalcanal* on 4 June 1944. While "Wildcat" fighters tracked the *U-505, Chatelain* attacked and blew the sub to the surface. A brief gun battle ensued with *Chatelain, Jenks* and *Pillsbury* firing 40mm and 20mm shells into *U-505* (these holes are still apparent in 1985). As plans had already been made to attempt the capture of a German submarine in order to investigate technological innovations aboard the undersea raiders, only the light 40mm and 20mm guns were used to respond to German gunfire. This fusilade "encouraged" the German submariners to abandon. While *Chatelain* and *Jenks* picked up the German crew, *Pillsbury* chased the still moving German sub. With difficulty, a small crew from *Pillsbury* boarded the evasive *U-505,* stopped the engines and closed the seacocks to cease flooding. Although there had not been time to set explosives, that danger was expected along with the attempt to flood the sub. Task Group 22.3 received the Presidential Unit Citation, boarders received individual awards and the U.S. Navy received a long-sought technological prize.

The *U-505* boarding was a unique achievement, but there were other incidents of boarding. The major difference was that the *U-505* boarders were attempting to save the sub. On 1 November 1943 the old flushdecker *Borie* (DD-215) engaged a U-boat in a surface gun battle, and in this battle there was no thought of saving anything. After both destroyer and sub had taken several hits, *Borie* rammed the U-boat so hard that for approximately 10 minutes the two vessels were one. While "aboard" the *U-405,* rifles, pistols, knives and empty shell casings replaced main armament, torpedoes and depth charges as the "weapons de jour." And, the idea of boarding was not restricted just to Americans. On 6 May 1944 *Buckley* (DE-51) and *U-66* fought a battle similar to the *Borie-U-405* action. On this moonlit night *Buckley* and *U-66* traded "broadsides" while running alongside each other before *Buckley* rammed the sub. While the two vessels were locked together, German submariners attempted to board *Buckley,* and a few were successful. Just as the hand-to-hand, pistol, rifle and whatever-was-handy fight began, the two vessels separated but were close enough that main batteries still would not bear. After each had attempted to ram, the submarine dove and *Buckley* finished the contest with depth charges. Badly in need of hull repairs, *Buckley* left for repairs and returned to duty in July. *Borie,* however, did not survive the war. On 2 November 1943, the day after her victory over *U-405,* the old four piper sank as a result of hull damage (from ramming) and a storm. *Borie* was awarded the Presidential Unit Citation; *Buckley* received the Navy Unit Commendation.

Because of their relatively small size and paucity of armor, destroyers and destroyer escorts usually did not fare well against either a torpedo or bomb. This statement cannot be made axiomatically, however,

As the U.S. Navy approached the shores of Japan, scenes such as this became common. Many an enemy plane met its end as the result of gunfire from destroyers. Although out of control, the burning plane in this photo narrowly missed the destroyer at left. USN

because *Laffey* (DD-724), *Evans* (DD-552) and *Hugh W. Hadley* (DD-774) took multiple hits and steamed away from battle. One, *Laffey*, not only still exists as a memorial, but served a lengthy period in the post-World War II U.S. Navy. *Laffey* was commissioned 8 February 1944 and was named to honor the memory of Presidential Unit Citation winner *Laffey* (DD-459) which was lost during the momentous Naval Battle of Guadalcanal in November 1942. On 15 April 1945 off Okinawa, *Laffey* (DD-724) was attacked by 22 planes. The *Sumner*-class destroyer shot down nine of her attackers, but was crashed by five planes and hit with four bombs. The topside of the destroyer was extensively damaged (see photos) and 32 were killed. Like the earlier destroyer that carried the same name, *Laffey* (DD-724) earned a Presidential Unit Citation.

Evans and *Hugh W. Hadley* each earned a Presidential Unit Citation on 11 May 1945 when they engaged a host of Japanese bombers and kamikazes. This was the same day that the carrier *Bunker Hill* was hit so hard. Some writers have offered the perspective that the Japanese kamikaze effort might have succeeded if their total effort had been directed at carriers instead of concentrating on the radar-picket destroyers. With this thought in mind, one wonders if *Bunker Hill* would have survived at all had the 100 planes that dove on *Evans* and *Hugh W. Hadley* attacked the big carrier. That speculation aside, one can perhaps speculate that nearly half of these planes might have had more success anywhere else instead of over these two destroyers. The *Fletcher*-class *Evans* was hit by four kamikazes and lost 32 killed while *Hugh W. Hadley*, a *Sumner*-class destroyer, lost 28 officers and men to four kamikazes. But, between them, the two destroyers were responsible for 38 to 46 enemy planes. The two destroyers began the battle nearly side-by-side, but were far apart by the end of the protracted fight. Although *Evans* and *Hadley* survived the 11 May battle, both were so badly damaged that neither served in the post-war Navy.

Another common scene from two months prior to the attack on Pearl Harbor until the end of the war was the sight of water and debris rising high into the air as a result of destroyer and destroyer escort depth charges. Germany lost 768 submarines in World War II and Japan lost 130. Although Britain accounted for most of the German U-boats sunk, U.S. Navy destroyers and destroyer escorts acccounted for apporximately 120 Axis submarines. USN

The battleship *North Carolina*, carrier *Wasp* (CV-7) and destroyer *O'Brien* (DD-415) were all hit by the same spread of torpedoes fired by Japanese submarine *I-19* on 15 September 1942. *Wasp* sank the same day, *North Carolina* steamed away under her own power for repairs and so did *O'Brien*. However, on 19 October *O'Brien* broke up and sank. Note the damaged bow. Japanese submarine *I-19* was sunk by destroyer *Radford* (DD-446) in the Gilbert Islands area, November 1943. USN

When World War II began in Europe in 1939, horses were still a part of the military scene (Poland). By the end of the war in 1945 jet planes, rockets, computers, radar and a host of other technological innovations were in use. In 1943 the Germans employed radio-controlled bombs, and in the Mediterranean two U.S. Navy destroyer escorts added a new dimension to warfare by jamming radio signals that controlled German rocket-propelled glider bombs. One of these nearly sank the light cruiser *Savannah* in September 1943 (197 killed), and the potential of these weapons was quickly recognized. In January 1944 *Herbert C. Jones* (DE-137) and *Frederick C. Davis* (DE-136) were stationed off the Anzio beachhead with the special assignment of jamming German radio signals. For nearly two months the two destroyer escorts were eminently successful in deflecting the enemy glider bomb, but their technological success was deduced by the Germans and both ships received special attention from enemy planes. Near missed too many times to count, both *Jones* and *Davis* survived the multiple attacks with only scratches, and set a precedent for future electronic warfare.

Few surface battles of any consequence were fought without destroyers being significantly involved. Of all the naval units to serve Japan, no type served with any greater distinction than destroyers. In retrospect, Japanese destroyers inflicted more significant damage upon American cruisers and destroyers than did battleships. Forty years after the war, U.S. Navy veterans continue to tip a hat to the performance of Japanese destroyers—especially veterans of the *Northampton, Pensacola, Minneapolis* and *New Orleans*, all victims of Japanese destroyer-launched torpedoes during the Battle of Tassafaronga. But, Japanese destroyer performance in battle was paralleled by U.S.Navy destroyers, particularly in the battles of Balikpapan, Komandorski Islands, Vella Gulf and Cape St. George.

The success of the old flush-decker destroyers *John D. Ford (DD-228)*, *Pope* (DD-225), *Parrott* (DD-218), and *Paul Jones* (DD-230) in the Battle of Balikpapan (Borneo) was overshadowed by a succession of mistakes, failures and lost battles in the early months of the Pacific war.

The tactical victory of these four destroyers on the night of January 24, 1942, had little, if any, effect on the strategic situation in the southwest Pacific, but the destruction of four transports and a patrol boat was great encouragement to a navy greatly in need of it.

On 15 April 1945, *Laffey* (DD-724) took three bombs, two near misses and five kamikaze planes, but survived and eventually fought again off Korea. Perpetuating the name of the destroyer lost during the Naval Battle of Guadalcanal in November 1942, *Laffey* (DD-459) and *Laffey* (DD-724) each won the Presidential Unit Citation. In the bottom photo, six men died in the aft 5-inch gun mount; one survived. Presently, *Laffey* is preserved as a memorial near Charleston, S.C. USN

Shore bombardment and call-fire resulted in damage to numerous U.S. Navy ships as enemy shore batteries often got in hits before they could be silenced. Here, *Hall* (DD-583) is hit off Iwo Jima. Not badly hurt, the destroyer went on to participate in the Okinawa invasion two months later. Eventually, *Hall* was transferred to Greece. USN

This close-up of *Claxton* (DD-571) in dry dock in December 1944 provides a good look at the thin skin of a "tin can." A member of the famous Destroyer Division 23, *Claxton* shared her Presidential Unit Citation with four other members of the division. USN

Lindsey was launched as a *Sumner*-class destroyer but commissioned as a destroyer minelayer (DM-32). On 12 April the ship was hit by two kamikazes and lost 57 men killed and nearly 60 feet of her bow. The ship is seen here off Okinawa shortly after the attack. USN

The all-time champion single-battle kamikaze-killer was *Hugh W. Hadley* (DD-774). Fighting beside another sharp shooting destroyer, *Evans* (DD-552), *Hadley* shot down 23 planes in a two-hour battle off Okinawa. Damaged by four hits, the destroyer suffered the loss of 28 killed, but was able to steam away under her own power. Both *Hugh W. Hadley* and *Evans* won the Presidential Unit Citation, and both were scrapped soon after the war as a result of damage incurred on 11 May 1945. USN

Liberal use of torpedoes by the four raiding destroyers in Balikpapan Bay accounted for most of the damage to enemy ships, but gunfire was employed to good advantage as the ranges to targets were nearly "point blank." Although the Japanese had a dozen destroyers and a cruiser in the bay, the four American destroyers made good their escape without serious injury. A few weeks later on 1 March 1942, however, *Pope* would become the last American warship to be lost to the Japanese in their initial push into southwest Asia. *Pope* was lost in a battle against a much larger Japanese force, and the survivors of her crew would have to await release from a prison camp at war's end to learn that their valiant efforts in Balikpapan Bay and in the Java Sea had won for *Pope* the Presidential Unit Citation.

The Battle of the Komandorski Islands was discussed in chapter three and the role of cruisers *Salt Lake City* and *Richmond* were noted therein. As *Salt Lake City* was the largest and most powerful American ship, she naturally drew most of the enemy's attention and gunfire. But, when the heavy cruiser lost power as a result of several shell hits, it was the attack of destroyers *Monaghan* (DD-354), *Bailey* (DD-492) and *Coghlan* (DD-606) that helped discourage the much stronger enemy force from continuing the already three-hour-plus battle. And, although none of the torpedoes released by the three charging destroyers hit enemy targets, the Japanese retirement gave *Salt Lake City* time to patch up enough to restore power and prepare for more battle, or escape. Only *Monaghan* survived this charge without damage, and the damage incurred by the three was more than made up for by numerous gunfire hits on enemy cruisers and destroyers.

By the time of the August 1943 Battle of Vella Gulf, the U.S. Navy had learned most of the lessons made necessary by faulty torpedoes, lack of torpedo flash hiders, and the lack of success of tying destroyers to cruisers in night battles. A number of lessons in night tactics were learned from tragic experiences with Japanese destroyers, and it seemed that nearly all lessons learned in combat were put to the test on the night of 5 August 1943. On this date six U.S. Navy destroyers steamed to intercept a Japanese force of unknown composition, but known to be transporting troops in the central Solomons region. Discovered by radar, the enemy force consisted of four destroyers, three heavily laden with troops. Before the Japanese destroyers could effectively react, torpedoes fired by *Maury* (DD-401), *Craven* (DD-382) and *Dunlap* (DD-384) found their marks and *Kawakaze,*, *Hagikaze* and *Arashi* went to the bottom. In considerable measure, this victory was the November 1942 Battle of Tassafaronga in reverse. Unhindered by cruisers, the destroyers held gunfire while their torpedoes were running and steamed away with one of the more notable wartime victories for destroyers.

The Battle of Cape St. George was similar to the Battle of Vella Gulf both in tactics and result. Steaming at high speed to intercept ships evacuating enemy pilots and mechanics, *Charles Ausburne* (DD-570), *Claxton* (DD-571), *Dyson* (DD-572), *Spence* (DD-512) and *Converse* (DD-509) caught two Japanese destroyers off Bougainville in the early morning hours of 25 November 1943, and torpedoes from *Ausburne, Claxton,* and *Dyson* destroyed one and fatally crippled the other. *Spence* and *Converse* remained to finish the cripple while the other three American destroyers sped off in pursuit of three other enemy destroyers. Evading Japanese torpedoes, the three American ships fought a long-range gun duel with the three fleeing enemy ships. Two Japanese destroyers escaped, but one was sunk as the result of repeated 5-inch shell hits. Three Japanese destroyers were lost at no cost in lives to American personnel. If American destroyer performance at Vella Gulf in August evened the score for Tassafaronga, success at Cape St. George threw the pendulum far in favor of the U.S. Navy. Not surprisingly, all five U.S. Navy destroyers that fought in this action received the Presidential Unit Citation.

One thought that must have been comforting to the destroyermen who fought in the battle of Vella Gulf and Cape St. George was that they at least had the option of using the destroyers' high speed to put distance between themselves and their opponents if necessary. Such was not the case for *Cole* (DD-155) and *Bernadou* (DD-153) on the evening they won their Presidential Unit Citations. In the early morning darkness of 8 November 1942 these two flush-deckers attempted to slip past enemy defenses during the invasion of North Africa. Cole's assignment was to enter Safi harbor and deposit specially trained assault troops on a pier where the troops were to seize and hold loading cranes that would be needed to unload tanks and other heavy equipment essential for the success of the invasion. *Bernadou* was to steam literally onto the beach to quickly place her assault troops ashore in position to secure vital harbor installations. Both ships were successful in delivering troops to their objectives, and both survived the operation despite being discovered on their way in and having to run a gauntlet of gunfire from enemy shore batteries. In this same operation *Alexander Dallas* (DD-199) earned a Presidential Unit Citation for steaming up the Sebou River to carry assault troops to capture the important airfield at Port Lyautey. This was no minor task as the *Dallas* had to contend with enemy guns as well as nets in the barely navigable stream. After running aground once and blasting her way through a net, the determined destroyer pressed on to the airfield.

Although the Battle of Surigao Strait in the waters of Leyte Gulf is more often recalled as the last battle wherein battleships fought each other, destroyers may

O'Bannon (DD-450) was not preserved as a memorial, but a strong argument can be made that she should have been. *O'Bannon* earned more battle stars than any other destroyer or destroyer escort (17) and the Presidential Unit Citation in World War II. The venerable destroyer fought off Korea (three battle stars) and served into the 1970s. She is shown here in Pearl Harbor late in her career, and changes from her original configuration are evident. USN

well have accounted for more of the damage done to the Japanese force, which included two battleships. Over two dozen destroyers fired torpedoes and 5-inch gunfire into the enemy force, which had already encountered PT-boats and was steaming toward American cruisers and battleships. Documentation of killing hits is impossible when so many ships are involved and when a battle is fought in darkness, but on 25 October 1944, U.S. Navy destroyers launched several dozen torpedoes and post-war evidence indicated that destroyer *Killen* may well have been largely responsible for the fatal damage to battleship *Yamashiro*.

A number of individual destroyers compiled great battle records during World War II, and while space and the major thrust of this book (memorials) does not permit an elaboration on all, this section devoted to destroyer success cannot close without mention of a few. Among battleships, carriers, cruisers, destroyers and submarines that fought in World War II, there was at least one in each category that deserved preservation as a memorial. A top candidate among destroyers would have been, and should have been, *O'Bannon* (DD-450). Winner of the Presidential Unit Citation, this *Fletcher*-class destroyer led all destroyers and destroyer escorts with 17 battle stars for World War II, and she added three more for Korea before steaming into action off the coasts of Vietnam. *O'Bannon* began shooting at the Japanese in surface battles off Guadalcanal and continued through the battles of Kula Gulf and Vella Lavella. In the October Battle of Vella Lavella she was one of three U.S. Navy destroyers that engaged nine Japanese destroyers; both sides lost one ship and *O'Bannon* suffered her most serious wound of the war when she rammed sister ship *Chevalier*, which swerved into O'Bannon's path after taking a fatal torpedo hit. A second candidate for preservation would have been another *Fletcher*-class destroyer, *Nicholas* (DD-449). Like *O'Bannon, Nicholas* fought her way up the Solomons (off Guadalcanal, Kula Gulf and Kolombangara), won the Presidential Unit Citation and registered 16 battle stars for World War II and six for Korea before serving off Vietnam. *Nicholas* and *O'Bannon* demonstrated their versatility as both sank Japanese submarines in addition to hurting the enemy with their guns.

A third candidate for preservation would have been the lead ship of the most successful class of destroyers in World War II, *Fletcher* (DD-445). *Fletcher* garnered 15 battle stars in World War II, five for Korea, sank a Japanese sub on 11 February 1943, and forever won the gratitude of *Northampton* survivors for her rescue work on their behalf 1 December 1942. Another strong candidate would have been *Radford* (DD-446), a *Fletcher*-class destroyer that won 12 battle stars and the Presidential Unit Citation, and had the distinction of sinking Japanese submarine *I-19* which had sunk *Wasp* (CP-7), fatally damaged *O'Brien* (DD-415) and wounded battleship *North Carolina* in September 1942. *Maury* (DD-401), a *Benham*-class destroyer, won the Presidential Unit Citation, 16 battle stars and distinguished herself during the Battle of Vella Gulf. However, members of her class were discarded soon after the war and she was long gone (1946) before plans to establish destroyer memorials were implemented.

Among destroyer escorts that deserved to be preserved, Presidential Unit Citation winner *England* (DE-635), of course, heads the list for her unprecedented kill of six Japanese submarines in less than two weeks. Other candidates would have included *John C.*

Butler (DE-339) with five battle stars, recipient of the Presidential Unit Citation and the Navy Unit Commendation and survivor of "Taffy 3" in the 25 October 1944 Battle off Samar; *Bronstein* (DE-189) with a Presidential Unit Citation, four battle stars and primarily responsible for the sinking of three German submarines; and *Lawrence C. Taylor* (DE-415). *Lawrence C. Taylor* did not win any major awards and recorded only seven battle stars, but she did sink the last Japanese submarine lost in World War II (July 1945), and in November 1944 she sank the Japanese submarine (*I-26*) that sank the U.S. Navy cruiser *Juneau* in November 1942.

The reader should note that the "recommendation-for-preservation-as-a-memorial" is only the presumption of the author. And, destroyers and destroyer escorts lost during the war were not "recommended" for the obvious reason.

Nicholas (DD-449), like *O'Bannon,* also had a strong claim for preservation. Often in company with *O'Bannon, Nicholas* fought her way up the Solomons and on to Japan winning 16 battle stars and a Presidential Unit Citation. Her name is presently in use in the U.S. Navy as a frigate, FFG-47, carries on her tradition of excellence. *Nicholas* is pictured here in World War II configuration. USN

The identity of this destroyer is not known, but the picture speaks for itself. The danger to a destroyer posed by a storm is evident, and any destroyer operating in a storm with partially empty tanks is subject to disaster. Although the infamous typhoon of 18 December 1945 is well remembered, other ships were lost during World War II in storms, including *Warrington* (DD-383). USN

MEMORIES OF SACRIFICE

During World War II a total of 71 destroyers and 11 destroyer escorts were lost to all causes. However, these totals do not include another 17 destroyers and one destroyer escort that were lost while serving under other designations. In the Presidential Unit Citation listings and Navy Unit Commendation awards, and in the listings of ships lost (Ultimate Sacrifice), destroyers and destroyer escorts are included that carried different official designations before, during or after the period of their award or demise. In this book the contention is "once a destroyer or destroyer escort, always one."

This contention is not officially compatible with U.S. Navy records, but it is compatible with the reality that change in official designation did not totally alter the functions of "former" destroyers and destroyer escorts. Many of these ships continued to sink enemy submarines, fight surface battles, shoot down enemy planes and bombard enemy shore positions even though they had officially become minelayers, minesweepers, seaplane tenders, fast transports or auxiliaries.

The 100 destroyers, destroyer escorts and former DDs and DEs were lost to enemy aerial and submarine torpedoes, bombs and gunfire, but they were also lost to storms, collisions, mines and even by running aground. On at least three occasions, all hands went down with their ship–*Edsall* (DD-219) and *Pillsbury* (DD-227) in the Java Sea area on 1 March 1942, and *Jarvis* (DD-393) on 9 August 1942 south of Guadalcanal. *Edsall, Pillsbury* and *Jarvis* were lost to Japanese guns and bombs. Other particularly tragic combat losses included *Sims* (DD-409) in the Coral Sea with only 14 survivors; *Barton* (DD-559) and *Laffey* (DD-459) off Guadalcanal in November 1942 with personnel losses of over 90 percent for both destroyers; and *Jacob Jones* (DD-130), with only 11 survivors after being torpedoed off New Jersey in February 1942. But, nearly equal losses were sustained by destroyers to non-combat causes. *Ingraham* collided with a fleet oiler during an Atlantic convoy run on 22 August 1942 and only 11 lived, while 90 percent of the officers and men aboard *Spence, Hull* and *Monaghan* were lost in the infamous 18 December 1944 typhoon. The capricious storm matched the fleet's evasive course changes and capsized the *Fletcher*-class *Spence*, which, along with other members of the famous "Little Beavers" of Destroyer Squadron 23, was a Presidential Unit Citation Winner. Only 23 of Spence's crew survived. Sixty-two survived the sinking of *Hull*, but only six lived to tell the story of Monaghan's last moments. *Hull* and *Monaghan* were both *Farragut*-class destroyers with known stability problems due to wartime weight additions topside. The *Fletcher*-class *Spence* did not have the problem to the same degree, but to the storm it made no difference. Unlike the losses of *Edsall, Pillsbury* and *Jarvis*, whose fates were not immediately known, the loss of *Spence, Hull* and *Monaghan* was promptly announced to the American public before next of kin knew exactly who had survived and who had not. Controversy over this tragedy still exists.

Despite the fact that Guadalcanal and Okinawa were American victories, the price paid for both was painfully high. And in both places, the number "15" was unlucky for the U.S. Navy. The armada that steamed toward Okinawa in early 1945 was tabbed "the fleet that came to stay." This expression has come to have a double meaning as the U.S. Navy not only

Spence (DD-512), a winner of the Presidential Unit Citation with other members of Destroyer Division 23, was lost in the infamous 18 December 1945 typhoon. Whereas *Hull* and *Monaghan*, both *Farragut*-class destroyers sunk in the same storm, were known to have topside weight problems which affected stability, the loss of the *Fletcher*-class *Spence* indicated that design alone could not be blamed for the capsizing of the three destroyers. Only 23 survived the sinking of *Spence*. USN

stayed off the shores of Okinawa despite kamikazes and resolute resistance, but also left 15 destroyers and destroyer escorts beneath the waters around that island. Beneath the waters off Guadalcanal, another 15 destroyers still remain.

It has been said that Guadalcanal was not only a place but an emotion. For destroyermen, both Guadalcanal and Okinawa are emotions.

Memories of destroyer and destroyer escort sacrifices are longer than the list of those that made the ultimate sacrifice as scores were damaged but not sunk. Some of the more publicized stories of damaged DDs and DEs, in addition to accounts of *Evans, Hugh W. Hadley* and the second *Laffey*, are those of the *Hazelwood* (DD-531), which lost 77 to a kamikaze off Okinawa; supreme sub-killer *England*, which lost 37 to a kamikaze on 9 May 1945 off Okinawa; and the accounts of losses sustained by the still surviving memorialized destroyers *Kidd* (DD-661) and *Cassin Young* (DD-793).

Of all the stories that will continue to be told and retold from World War II that concern destroyers and destroyer escorts, one will endure beyond all others. Not even the unparalled success of the *England* will grasp the attention of future generations in the same manner as will the charge of the *Johnston, Hoel* and *Samuel B. Roberts* (DE-413) off Samar on 25 October 1944. The circumstances of the battle were related in chapter two in connection with the escort carrier *Gambier Bay*. Here, attention is directed to an event that could well serve as the epitome of both sacrifice and success in the same action.

Destroyer *Heermann* (DD-532) and destroyer escorts *John C. Butler* (DE-339), *Raymond* (DE-341) and *Dennis* (DE-405) accompanied *Johnston, Hoel* and *Samuel B. Roberts* in both the effort to conceal the thin-skinned escort carriers with smoke and in the headlong charge against Japanese battleships, cruisers and destroyers. All seven American ships were awarded the Presidential Unit Citation for this action, but *Johnston, Hoel* and *Samuel B. Roberts* will be remembered the longest because thay paid the highest price. *Johnston* earned an eternal reputation for steaming at the enemy to make a torpedo attack *with no torpedoes. Hoel* took some 40 hits and fought until 90 percent of her complement was dead, and destroyer escort *Samuel B. Roberts* – which would not have been faulted for concentrating on making smoke instead of attempting to fight a battleship with just two 5-inch guns – continued to fire her guns until waves swept over her decks.

Sacrifice? Yes. The men who served in these seven ships knew the odds and their chances of survival. But, they pointed their bows and guns toward the enemy and did not seek quarter. Success: Yes. The Japanese force was hurt by torpedoes and gunfire, and even if they had not suffered hits, they were delayed in their push toward the American transports and beachhead by dodging torpedoes. Japanese withdrawal was in part spurred by concern about additional air attacks, but a second consideration was the tenacity of the destroyers and destroyer escorts attacks. Surely, such ferocity could only be inspired by the near presence of American battleships and cruisers! To the contrary, men aboard the American "tin cans" knew they were the last line of defense, and they fought accordingly.

Lost in the 18 December 1945 typhoon was *Hull* (DD-350) (shown here) and *Monaghan* (DD-354), two *Farragut*-class destroyers. Sixty-two survived the sinking of *Hull* but only six survived the loss of *Monaghan*. Before sinking, *Hull* earned 10 battle stars; *Monaghan* earned 12 along with downing Japanese submarine *I-7* in June 1943. Of the eight members of the *Farragut*-class – the first "modern" destroyer class – seven won 10 or more battle stars in World War II. USN

To see one was nearly to see all. A variance in main armament (two 5-inch guns or three 3-inch guns) was about all that distinguished one class of destroyer escorts from another. Four hundred and ninety-eight destroyer escorts were built during World War II; 86 of these were leased to Allied countries. Eighteen destroyer escorts serving with the U.S. Navy won the Presidential Unit Citation, and operating with CVEs in hunter-killer teams, destroyer escorts played a paramount role in winning the Battle of the Atlantic. In the Pacific their performance was equally distinguished. USN

Despite outstanding war records by a number of destroyer escorts, two are destined to be remembered more often than their sisters: *England* (DE-635) and *Samuel B. Roberts* (DE-413) (shown here). *England* sank six Japanese submarines in less than two weeks. *Samuel B. Roberts* charged enemy battleships and cruisers off Samar on 25 October 1944, and even though sunk in this action, she will be remembered for courage the size of a battleship, and a fighting spirit equally large. USN

They were only 77 to 80 feet long and they were made of wood, but to Japanese troops transported in barges and other inter-island craft, they were the most fearsome vessels afloat. The fastest fighting machines on water they necessitated the development of the destroyer–originally "torpedo boat destroyers." PT boats performed a host of functions, and attacked all classes of combat ships and auxiliaries in World War II. USN

DESTROYER MEMORIALS

As destroyers and destroyer escorts have been named for U.S. Navy heroes, it is therefore understandable that memorials do not exist in the manner one finds for battleships, which are named for states, and cruisers, mostly named for cities. Memorials honoring destroyers and destroyer escorts that have been scrapped or transferred to other countries do not exist in abundance. In consideration of the fact that close to a thousand destroyers and destroyer escorts were associated with World War II, very little remains relative to what exists from the small number of battleships that served. Still, there is a wealth of World War II destroyer history available in the form of several memorialized destroyers and one destroyer escort.

It is the Northeast and South that possess the wealth of destroyer and destroyer escort history by virtue of memorialized ships. The Boston area is particularly fortunate to have two memorialized destroyers. The *Gearing*-class *Joseph P. Kennedy, Jr.* (DD-850) commissioned on 15 December 1945, three months after World War II ended, and therefore did not win any battle stars for World War II. However, the *Kennedy* did win two battle stars for action off Korea, and drew considerable notoriety for her role in President John F. Kennedy's inauguration, and for her interception of a Soviet ship during the 1962 Cuban missile crisis. Today, she rests in Battleship Cove at Fall River, Mass., along with the Battleship *Massachusetts*, submarine *Lionfish*, two PT boats and other historical artifacts. The *Kennedy* is particularly significant to World War II history in the sense that she is the home of the Tin Can Sailors national organization. Twice a year destroyer veterans gather aboard the ship to visit, clean and paint the *Kennedy*. As time continues to pass, it is expected that destroyer veterans born long after 1945 will continue this tradition in helping to preserve the *Kennedy*. In 1986, about the time this book is due off the press, a planned Destroyermen's National Museum is to open aboard the *Kennedy*.

The World War II history that exists aboard the *Kennedy* will have been placed there. As it is still being placed, no assessment can be made, although there were numerous items of interest on display in 1985. World War II history is aboard the *Allen M. Sumner*-class *Laffey* (DD-724) (five battle stars for World War II, two for Korea) at Patriots Point near Charleston, S.C., even though present displays are few. Commissioned 8 February 1944, *Laffey* saw action off Normandy on D-Day (hit by a shore battery with only minor damage) before moving on to the Pacific where she was active off the Philippines and Okinawa. While serving as a radar picket off Okinawa, *Laffey* took three bombs, two near misses and five kamikazes that killed 32 and wounded 71. In this battle Laffey's crew shot down nine planes and saved their badly damaged ship. For this action *Laffey* was awarded the Presidential Unit Citation.

The Presidential Unit Citation awarded to *Laffey* (DD-724) is presently on display inside the destroyer. In the same compartment is the Presidential Unit Citation awarded to the earlier destroyer *Laffey* (DD-459), which was sunk during the Naval Battle of Guadalcanal in November 1942. *Laffey* (DD-459) traded broadsides with Japanese battleship *Hiei* and was sunk by the combination of the battleship's 14-inch guns and a destroyer-launched torpedo. In an effort to capture the mood of the compartment in which both *Laffeys* are honored, a photo has been placed in the Color section of this book. The effort will not succeed totally because it does not include the entire compartment, and because the photograph contained here does not adequately convey the compartment's ambiance. The entire compartment is painted flat black, and red lights are placed in a manner to allow the visitor to see the large color paintings of the two destroyers

The *Joseph P. Kennedy, Jr.*, (DD-850) was built during World War II but commissioned three months after the end of the war. The *Kennedy*, however, did earn two battle stars off Korea, was centrally involved in the Cuban Missile Crisis, and today serves in memorial status at Fall River, Mass. The *Kennedy* is home for the national Tin Can Sailors Association. Author's Collection

Two U.S. Navy destroyers carried the name *Laffey* in World War II and both won the Presidential Unit Citation. *Laffey* (DD-459) won her award during the Naval Battle of Guadalcanal in November 1942 while *Laffey* (DD-724) won her's off Okinawa for battling 22 attacking enemy planes. Author's Collection

In 1985 *Laffey* (DD-724) is preserved as a memorial within the Patriot's Point Naval and Maritime Museum across the river from Charleston, S.C. In this picture, *Laffey* is seen beside submarine *Clamagore* with the bow of the nuclear merchant ship *Savannah* at upper right. In the distance at upper left is a unit of the contemporary Navy and historic Fort Sumter. This picture was taken from the flight deck of the carrier *Yorktown* (CV-10). Author's Collection

in their finest hours, and to see the large Presidential Unit Citation plaques awarded to each ship. The attempt to use black paint, direct lighting and wreaths honoring those killed, succeeds in creating the somber ambiance which is most appropriate to call attention to the success and sacrifice to two U.S. Navy destroyers greatly deserving of remembrance.

Without question, the compartment off the main deck just described is the highlight of a visit to the *Laffey*. The other areas of the destroyer that help one return to the World War II era are the three 5-inch gun mounts. These appear essentially as they did during World War II. However, most of the topside superstructure is different now as *Laffey* was "FRAMED" (Fleet Rehabilitation and Modernization) in 1962. The torpedo tubes aboard now are not those aboard in 1945, and the bridge and masts are different; the stacks are essentially the same. World War II 40mm and 20mm anti-aircraft guns are gone and overall appearance is not the same, but these are considerations that would distract only the visitor seeking World War II history exclusively. With the exception of the battleship *Massachusetts*, preserved World War II warships do not highlight the specific areas where they were hit by enemy bombs, shells, torpedoes or planes. Pictures, charts and narrative near the places aboard

Thanks to patriotic citizens in Louisiana, the USS *Kidd* (DD-661) has been and continues to be restored to its World War II configuration. Preserved as a memorial in 1983, the *Kidd* succeeds in displaying the famous *Fletcher*-class destroyer in 1945 appearance. On 11 April 1945 this destroyer was hit by a kamikaze just aft of the bridge on the starboard side. Courtesy of Tim Rizzuto

In order to document the condition of the *Kidd* when it was transferred to the Louisiana Naval War Commission, one compartment was left "as is." The remainder of the destroyer has been cleaned, painted and polished to appear in 1985 as though she is going back into commission. Courtesy of Tim Rizzuto

A unique feature of the *Kidd* is a specially built docking and restraining system. The ship is seen in these two photographs mostly out of the water in June 1985. The *Kidd* is completely afloat about six weeks of the year, and completely out of the water resting on keel blocks much of the year (summer and fall). When partially or completely out of the water, the underside of the destroyer is available for study. Author's Collection

where a ship was damaged would be especially interesting and meaningful in the opinion of this writer. Perhaps this will be undertaken in the future if others feel the same and communicate these thoughts to respective curators.

The *Fletcher*-class destroyers are often reputed to be the "backbone" of the American destroyer force during World War II. Commissioned soon after the United States entry into World War II, the 175 *Fletchers* were well suited to wartime conditions and they compiled enviable records. Three *Fletchers* have been preserved as memorials: the *Kidd* (DD-661) at Baton Rouge, La.; the *Cassin Young* (DD-793) at Boston, Mass.; and *The Sullivans* (DD-527) at Buffalo, N.Y.

Of the destroyers that have been preserved as memorials, the *Kidd*, on the Mississippi River at Baton Rouge, has been restored closest to World War II appearance. And, with the possible exception of the USS *Constitution*, no ship memorial of any kind from any era presents a more historically accurate appearance or a more pleasing one than the *Kidd*. The citizens of Baton Rouge, city officials, state officials and those directly responsible for maintaining the *Kidd* have set a standard of excellence that could well serve as a model for others. The destroyer is unbelievably clean even to the point of keeping brass polished and the upholstery of chairs in seemingly new condition (see color photo on back cover). The country has been searched for ashcans, hedgehogs, tear-drops, 20mm and 40mm gun mounts in an effort to present *Kidd* as she was in 1945. The use of paint on the hull is what one would have found on DD-661 at one period during the war, and the freshness of paint and overall appearance inside and out gives the impression that *Kidd* is going back into commission within a matter of

days. The amount of work that has gone into the ship is documented by having left one small compartment as it was when the ship was acquired from the U.S. Navy after being in mothballs for nearly 20 years (see photo).

Named for Rear Adm. Issac C. Kidd, who was lost on *Arizona* 7 December 1941, *Kidd* was awarded four

The restoration of the *Kidd* has been successful to such a degree that the only improvement that could be made to this wardroom would be to place food on the plates. The now peaceful *Kidd*, which flew the "Jolly Roger" pirate flag in the Pacific, won four battle stars in World War II. Author's Collection

battle stars for World War II and four for action off Korea. Commissioned 23 April 1943, the destroyer was struck on the starboard side by a kamikaze on 11 April 1945, suffering 38 killed and 55 wounded. Although struck on the starboard side between the forward stack and the bridge superstructure, the bomb passed through the port side of the destroyer before exploding. As the area of damage is not marked on the *Kidd* (there is a plaque honoring the men lost), when visiting note that the point of initial impact was about main deck level just forward of the number one stack, and that the bomb left the ship at main deck level under the aft portion of the bridge superstructure.

Those responsible for acquiring and preserving the *Kidd* are justifiably proud of the unique docking system that allows the destroyer to rise and fall with the 40-foot rise and fall of the Mississippi River. In the late summer and fall, the *Kidd* is completely out of the water and rests on keel blocks similar to what she would find in a dry dock. In the spring and early summer the destroyer is afloat. There is no "at sea" feeling even when the ship is afloat as the Mississippi River is not very wide at Baton Rouge. But that is a very minor consideration because the World War II historian will be far too occupied with the wealth of history to be seen and experienced, and too impresssed with the 1945 restoration effort still in progress. Indeed, no tour of the country to visit World War II memorials is complete without a stop here.

The *Cassin Young* (DD-793), in Boston's Charlestown Navy Yard, is very close to the *Kidd* in both historical restoration and in overall appearance. Acquired by the National Park Service in 1978, efforts to maintain and restore the destroyer have been notably successful. Resting only a few feet from the long-

The narrow beam of destroyers is apparent in this view of the *Fletcher*-class destroyer *Cassin Young* (DD-793), preserved as a memorial in the old Charlestown Navy Yard, Boston. A total of 88 destroyers – including destroyers converted to other official designations such as fast transports and minesweepers – were lost in World War II. Author's Collection

The *Cassin Young* won the Navy Unit Commendation and four battle stars during World War II. Like the *Kidd*, the *Cassin Young* is now presented to the public in near original configuration, and is maintained in excellent condition by the National Park Service. Author's Collection

The Sullivans (DD-537), named for the five brothers lost aboard the cruiser *Juneau* in November 1942, is preserved as a memorial along with the cruiser *Little Rock* in the Buffalo and Erie County Naval & Servicemen's Park. *The Sullivans* earned nine battle stars for World War II and two for service off Korea. Author's Collection

preserved USS *Constitution* and only a short distance from Bunker Hill and many other historical sites, the *Cassin Young* offers the historian World War II-era 20mm and 40mm gun mounts, depth charges and torpedo tubes. Like the experience with the *Kidd*, it has been difficult to find all the World War II electronic gear that was removed in the post-war era. And, like the *Kidd*, no markings existed in 1985 to show where this destroyer was hit by a kamikaze (starboard amidships).

Named for Medal of Honor winner Capt. Cassin Young, who distinguished himself at Pearl Harbor as commanding officer of *Vestal* and as commanding officer of the cruiser *San Francisco* before being killed on her bridge during the Naval Battle of Guadalcanal, *Cassin Young* (DD-793) received the Navy Unit Commendation and four battle stars for action in World War II. Commissioned 31 December 1943, she suffered 22 killed and 45 injured when hit by a kamikaze off Okinawa 29 July 1945.

The Buffalo & Erie County Naval & Servicemen's Park features the cruiser *Little Rock* and destroyer *The Sullivans* (DD-537). Like the *Kidd* and *Cassin Young*, *The Sullivans* is a *Fletcher*-class destroyer, but the now-preserved ship has lost some significant portions of her original configuration. Noticeably absent is the number three 5-inch mount and in place of her original torpedo tubes are more recent Mark 44s. Despite this, the World War II history is still here, especially in the compartment given over to the remembrance of the five Sullivan brothers and their lost cruiser, *Juneau* (see Cruiser chapter). This compartment, along with another memorial to the five brothers in Waterloo, Iowa, will continue to honor the memory of one family's great sacrifice in defense of the nation.

The Sullivans began life as *Putnam*, but the name was changed before the destroyer was complete, and on hand to sponsor the ship at her launching was Mrs. Thomas F. Sullivan, mother of the five brothers. Carrying a "lucky shamrock," *The Sullivans* was commissioned 30 September 1943 and served to war's end, earning nine battle stars. Reactivated for Korea, the destroyer earned two more battle stars. The "lucky shamrock" served *The Sullivans* well as she did not receive serious injury during World War II or off Korea. Today, the large, green shamrock is painted on the forward stack and it is a remembrance that stays with a visitor long after leaving Buffalo. Of all the interesting artifacts at Servicemen's Park, however, the longest lasting remembrance is the motto "We Stick Together," which is printed on a ramp leading to the destroyer.

The Sullivans resembles her World War II configuration less than either *Kidd* or *Cassin Young*. The number three 5-inch gun mount has long since been removed and the torpedo tubes shown in this picture are a later design than what the ship carried from 1943 to 1945. Note the slogan "We Stick Together." Author's Collection

There is only one destroyer escort that has been preserved as a memorial, and that is the *Stewart* (DE-238). Commissioned 31 May 1943, *Stewart* steamed into the Atlantic looking for German submarines and any other trouble the enemy might provide. However, *Stewart* was not awarded a battle star. Considering the fact that she served in a dangerous combat zone, she is deserving of remembrance as a combat veteran..

Inheriting the name of a flush-deck destroyer (DD-224) that had earned two battle stars before being damaged in early 1942 in the Java Sea area and captured by the Japanese for their use, *Stewart* (DE-238) will continue to have a unique history as the last surviving member of her type. Located in Seawolf Park on the Houston Ship Channel at Galveston, Texas, the memorialized destroyer escort sits high and dry *on land* as does the famous World War II submarine *Cavalla* enshrined beside her. Barring a terribly severe hurricane, she will not again touch water.

The view from the bridge of the *Stewart* is fantastic. Large ships pass before the *Stewart* and *Cavalla*, "aided" in their navigation to and from the blue and green Gulf of Mexico by scores of seagulls. Aboard the *Stewart*, the history buff can be satisfied that most of what he or she can see is just as it was in World War II. *Stewart*, like most destroyer escorts, was decommissioned soon after the war, so there was no modernization program. *Stewart* carried three 3-inch guns instead of two 5-inch guns as main armament, but other than this characteristic, the *Stewart* looked–and looks –like any other destroyer escort to serve with the U.S. Navy in World War II.

Inside the *Stewart* there is very little in 1985 in the manner of memorials to honor other destroyer escorts. However, there are plans to change this, and a significant museum may be created there. In view of the great contributions rendered by destroyer escorts (see Presidential Unit Citation and Navy Unit Commendation lists), a lasting, appropriate, extensive memorial exhibit needs to be created. And, such an exhibit should contain library facilities for future generations that will come searching for the history of these great ships.

All of the preserved ships discussed above deserve and need support either by volunteer service for maintenance or by financial support. All are still relatively new memorials (*Stewart* 1974, *The Sullivans* 1977, *Laffey* 1978, *Cassin Young* 1981 and *Kidd* 1983), and what they will be to future generations depends upon what is done in the next few years.

Veterans of the destroyer escort *Merrill* (DE-392) are well aware of this need, and have been working hard of late to find a final, permanent home for several significant portions of their ship that escaped destruction when the DE was scrapped. Artifacts from the bridge of *Merrill* were loaned by the Navy to the Louisiana Maritime Museum in the early 1970s, and in 1985 these items were tracked down by one of Merrill's veterans while searching for the builder's plaque (seek and be surprised at what you will find). Other destroyer escort veterans will probably search

Only one destroyer escort of 498 built during World War II has been preserved as a memorial. The USS *Stewart* (DE-238) did not win any battle stars in World War II, but she did serve in a combat zone for many months. Located at Galveston, Texas, the *Stewart* has been enshrined alongside the famous World War II submarine *Cavalla*. Both sit on dry land, and barring a first magnitude hurricane, neither will touch the sea again. Note the two 3-inch guns forward of the bridge. Author's Collection

In 1985 the *Gearing*-class destroyer *Southerland* (DD-743) was still in mothballs at Bremerton, Wash. *Southerland* won one battle star in World War II, eight off Korea and 10 off Vietnam. Her destiny appears to be the scrap pile. Few World War II-era destroyers still exist in mothballs or in foreign navies. Before the turn of the century, all that will exist will be the five memorialized destroyers now open to the public. Author's Collection

In a battle on 12 April 1945 the *Sumner*-class *Hugh W. Hadley* and *Fletcher*-class *Evans* (DD-552) shot down 38 to 46 Japanese planes. Both earned the Presidential Unit Citation for the action. Aboard the battleship *Alabama* is a compartment honoring the memory of the destroyer *Evans* and her heroic day off Okinawa. The *Evans* was built only a few miles from the memorialized battleship. Author's Collection

in vain as the Navy kept very little from these ships before they were towed to the ship breakers.

Most curators are greatly concerned with the aesthetic appeal of their museum. This is standard. One of the problems with this, however, is that an important artifact may not be on display because of aesthetics. This may or may not have been the reason (just didn't think to ask) that one of the most significant parts of any ship to fight in World War II was chained to a wall *in the basement* of the Naval Academy Museum. Stumbled upon by accident in 1984, still there in the early months of 1985, was the scoreboard from the bridge of the destroyer escort *England* (see photos in this chapter and in Color section). A small plaque above the approximately 4-foot by 5-foot piece of steel identifies the scoreboard as being from the *England*, but a quick glance is all that is necessary for a historian to recognize that six painted flags under a rendering of a submarine could only be from *England*.

Other than a small compartment aboard the *Alabama* that honors the memory of the *Evans* (DD-552), the remaining parts of destroyers and destroyer escorts are scattered around the country in somewhat random fashion rather than appearing in a status directed toward fully memorializing a respective destroyer. The compartment aboard the *Alabama* honoring the *Evans* (see picture) is primarily a photographic display. *Evans*, a *Fletcher*-class destroyer built not far from

One of the highlights of the destroyer *Foote* (DD-511) was her participation in the 1943 Battle of Empress Augusta Bay. Presently, the mast from the destroyer is displayed on the grounds of the Admiral Nimitz Museum in Fredericksburg, Texas. The American flag and flag of the admiral now fly from the mast. Author's Collection

where the *Alabama* now rests, is quite deserving of remembrance for her battle against kamikazes off Okinawa. Equally deserving is a major memorial for *Hugh W. Hadley*; presently, however, one similar to that of the *Evans* does not exist.

Parts of World War II destroyers exist mainly in storage or on display in recruiting centers and naval reserve centers. For example, the steering wheel of the *Fletcher* has been on loan to the Navy Recruiting Service in Puyallup, Wash.; the steering stand of the *Gearing* has been on loan at Mayport, Fla., while the destroyer's annunciator is located in Newark, N.J.; Buckley's wheel, stand, and rudder indicator were loaned to the Naval Training Center at Orlando, Fla., while the helm stand and wheel of destroyer escort *Ricketts* has resided at the University of Florida ROTC Department. Other artifacts have been placed on loan by the Navy or given to museums for display. Examples are the mast of the *Foote* and searchlight from *Frankford* (DD-497) at the Admiral Nimitz Museum in Fredericksburg, Texas, and the number three, 4-inch gun from the *Ward* (DD-139) in St. Paul, Minn. In the early morning hours of 7 December 1941, the *Ward* attacked and sank one of the Japanese midget submarines attempting to get inside Pearl Harbor before Japanese carrier planes arrived.

If the Tin Can Sailor's Association did no more than they have already done, there is enough left to document for future generations the contributions they and their ships made in World War II. And, a few veterans' groups have sponsored memorial plaques like those honoring *Melvin* (DD-680) and *Reid* (DD-369) at the Nimitz Museum. Of course, it is hoped that more will be done, and that more information, artifacts and memorabilia will be placed on display in

On the grounds of the state capitol in St. Paul, Minn., is the number three 4-inch gun removed from the destroyer *Ward* (DD-139) during her conversion to fast transport APD-16. A round fired from this gun struck and sank a midget submarine attempting to enter Pearl Harbor before Japanese planes arrived on 7 December 1941. Courtesy of Minnesota Historical Society

In March 1985 the scoreboard of the destroyer escort *England* (DE-635) was chained to a wall in the basement of the Naval Academy Museum at Annapolis, Md. In the second picture of the *England*, taken in May 1945 just after she was hit by a kamikaze, the port side scoreboard is clearly visible. Examination of the two photos reveals that the preserved scoreboard was taken from the starboard side of the bridge structure. Author's Collection and USN

the near future aboard the *Kennedy, Laffey, Kidd, Cassin Young* and *The Sullivans.* Some destroyers such as the *O'Bannon, Reuben James,* and *Hugh W. Hadley* need some special memorial. The Navy continues to perpetuate some names – i.e., *Nicholas* (FFG 47) – and as appropriate as this is, something more needs to be placed to ensure the remembrance of great ships, great crews, and great examples of success and sacrifice.

The men who served on destroyer escorts have already proven themselves more than equal to the challenge of war. In war they were courageous and resourceful. As part of the hunter-killer teams, they swept the German U-boats into oblivion and won the Battle of the Atlantic. In the Pacific, they were no less courageous or resourceful, and the challenge there was met and won. Since the war, these veterans have proven their mettle by raising families in an uncertain age, and they have helped provide the United States with a paramount place among nations. At reunions they continue to prove that age has not diminished their vitality, camaraderie or thirst. But, there is still one challenge remaining that confronts these men as individuals, as members of their respective reunion groups and as members of the Destroyer Escort Sailors Association. That challenge is to provide future generations with some tangible reminder that *England* meant more than the name of a country; that *Samuel B. Roberts* was not an unsuccessful candidate for president; that *Bronstein* was not a Wall Street broker and that *Chatelain, Frost, Pillsbury, Pope, John C. Butler, Dennis, Merrill, Menges* and *Riddle* were not members of some long-forgotten baseball team.

Whether it is done at Fall River, Galveston, Charleston or some other location, it is incumbent upon those who can best tell their own story to create a photographic-narrative-memorabilia museum exhibit, and establish as full a library as possible to document the story of the World War II destroyer escort. It is a magnificent story, and its equal in scope will most likely never occur again. And time is slipping away...*

In the modern age the ships that have come to be named and known as "destroyers" trace their history back to the invention and development of the self-propelled torpedo and the small, fast "torpedo boats" that launched the torpedoes. This weapon was a threat to the largest capital ships and to counter it, "torpedo boat destroyers" were built. In time only the term "destroyers" was used and their functions were expanded beyond defending against the quick torpedo boats by becoming a platform themselves for the launching of torpedoes. In essence, the World War II destroyer was a large "torpedo boat," among other things. At this place, then, it is proper to note the few remaining PT boats that have been preserved as

*See addendum.

Battleship Cove at Fall River, Mass., is not only home to the battleship *Massachusetts*, destroyer *Kennedy* and submarine *Lionfish*, but is also home for two PT boats and the most extensive memorial in the country honoring veterans of PT boats. An Elco PT boat (619) is on display across from the *Massachusetts* while compartments within the battleship house a PT boat museum and library that rivals the space and quality of the battleship's exhibit. Author's Collection

Inside a World War II Quonset hut is the 78-foot Higgins PT boat 796, the last known PT boat known to have served with the U.S. Navy in World War II. In addition to what can be seen in these two pictures, other artifacts such as engines and squadron insignia are on display. Author's Collection

Along with destroyer *The Sullivans* and the cruiser *Little Rock* is this PT boat at the Buffalo and Erie County Naval and Servicemen's Park. Made of wood, these very fast boats depended upon their speed to carry them into and out of trouble. During World War II PT boats attacked every type of Japanese vessel from barge to battleship. Author's Collection

memorials.

PT boats were mostly made of wood, and any individual who has owned a wood boat knows that after 10 years any service rendered by that boat is "gravy." After 40 years, it is not surprising that so few of the fast (over 50 knots) PT boats survive. The major PT boat exhibit is within Battleship Cove at Fall River, Mass. Inside the battleship *Massachusetts* are several large compartments, with an excellent exhibit honoring PT boats and their crews. All the artifacts and memorabilia one would expect to find in such an exhibit are there–including models and pictures of former PT boat commander John F. Kennedy. One large model on display was used in the John Wayne movie "In Harm's Way." The large exhibit rivals the exhibit devoted to the battleship itself and cannot be fully seen without allowing more than an hour. An hour would allow one just to see the museum, not study it or visit the library. A few feet from the battleship are two PT boats, one inside a protective Quonset hut and the other, an 80-foot Elco (PT-617) outside (see photos). The "housed" PT-796, a 78-foot boat with 21-foot beam and displacing 55 tons, is the last known operable Higgins' type boat used by the U.S. Navy in World War II. The history of the World War II PT boats is documented here about as well as any historian could expect.

On the grounds of Buffalo's Naval and Servicemen's Park a visitor will find another preserved PT boat sitting on land beside the cruiser *Little Rock*. This boat cannot be viewed as well as the two at Fall River, but it is well maintained and serves to remind that service on a PT boat was only for a man who could not understand the meaning of the word "fear."

In 1976 a historical marker was placed to honor veterans of PT boats at Melville, R.I., the Motor Torpedo Boat Squadron's Training Center. Like destroyer veterans, veterans of the "Mosquito Fleet" deserve a "well done" for documenting their history for future generations.

Although there are preserved destroyers, all are *Fletcher, Sumner* or *Gearing*-class ships. Very little remains in museums or other displays to honor the several pre-war destroyer classes. Therefore, this photograph is placed here to call into remembrance the hundreds of battle stars earned, awards won and sacrifices of the pre-war destroyers. USN

BELLS

Nearly all of the bells aboard World War II battleships, carriers and cruisers still exist even though the ships have long since been dismantled, sunk as targets or otherwise discarded. Many battleship bells are now located in museums in their respective state capitols and cruiser bells are often found in namesake cities. Most carrier bells that still exist are held in storage by the Navy, but many are on display at various museums across the country.

Of particular interest are three bells that survived despite the wartime sinking of their respective ships. A bell from the USS *Northampton* (CA-26) survived as it was removed from the cruiser due to a crack before CA-26 was sunk at Tassafaronga in 1942. For similar reasons a bell was removed from the ill-fated USS *Indianapolis* (CA-35) before the ship was lost only days before World War II ended. The *Northampton* bell follows "Nora" reunions; the *Indianapolis* bell is in the namesake city.

In Chicago's Museum of Science and Industry is a bell from the USS *Chicago* (CA-29) (see photo), which was sunk off Rennell Island in January 1942. The bell is unquestionably genuine. However, a plaque below the bell indicates it was removed from the cruiser in a "strip ship" operation *after* the ship went down. As the *Chicago* sank to a depth of 10,000 feet–submarines could dive to a maximum of 600 in 1942–it would seem there is more to the history of this bell than is apparent.

The pictures in this section generally do not require identification as the ship's name is engraved on the bell. On three, however, the names are not clear: the bell of the *West Virginia* (BB-48) is shown in front of the ship's wheel; the bell of the *Biloxi* (CL-80) rests beside an art print; and the bell of the *Portland* (CA-33) is attached to the ship's mast. The *West Virginia* bell is in the state capitol museum complex, Charleston, W. Va.; Biloxi's bell is in the City Hall building, Biloxi, Miss.; and the bell of the *Portland* is part of the CA-33 memorial at Fort Allen Park, Portland, Me.

The ship's bells of the *Intrepid* and *Yorktown* are aboard these two preserved carriers in 1985. Earlier in this book, one can view the bell of the *Massachusetts* (BB-59) (Chapter One), the bell of the *Ranger* (CV-4) (Chapter Two) and the bell of *Helena* (CA-75) (Chapter Three). The bell of the *Massachusetts* is aboard ship in 1985 as she has been preserved. However, "the" bell of the *Alabama* seems to be everywhere: one is on board, another rests in front of the gift shop (see photo), and another is within the Hampton Roads Naval Museum (see photo in Chapter Three–*Alabama* bell is above *St. Louis* builder's plaque). Of course, all the large ships had more than one bell.

In addition to those already mentioned, the other bells pictured here in 1985 were located as follows: USS *Maryland* at Annapolis, Maryland State Capitol; USS *Oklahoma City* at Kirkpatrick Center, Oklahoma City, Okla.; USS *Pensacola* at the old City Hall, Pensacola, Fla.; USS *California* at the State Capitol, Sacramento, Calif.; USS *South Dakota* at "SoDak" memorial, Sioux Falls, S.D.; USS *Enterprise* in front of Bancroft Hall, U.S. Naval Academy, Annapolis, Md. (rung when Navy beats Army); USS *Mobile* aboard the *Alabama* at Mobile, Ala.; USS *New Orleans* at the Louisiana Maritime Museum, New Orleans, La.; and USS *Panay* at the Naval Academy Museum, Annapolis, Md.

Several ship's bells not pictured here deserve mention. The bell of the USS *San Francisco* was originally part of the memorial to the ship, but was later removed when the mast rusted through. The bell of the *Arizona* has been dedicated in memorials several times, as might be expected. On display at the Nimitz Museum in 1985 is the bell of the submarine *Hake*. During the war it was blown off its mounting in a depth charge attack but was still sitting on deck when the sub surfaced. And, the bell of the destroyer *Balch* (DD-363) was reunited with the ship's veterans nearly 40 years after DD-363 was scrapped.

WARSHIPS NAMED YORKTOWN
1840 SLOOP-OF-WAR
Sunk by hitting a reef 1850
1889 GUNBOAT (NO. 1)
Decommissioned 1919
1937 AIRCRAFT CARRIER (CV-5)
Three Battle Stars - World War II
Sunk at the Battle of Midway 1942
1943 AIRCRAFT CARRIER (CV-10)
"The Fighting Lady"
Eleven Battle Stars - World War II
Five Battle Stars - Vietnam War
Decommissioned 1970
U.S.S.
1943

U.S.S.

U.S.S.
SOUTH DAKOTA
1942

U.S.S.
PANAY
1928

U.S.S. MOBILE
U.S.S.
MOBILE
1943

U.S.S.
1944

PENSACOLA

U.S.S. NEW ORLEANS
PRESENTED TO THE U.S.S. NEW ORLEANS
BY THE PEOPLE OF NEW ORLEANS
OF THEIR APPRECIATION OF THE
A VESSEL OF THE U.S. NAVY NAMED

U.S.S.
INTREPID
1943

U.S.S. MARYLAND -1946

CHAPTER FIVE
SUBMARINES

PRESIDENTIAL UNIT CITATION

Albacore	SS-218
Archerfish	SS-311
Barb	SS-220**
Batfish	SS-310
Bowfin	SS-287**
Cavalla	SS-244
Flasher	SS-249
Gato	SS-212
Greenling	SS-213
Guardfish	SS-217*
Gudgeon	SS-211
Haddock	SS-231
Harder	SS-257
Jack	SS-259
Nautilus	SS-168
Parche	SS-384
Pintado	SS-387
Queenfish	SS-393
Rasher	SS-269
Redfish	SS-395
Sailfish	SS-192
Salmon	SS-182
SandLance	SS-381
Seahorse	SS-304
Sealion	SS-315
Silversides	SS-236
Spadefish	SS-411
Tang	SS-306*
Tinosa	SS-283
Tirante	SS-420
Trigger	SS-237
Trout	SS-202
Tunny	SS-282*
Wahoo	SS-238

**Navy Unit Commendation
*2 awards

NAVY UNIT COMMENDATION

Aspro	SS-309
Atule	SS-403
Barb	SS-220
Bergall	SS-320
Bluegill	SS-242
Bonefish	SS-233
Bowfin	SS-287
Crevalle	SS-291
Croaker	SS-246
Dace	SS-247
Darter	SS-227
Grayback	SS-208
Growler	SS-215
Guitarro	SS-363
Gurnard	SS-254
Haddo	SS-255
Halibut	SS-232
Hammerhead	SS-364
Hawkbill	SS-366
Lapon	SS-260
Pargo	SS-264
Permit	SS-178
Picuda	SS-382
Plunger	SS-179
Pogy	SS-266
Puffer	SS-268
Raton	SS-270
Ray	SS-271
S-44	SS-155
Sea Devil	SS-400
Seawolf (2 awards)	SS-197
Skate	SS-305
Sunfish	SS-281
Swordfish	SS-193
Tautog	SS-199
Thresher	SS-200
Trepang	SS-412
Trigger	SS-237

SUBMARINE BATTLE STARS

Narwhal	SS-167....15
Thresher	SS-200....15
Nautilus	SS-168....14
Tautog	SS-199....14
Plunger	SS-179....14
Gato	SS-212....13
Finback	SS-230....13
Seawolf	SS-197....13
Drum	SS-228....12
Flying Fish	SS-229....12
Silversides	SS-236....12
Stingray	SS-186....12
Guardfish	SS-217....11
Haddock	SS-231....11
Whale	SS-239....11
Saury	SS-189....11
Seadragon	SS-194....11
Tambor	SS-198....11
Trout	SS-202....11
Gar	SS-206....11
Gudgeon	SS-211....11
Trigger	SS-237....11
Greenling	SS-211....10
Grouper	SS-214....10
Bluefish	SS-222....10
Permit	SS-178....10
Pollack	SS-180....10
Seal	SS-183....10
Sturgeon	SS-187....10
Spearfish	SS-190....10
Searaven	SS-196....10

ULTIMATE SACRIFICE

Albacore	1944
Amberjack	1943
Argonaut	1943
Barbel	1945
Bonefish	1945
Bullhead	1945
Capelin	1943
Cisco	1943
Corvina	1943
Darter	1944
Dorado	1943
Escolar	1944
Flier	1944
Golet	1944
Grampus	1943
Grayback	1944
Grayling	1943
Grenadier	1943
Growler	1944
Grunion	1942
Gudgeon	1944
Harder	1944
Herring	1944
Kete	1945
Lagarto	1945
Perch	1942
Pickerel	1943
Pompano	1943
R-12	1943
Robalo	1944
Runner	1943
S-26	1942
S-27	1942
S-28	1944
S-36	1942
S-39	1942
S-44	1943
Scamp	1944
Scorpion	1944
Sculpin	1943
Sealion	1941
Seawolf	1944
Shark (SS-174)	1942
Shark (SS-314)	1944
Snook	1945
Swordfish	1945
Tang	1944
Trigger	1945
Triton	1943
Trout	1944
Tullibee	1944
Wahoo	1943

There is often a hesitancy among historians to attempt to record the contributions of United States Navy submarines in World War II. First, there is a continuing disagreement concerning number of ships sunk and gross tonnage put under the waves by U.S. Navy submarines. For instance, veterans of the *Bowfin* (SS-287) openly acknowledge that their sub officially ranks 15th in enemy vessels sunk and 17th in gross tonnage sunk. But, they are equally emphatic that the Japanese kept very poor records and did not admit to all the ships they lost during the war. Therefore, many *Bowfin* veterans believe their true record was what they claimed: 44 vessels sunk and 179,946 tons sunk – totals that would place *Bowfin* first among subs in both categories. A monument only a few feet from the enshrined battleship *Texas* honors the submarine *Seawolf* (SS-197), and engraved upon the impressive bronze plaque is the claim that this sub sank 27 ships and downed 108,600 tons. Officially, *Seawolf* is credited with 18 ships sunk and 71,609 tons. And, the preserved *Cod* (SS-224) at Cleveland, Ohio, claims 40 ships sunk on her conning tower and in the brochure provided to visitors. Officially, *Cod* was credited with far fewer *ships* sunk as 500 tons was the criteria for a "ship"; most of Cod's victims were junks, motor sampans and barges which were well under 500 tons.

A second reason for hesitancy in attempting to write the story of U.S. Navy submarines in World War II is the apprehension concerning anyone's ability to adequately convey the courage necessary to go into battle in a submarine. When one walks the decks of a destroyer or destroyer escort, one is impressed by the narrow beam of these ships, and there is an immediate concern – justified by experience – as to the possibilities of surviving a torpedo hit. A submarine has an even smaller beam, and if one feels apprehensive about personal safety while standing on the deck of a destroyer or destroyer escort, then one most certainly will call into question the motivations that inspire a man to serve in a submarine.

The above "hesitancies" noted, this writer will press on because, first, there is always the possibility that the veterans' claims are as valid or even more valid than official records; secondly, *Bowfin*, *Seawolf* and *Cod* do not require unofficial claims to document their fame or places in history. *Bowfin* was one of only five U.S. Navy combatants to win both the Presidential Unit Citation *and* the Navy Unit Commendation during World War II,[1] while *Seawolf* was one of only three major combatants to win two Navy Unit Commendations during World War II,[2] and *Cod* had the unusual distinction of having all seven of her war patrols designated successful as she was officially credited with 26,985 tons sunk including a destroyer. Third, words cannot and will not adequately convey the courage necessary to go into battle in a submarine, but one must nonetheless make the effort.

Escort carriers, destroyers and destroyer escorts won the Battle of the Atlantic by defeating German submarines and keeping open the economic lifelines between the United States – the arsenal of democracy – and Europe. The Pacific war was won in large part because U.S. Navy submarines closed the shipping lanes that were the economic lifelines of Japan. There is considerable evidence to support the contention that the greatest single blow to Japan's war fortunes was the loss of merchant ships. Whereas the contributions of destroyers and destroyer escorts are sometimes seemingly taken for granted, it is rare that the success of American submarines in World War II is overlooked, taken for granted, understated or diminished in significance.

If any aspect of the submarine contribution is occasionally overlooked, it is versatility. This is forgivable because American submarines were so overwhelmingly successful in their primary mission of sinking enemy merchant and naval vessels. Still, the U.S. Navy submarine was utilized for numerous functions that had to be at least the equal to sinking enemy ships or they would not have been thus employed. Before major amphibious landing, submarines were detailed to potential landing areas for reconnaissance; planes would alert the enemy, and the snooping submarine had better possibilities of remaining undetected. Late in the war, the submarine – out of surface targets to hunt – became the favorite of all vessels among pilots and aircrews for their rescue and lifeguard work. From the beginning to near the end of the war, submarines served as transports for commando raids and for supplying guerrillas in the Philippines and in other enemy-held territories. Special missions, including delivery of coast-watchers and evacuation of refugees, were never-ending, and a submarine was often called upon for scouting, mine laying or detection, picket boat destruction, weather forecasting and even shore bombardment (the big older submarines *Nautilus* (SS-168) and *Narwhal* (SS-167), which carried two 6-inch deck guns, were especially prominent in this capacity). The only function that did not seem to be successful was the effort to tie the submarine to surface ships for a major battle. When employed in this role, the submarine did an excellent job as a scout, but when the shooting began the submarine was more effective when able to move about freely.

Unlike the large number of destroyers built during World War I that served with distinction in World War II, U.S. Navy submarines that saw combat service from 1941 through 1945 were built after World War I. The "S" boats built in the 1920s saw service in World

1. *Enterprise* (CV-6), *John C. Butler* (DE-339), *Barb* (SS-220), *Trigger* (SS-237) and *Bowfin* (SS-287).

2. *Hopkins* (DMS-13) [formerly (DD-249)], *Morrison* (DD-560) and *Seawolf.*

Bottom: A later U.S. Navy submarine with the same name would gain fame as the world's first nuclear submarine, but *Nautilus* (SS-168) earned her fame in combat. During World War II *Nautilus* earned a Presidential Unit Citation, 14 battle stars, sank five ships, carried commandos to Makin Island and Attu, and performed the first major photo-reconnaissance mission for a submarine (Gilbert Islands, 1943). *Nautilus* is seen here before America's entry into the war. Twenty-three of the 52 subs lost in World War II were commissioned before 7 December 1941. USN

The *Gato* class and near-sister *Balao* class were considered the workhorses of the submarine fleet in World War II. Seventy-three Gato's were built and 132 "thick-skinned" Balao's were ordered. All 10 of the top 10 U.S. Navy submarines in official tonnage sunk were Gatos or Balaos as were seven of the top eight in number of ships sunk. Pictured is the *Balao* (SS-285). USN

War II, but were not well suited to the demands of the Pacific war. Six were lost during the war and one, *S-44*, won the Presidential Unit Citation for sinking the Japanese heavy cruiser *Kako* in August 1942 before she herself was lost in October 1943.

The "S" boats were followed by the unsuccessful *Barracuda* class – the *Argonaut*, the two Narwhals, the *Dolphin*, and the two Cachalots. In 1935 and 1936, the 10 Porpoise-class (P class) submarines were commissioned, and these were the first successful fleet boats in terms of design; they were also successful in combat. In 1938 and 1939, the 16 *Salmon-Sargo*-class boats were commnissioned, and these famous boats were followed in 1940 and 1941 by the 12 equally famous *Tambor*-class boats. When war began 7 December 1941, the *Gato*-class boats were just beginning to commission. These boats – along with the later very similar *Balao class – would become the workhorses of the submarine fleet. During the war 73 Gatos were built and 132 Balaos and 134 Tench*-class boats were ordered. Most of the deep-diving Balaos commissioned in time to see service, but less than a dozen *Tench*-class boats made war patrols due to their late arrival.

The quickest way to distinguish the pre-war submarine classes from the newer classes is to remember that numerical designations up through 211 were prewar. The *Gato* class began with the class leader carrying the number 212 (one *Gato* class member, *Drum* (SS-228), did commission a month before Pearl Harbor), *Balao* was SS-285 and *Tench* was SS-417. As technical considerations are beyond the scope of this book, only the specifications of the Gato-class boats are presented here. It should be noted, however, that the specifications for the Gatos were similar to all the fleet submarines from the P class to the *Tench* class.

Gato-Class Specifications

Displacement	1525 standard (surface)
Length	312 feet
Beam	27 feet
Torpedo tubes	6 bow, 4 stern
Torpedos carried	24
Speed	20 knots surface, 9 submerged
Complement	60 to 80
Operating depth	300 feet (*Balaos* 400 feet)
Range	10,000 miles (about 2½ months)

Before the war was over, the members of the "S" class were removed from combat as well as other survivors of several earlier classes. That the Gatos and near-sister Balaos were considered the workhorses of the submarine fleet is documented by the fact that these boats were awarded 28 of the 34 Presidential Unit Citations and 30 of the 38 Navy Unit Commendations. And, seven of the top eight submarines in ships sunk and all 10 of the top subs in tonnage sunk were Gato-Balaos. The contributions of submarines of earlier classes, however, can be substantiated by noting that 19 of the top 31 subs in battle stars were pre-*Gato*, and that 23 of the 52 subs lost during the war were pre-*Gato*.

MEMORIES OF SUCCESS

When World War II began for the United States in December 1941, the U.S. Navy had 111 submarines in commission, 51 of which were in the Pacific. When the war ended in the late summer of 1945, 288 submarines had served including 52 which had been lost during the conflict. With only 1.6 percent of the Navy's personnel in submarines, this force accounted for approximately 55 percent of all Japanese merchant and naval shipping, and approximately 30 percent of all Japanese warships sunk. All of this was accomplished in spite of significant problems with torpedoes. After nearly two years of war the torpedo defects were corrected, but historians will always speculate on how the war would have been different had American submarines possessed effective torpedoes from the first day of the war.

Forty years after the end of World War II it would appear that memories of success relevant to submarines would fall into four categories: 1) the legendary boats; 2) the "great moment" boats; 3) the "great record" boats; and 4) the "forgotten famous" boats. Three boats belong in the category of the legendary boats: the *Wahoo* (SS-238), *Tang* (SS-306) and *Harder* (SS-257). *Wahoo* was the first submarine legend in the sub force. Blessed with great leadership by having Cmdr. Dudley W. "Mush" Morton as CO and Lt. Cmdr. Richard "Dick" O'Kane as exec., this sub sank 20 ships in 1942 and 1943. Awarded the Presidential Unit Citation for her success, *Wahoo* was an extremely aggressive boat that set the pace for contemporary and later boats. For operating in shallow water, attacking at every opportunity, and on one occasion even surfacing to allow crew members to throw incendiaries at a trawler not worthy of a torpedo, *Wahoo* had become a legend by the time of her loss in October 1943. Even her loss reflected her aggressive spirit as she was one of the first boats to enter the Sea of Japan with its unknown dangers.

Before *Wahoo* began her last patrol, Cmdr. Dick O'Kane was detached to take command of *Tang* (SS-306). Tang's success was no surprise as Morton had assigned periscope duties to O'Kane during Wahoo's attacks. Although Tang's operational career was relatively short, like *Wahoo*, she made the most of her opportunities. Once sinking 10 ships in two weeks during the summer of 1944, Tang's abrogated career was still good enough to find her at war's end in second place in ships sunk (24) and fourth in total tonnage (93,824). One of only five U.S. Navy combatants to win two Presidential Unit Citations during the war, *Tang* was also renowned for her rescue work, having saved the lives of 22 airmen.

Harder, like *Wahoo* and *Tang*, was blessed with an extremely proficient and aggressive CO, Cmdr. Sam Dealey. *Harder* was officially credited with 16 ships sunk and three of these were destroyers, the submarine's natural enemy. Harder's assault on destroyers – two others were damaged – helped influence an entire Japanese fleet to move to a safer haven late in the war. Like *Tang, Harder* took rescue work seriously, and one of the more famous pictures of the war is an aerial photo showing *Harder* just off a beach braving enemy fire while attempting to rescue downed aviators (the effort was successful despite enemy interference and complications from an uninvited "friendly" float plane). *Harder*, too, won a Presidential Unit citation, but like *Wahoo* and *Tang*, official awards did not bring legendary status. The Presidential Unit

The first submarine to become a legend in World War II was *Wahoo* (SS-238) commanded by Cmdr. Dudley "Mush" Morton. Morton's executive officer was Dick O'Kane who went on to become CO of another legendary sub, *Tang*. Despite being lost to air attack off Japan in October 1943, *Wahoo* was so aggressive and effective that at the end of the war nearly two years later she still ranked sixth in ships sunk. This was the crew and sub that demonstrated the full potential of the Navy's fleet submarine. USN.

Albacore (SS-218) sank more Japanese naval ships than any other American submarine, won a Presidential Unit Citation and earned nine battle stars. However, her sinking of two destroyers and a light cruiser is overshadowed by her sinking of the new carrier *Tahio* in June 1944. *Albacore* was lost with all hands in November 1944, believed to have been the victim of a mine. USN

Tautog (SS-199), a pre-war *Tambor*-class sub, led all U.S. Navy submarines in number of enemy ships sunk (26). *Tautog* placed 11th in tonnage sunk, earned 14 battle stars and a Navy Unit Commendation. She is seen here in 1940. Note the absence of anti-aircraft guns. USN

Rasher (SS-269) had a great record during World War II having placed second in tonnage sunk (only 330 tons behind *Flasher*). She sank 18 ships and won a Presidential Unit Citation. Serving off Vietnam into the 1970s she deserved preservation but was scrapped. The most successful of the Manitowoc-built subs, *Rasher* is seen here in 1953 serving as a radar picket sub. A portion of *Rasher's* conning tower survives at the Columbia Maritime Museum. USN

One of the great World War II stories of both success and tragedy attends *Seawolf* (SS-197). *Seawolf* won two Navy Unit Commendations for sinking 18 ships (71,609 tons) but was mistakenly sunk in a "safety" zone by the combined efforts of U.S. Navy aircraft and the destroyer escort USS *Rowell* (DE-403). She was carrying 17 Army Rangers on a special mission to the Philippines when she was lost in October 1944; this incident documents what can happen when communications fail. USN

Citation awards – like the Medal of Honor awarded to O'Kane and to Dealey and Morton's four awards of the Navy Cross – were only pleasant footnotes. As long as there are submarines in the U.S. Navy, the names *Wahoo, Tang,* and *Harder* will have meaning far beyond the names of medals and awards.

At least 13 World War II submarines could be included in the "great moment" category. Although these boats may well have had outstanding careers, they will most likely be remembered as time passes for one specific day, moment, event or battle. *Albacore* (SS-218) sank more Japanese naval ships than any other American sub, won a Presidential Unit Citation and earned nine battle stars. However, her sinking of two destroyers and a light cruiser and receipt of awards is overshadowed by the day in June 1944 when she torpedoed and sank the new and powerful Japanese carrier *Taiho.*

The largest aircraft carrier of any nation ever to be sunk in action was the *Shinano,* originally intended to be the third super-battleship in the Japanese Navy. When *Archerfish* (SS-311) sank this leviathan on 21 November 1944, she earned a Presidential Unit Citation and a special place in naval history. *Cavalla,* now resting in memorial status at Galveston, Texas, earned her Presidential Unit Citation and niche in naval lore for the 19 June 1944 sinking of the Japanese carrier *Shokaku. Shokaku,* one of the six Pearl Harbor raiders, had survived the battles of the Coral Sea, Eastern Solomons and Santa Cruz. She and sister ship *Zuikaku* were perhaps the two best Japanese carriers of the war.

Sealion (SS-195) had her great moment eight days before *Archerfish* sank *Shinano.* On 21 November 1944, *Sealion* caught the Japanese battleship *Kongo* off Formosa and sank her along with an escorting destroyer. This was the only enemy battleship downed by a U.S. submarine during the war. One of the few heavy cruisers sunk by a U.S. Navy submarine was *Kako,* sunk by *S-44* in August 1942. *Kako* was one of the Japanese cruisers that helped sink three American and one Australian heavy cruisers off Savo Island a few days earlier. It took *Batfish* (SS-310) four days to experience her great moment. From 10 February to 13 February 1945 *Batfish* sank three Japanese submarines and thereby earned the unofficial title of "America's sub killer." Having sunk a destroyer (August 1944) along with several merchant vessels, *Batfish* was a candidate for a Presidential Unit Citation before her "sub performance" in February ensured the award.

All told, *Jack* (SS-259) was credited with 15 ships sunk, but her great-moment performance occurred on 19 February 1944 when she downed four tankers. Tankers rated high on the priority list of targets just behind carriers and battleships and ahead of several combatants. *Guardfish* (SS-217) won two Presidential Unit Citations, sank 19 ships and earned 11 battle stars, but will probably best be remembered for the occasion when she was so close to Japan that her men could watch a horse race through a periscope. *Darter* (SS-227) and *Dace* (SS-247) shared their great moments together when they torpedoed three Japanese cruisers, sinking two and damaging the third, in the early stages of the October 1944 Battle of Leyte Gulf. For their discovery of the approaching enemy formation and subsequent successful attacks, both subs were awarded the Navy Unit Commendation.

Tirante (SS-420) and *Parche* (SS-384) did not win their respective Presidential Unit Citations together in the same action, but their combat performances were similar. *Tirante,* commanded by Medal of Honor winner Lt. Cmdr. George L. Street, sailed boldly into one of the Yellow Sea's shallow harbors to sink three enemy ships in the spring of 1945. The commanding officer of *Parche,* Cmdr. Lawson P. Ramage, also won a Medal of Honor for holding his sub on the surface 31 July 1944 in a free-for-all action which resulted in the sinking of two Japanese ships and severe damage to a third. *Growler* (SS-215) earned a Navy Unit Commendation for an action fought on the surface, but her great moment is better related later in the Memories of Sacrifice section.

Most of the submarines of "legendary" and "great moment" status had outstanding careers and great records. The following 14 boats may have lacked that one momentous battle or sinking that would have assured historical notoriety, but over their many months of service, they compiled records too great for history not to remember them. At the top of the category of "great record" boats would have to be *Tautog* (SS-199), *Flasher* (SS-249), *Barb* (SS-220) and *Bowfin* (SS-287). *Tautog,* a pre-war *Tambor*-class boat, led all U.S. Navy submarines in number of enemy ships sunk with 26 officially credited. *Tautog* was 11th in tonnage sunk, and she earned a Navy Unit Commendation and 14 battle stars. *Flasher,* whose conning tower has been enshrined at Groton, Conn., was the leading U.S. Navy submarine in total tonnage sunk with an official 100,231 tons credited. *Flasher* earned the Presidential Unit Citation and, along with *Jack,* earned a reputation as a "tanker killer". *Barb* was one of only five U.S. Navy combatants to earn the Presidential Unit Citation *and* the Navy Unit Commendation; she officially sunk 17 ships and placed third in tonnage sunk. Some may wish to remember *Barb* for a "unique moment" when she sent a party ashore to blow up a train and then assumed the role of a cruiser by bombarding a Japanese village with her deck gun. *Bowfin,* also a winner of the Presidential Unit Citation and Navy Unit Commendation, and *Barb* claimed far more tonnage sunk than what was officially credited. Both subs may well have actually surpassed *Flasher* in tonnage sunk, but without supporting documentation from Japanese records, history will never know. What is known is that Japanese record keeping did not equal the

American effort, especially in negative aspects. To hear the name "Nautilus," the vessel that comes to mind is either Jules Verne's fictional vessel or the first nuclear submarine, commissioned in 1954. As this page is being written, final preparations are being made to enshrine the historic nuclear *Nautilus* just outside the submarine base at Groton, Conn. However, the world's first nuclear submarine inherited her name from a World War II sub that sank five ships, earned 14 battle stars and won a Presidential Unit Citation. *Nautilus* (SS-168) is primarily remembered for transporting commandos to Makin Island (August 1942) and Attu (May 1943), and for completing the first major photo-reconnaissance mission for a submarine in World War II (Gilberts 1943).

Snook (SS-279), *Spadefish* (SS-411) and *Tinosa* (SS-283) were all built during the war, but they had time to register great records. *Snook* sank 17 ships (unless otherwise noted, official statistics are used) for a total of 75,473 tons; *Spadefish* sank 21 ships for a total of 88,091 tons and earned a Presidential Unit Citation; while *Tinosa* sank 16 ships for 64,655 tons and also won a Presidential Unit Citation.

Other World War II submarines that would have claim to the "great record" category would be *Silversides* (SS-236), *Drum* (SS-228), *Sailfish* (SS-192), *Cod* (SS-224), *Narwhal* (SS-167) and *Seawolf* (SS-197). As all or significant parts of the first five subs listed have been preserved, their records are registered later in this narrative. Seawolf's outstanding record is presented with the story of her loss in Memories of Sacrifice.

The last category of this arbitrary division of successful submarine remembrance is the "forgotten famous" boats. The eight U.S. Navy submarines included in this category were certainly legends to those who served aboard. In some regards they had great moments, and most any observer would agree that all eight had great records. However, when submarine stories appear, these eight boats that earned fame seem to be forgotten. *Rasher* (SS-269) sank 18 ships and placed second among all U.S. Navy submarines in tonnage sunk, only 330 tons behind the official leader, *Flasher*. Still in service during the Vietnam War, this Presidential Unit Citation winner was greatly deserving of preservation, but she was scrapped. *Trigger* (SS-237) won both the Presidential Unit Citation and Navy Unit Commendation – a rare feat – sank 18 ships, placed seventh in tonnage sunk and earned 11 battle stars. *Tunny* (SS-282) shared with submarines *Tang* and *Guardfish*, escort carrier *Fanshaw Bay* (CVE-70) and submarine rescue vessel *Pigeon* (ASR-6) the very rare distinction of being awarded two Presidential Unit Citations for service during World War II.

Gato's (SS-282) claim to fame was based on being leader of her class and receipt of a Presidential Unit Citation, while *Gudgeon* (SS-211) made her mark by sinking 71,047 tons of enemy shipping, winning 11 battle stars and a Presidential Unit Citation. *Thresher* (SS-200) tied *Narwhal* (SS-167) for leadership among submarines in battle stars with 15, earned a Navy Unit Commendation and sank 17 ships for a tonnage total of 66,172. *Stingray* (SS-186) did not win either of the two major awards a submarine could earn, but she did make more war patrols than any other sub (16) and was credited with 12 battle stars. And, *Seahorse* is remembered for sinking 20 ships for a total of 72,529 tons.

One of the classic World War II incidents of personal sacrifice occurred on *Growler* (SS-215) just after she collided with a large enemy gunboat (damaged bow seen here). Ordering others below, the wounded commanding officer, Lt. Cmdr. Howard W. Gilmore, then ordered his sub to dive without waiting for him to reenter. USN

MEMORIES OF SACRIFICE

In the preceeding section, 38 highly successful boats were treated. Eleven of those 38 did not live to see the end of the war. *Darter* was lost, but her crew was saved. Of the other 10 submarines, eight were lost with all hands (*Wahoo, Harder, Seawolf, Trigger, Gudgeon, Albacore, Snook* and *Growler*) while nearly all the officers and men aboard *Tang* and *S-44* were lost.

Of the 288 U.S. Navy submarines ready for duty in World War II, 52 were lost to all causes, 41 to enemy depth charges, air attack, surface gunfire, mines and shore batteries. Even with Japanese records available at the end of the war, there is still a question concerning the exact cause of nearly a quarter of the boats sunk. It is known that 38 boats were lost with all hands, and that 374 officers and 3,131 men are still on "eternal patrol." Viewed in terms of average personnel numbers assigned to the submarine force, these losses were very high. Being a relatively small force, many submariners were well accquainted with crewmen aboard other boats. Therefore, every announcement of a lost submarine was a devastating blow to the force.

The closeness of the men who served on submarines is evident in what they have done since the end of the war. Walk into most any naval museum and there is a plaque honoring 52 lost submarines and 3,505 officers and men. Visit the memorialized ships across the country and chances are that a monument will exist somewhere on the ship or adjoining grounds honoring those "still on patrol." After V-J Day, the voices of Sub Vets spoke and their hands wrote and built to ensure remembrance of their friends whose voices and hands are forever stilled. Submarine veterans alone fully understand the courage and sacrifice necessary to serve on a submarine. And, they have been determined to ensure that the ultimate sacrifice of their elite force will not be forgotten.

None of the submarine losses were easily accepted during the war although it is fair to say that some losses were especially difficult to accept. The losses of *Wahoo, Harder* and *Trigger* with all hands (including Morton and Dealey) were particularly difficult. The loss of *Tang* at the acme of her service was hard to accept as she was sunk by one of her own torpedoes off Formosa in October 1944. This boat, which had been so successful in sinking enemy ships and rescuing downed pilots, went to the bottom with all but five of her crew. After the war, Tang's commanding officer, Dick O'Kane, reported that a defective torpedo circled back to hit only 20 seconds after it was fired at an enemy ship.

Just as the loss of *Tang* was a sacrifice that should not have been necessary, so it was with the loss of *Seawolf*. Like *Tang, Wahoo, Harder, Trigger* and so many other boats with great records, *Seawolf* had already established herself as one of the best warships ever to serve in the U.S. Navy when she was lost in October 1944. What makes the loss of *Seawolf* so difficult to accept was the fact that she was mistakenly sunk by the combined efforts of misfortune, poor communication, a U.S. Navy plane and U.S. Navy destroyer escort. Directed to carry a special Army unit to the Philippines, *Seawolf* was passing through a new submarine safety lane, but she was running behind schedule. Passing a group of U.S. Navy ships, *Seawolf* was nearby when a Japanese submarine torpedoed destroyer escort *Shelton*. A search for the Japanese intruder was initiated and a plane from an American escort carrier sighted a sub, dropped bombs and signaled his sighting. Destroyer escort *Rowell* (DE-403) arrived and dropped depth charges with the unhappy result of sinking *Seawolf*. One of the U.S. Navy's all-time great vessels was lost needlessly primarily due to a lack of communication. If there was anything positive in regard to this sacrifice, it was that communication was effective so often that tragedies such as this were exceedingly rare. That, however, is little consolation.

There were innumerable stories of individual sacrifice during the war, and one of the more classic incidents of personal sacrifice was that of Lt. Cmdr. Howard W. Gilmore aboard *Growler* (SS-215) in February 1943. Involved in a surface battle with Japanese vessels that possessed more firepower than originally thought, commanding officer Gilmore conducted the battle from the exposed bridge of the sub. Just after colliding with the enemy gunboat, machine gun fire peppered *Growler*, and Gilmore was hit. Ordering others below, the wounded commanding officer gave the order "Take her down!" Not wishing to delay Growler's dive to relative safety and not wishing to expose others to enemy fire in an effort to carry him back into the sub, Gilmore made the ultimate sacrifice of himself to save his crew and boat. As it is written in the holy scriptures, "No greater love can a man give than to lay down his life for others."

Gilmore's great sacrifice allowed *Growler* and her crew to live to fight another day. Unfortunately, in November 1944 *Growler* was lost with all hands to unknown causes.

Another memorable story of sacrifice involved Capt. John P. Cromwell who was aboard *Sculpin* (SS-191) in November 1943. One of the great ironies of the war was the fact that *Sculpin* was instrumental in locating and assisting in the rescue efforts of the accidently sunken *Squalus* (SS-192) off Portsmouth, N.H., in May 1939. Raised from over 40 fathoms four months later, *Squalus* came back to the surface with 26 dead. Thirty-three had been rescued soon after she sank. Rebuilt, SS-192 was recommissioned with the new name *Sailfish*, and she went on to win a Presidential Unit Citation. Instrumental in her receipt of the award was her sinking of the Japanese escort carrier *Chuyo* on

Accidently sunk in May 1939, *Squalus* (SS-192) carried 26 of her 59 officers and men to their deaths. Four months later SS-192 was raised (seen here breaking the surface), towed back to the Portsmouth, N.H., Navy Yard, rebuilt, and recommissioned as *Sailfish.* Ironically, on 4 December 1943, *Sailfish* sank Japanese escort carrier *Chuyo* which was carrying 21 survivors of *Sculpin* to Japan. *Sculpin* was a sister ship to *Sailfish* and had located the sunken sub in 1939 and assisted both in the rescue of 33 men and the later raising of SS-192. USN

4 December 1943. Unknown to the CO and crew of *Sailfish* was the fact that 21 survivors of her sister ship *Sculpin*, which had been sunk only a few days earlier, were aboard the enemy carrier as captives. Only one survived the sinking of the carrier, but nearly two dozen other *Sculpin* survivors were aboard another enemy ship. After the war they rendered the account of Sculpin's last battle and the sacrifice of Captain Cromwell. As *Sculpin* was being abandoned on 19 November 1943, Cromwell recognized that a number of Sculpin's survivors would be picked up by the Japanese destroyer that had fatally damaged the sub. Possessing vital information concerning plans for the invasion of the Gilbert Islands, Cromwell elected to go down with *Sculpin* rather than risk having critical information extracted from him.

Cromwell and Gilmore were both awarded the Medal of Honor posthumously. As significant as this award is, it does not match the devotion to duty and sacrifice made by these extraordinary officers.

SUBMARINE MEMORIALS

Without question, the veterans of World War II submarines have done the best job of preserving the memory of their vessels, fellow crew members and fallen friends. Granted it is easier to preserve a submarine than any other major combatant for reasons of cost. Still, submariners have made the most of opportunities to preserve and memorialize. As previously mentioned, few naval or maritime museums do not have a monument or major plaque placed by submarine veterans in memory of the lost 52 submarines and 3,505 officers and men. Further, numerous monuments – many with a torpedo embedded – exist under trees or on lawns far from any preserved submarine and far from any body of water.

Although the efforts of submarine veterans to preserve their history is highly commendable, in one respect they have perhaps overexerted themselves. After visiting the memorials, one finds that nearly all preserved submarines and even some submarine monuments have brochures or plaques that significantly overstate the official record. In Chicago, an otherwise well-written brochure informs the reader that *Silversides* won four Presidential Unit Citations (she won one). Near the battleship *Texas* a monument honoring *Seawolf* (SS-197) claims 27 ships sunk for a total of 108,600 tons (officially, *Seawolf* was credited with 18 ships and 71,609 tons). At Muskogee, Okla., a *Batfish* booklet claims 37,080 tons sunk, but official records credit only 10,558. Along with Seawolf's claims, those of *Bowfin* and *Cod* were noted at the beginning of this chapter. At least submarine veterans are consistent with their "fish stories." But, who really knows? Overstatements of official credits may not be off too far. Regardless, no one can ever overstate the value of U.S. Navy submarines in World War II.

Forty years after World War II, 12 U.S. Navy submarines that won battle stars have been preserved as memorials. Eight of the 12 still greatly resemble their World War II configuration. As nearly all submarines were considerably altered during the war, few ended the war looking like they did when they were commissioned. Still, *Drum, Silversides, Bowfin, Batfish, Cobia, Cod, Lionfish* and *Pompanito* look much the same in 1985 as they did in 1945. *Cavalla, Croaker, Becuna* and *Torsk* served for varying periods in the post-war Navy and were modernized, with their exterior appearance now greatly different than that of 1945.

Silversides (SS-236), seen here at Navy Pier on Lake Michigan in the heart of Chicago, officially ranked third in ships sunk (23) and fifth in tonnage sunk (90,080). This aggressive sub once went into battle accidently flying the Japanese flag. *Silversides,* one of the few truly famous memorialized subs, won 12 battle stars and a Presidential Unit Citation for World War II service. Author's Collection

Bowfin (SS-287), another famous submarine, was one of only five U.S. Navy warships to win both the Presidential Unit Citation *and* Navy Unit Commendation in World War II. Preserved as a memorial at Pearl Harbor not far from the *Arizona* Memorial, *Bowfin* sank 16 enemy ships. Courtesy of Stan Cohen

Enshrined at War Memorial Park in Muskogee, Okla., is the *Batfish* (SS-310) which sank three Japanese submarines in four days (10-13 February 1945). Originally intended to be towed to Tulsa, *Batfish*–tied to six barges–could not negotiate all the turns in the river and therefore the decision was made to "beach" the sub-killer in Muskogee. Author's Collection

The interior of a submarine is cramped but highly functional. The crews' mess inside the *Batfish* is seen here. An audio tape approximately 15 minutes in duration helps acquaint visitors with this sub. Author's Collection

In addition to the 12 submarines listed above, three other submarines built during the World War II era that did not see action or win battle stars have been preserved. These are *Clamagore* (SS-343) moored at Patriots Points, Mt. Pleasant, S.C.; *Ling* (SS-297) at Hackensack, N.J.; and *Requin* (SS-481) at Tampa, Fla. Of these three, only *Ling* still retains her World War II configuration. *Marlin* (SST-2) at Omaha, Neb., was not laid down until 1952 and therefore cannot be considered a World War II sub. As the emphasis of this book is combat veterans of World War II, these four subs are noted but not treated.

In addition to the submarines that have been preserved, several meaningful portions of famous submarines have also been enshrined. The conning towers of *Flasher, Squalus/ Sailfish, Balao*, and *Pintado* exist; these and other significant memorials are discussed later.

It is quite fortunate that the eight preserved submarines that still resemble their World War II configurations include several that were highly successful. At the top of this group would have to be *Silversides* which officially ranked third in ships sunk (23) and fifth in tonnage sunk (90,080). Winner of a Presidential Unit Citation and 12 battle stars, *Silversides* now rests at Navy Pier on Lake Michigan in the heart of downtown Chicago. The only U.S. Navy submarine to enter battle flying the Japanese flag (by accident she caught some fishnets that were topped with the rising sun), *Silversides* is being ardently restored. Even though restoration is continuing, the sub is very presentable at present and well worth traveling to see as she is one of the few truly famous World War II preserved vessels. And, it was aboard this submarine that an event occurred that Hollywood has used in several movies. While submerged off New Ireland, and beneath a Japanese destroyer, a pharmacist's mate performed an emergency appendectomy on a crewmember.

Bowfin, easily within sight of the Arizona Memorial at Pearl Harbor, is another of the truly outstanding famous vessels to be preserved. A constant sight aboard this boat is of visitors lining up photographs at an angle that will include *Bowfin* and the Arizona Memorial in the background. Just as explanation is required to interpret the battleflag and scoreboard of *Cod*, so it is with Bowfin's. On Bowfin's flag and scoreboard is the claim of a bus having been sunk. Near the end of the war *Bowfin* torpedoed two ships in Minami Daito harbor and also sank a floating dock with crane and bus. No other sub is known to have sunk a bus. Winner of both the Presidential Unit Citation and Navy Unit Commendation, *Bowfin* is in very good condition (among preserved submarines, *Bowfin* and *Drum* appear to be in the best condition; *Cod* is not far behind). Whereas there are concerns for some of the preserved submarines making unscheduled dives, those responsible for maintaining *Bowfin* don't worry about her going down. Her bow is already resting on the bottom.

One of the surprises in visiting the preserved World War II submarines in 1985 was the diversity of settings. It is not correct to say that "to have seen one, one has seen all." *Batfish* (SS-310) has a particularly unique setting at War Memorial Park in Muskegee, Okla. Like the *Cavalla* and destroyer escort *Stewart* at Galveston and the minesweeper *Hazard* at Omaha, Neb., *Batfish* is totally out of the water, resting high and dry in a meadow-like field. Actually, *Batfish* was not intended to retire in Muskogee. She was on her way to Tulsa tied to six barges, but at Muskogee she and her barges could not negotiate the curves of the river. After sitting for a time on the river bank, it was decided to "beach" the famous sub in Muskogee. After floating the sub into the area where she now rests, a dike was built around the sub and the water was pumped out. *Batfish* is now at least a hundred yards from the channel of the

Commissioned one month before the attack on Pearl Harbor, *Drum* (SS-228) earned 12 battle stars and placed eighth in tonnage sunk. Towed to Mobile, *Drum* was placed inboard of battleship *Alabama*. In 1985, the overall interior and exterior appearance of *Drum* is at or near the top for memorialized subs. And, *Drum* is in near perfect wartime configuration. However, her original conning tower was removed during the war after receiving considerable damage from depth charges. USN – Author's Collection

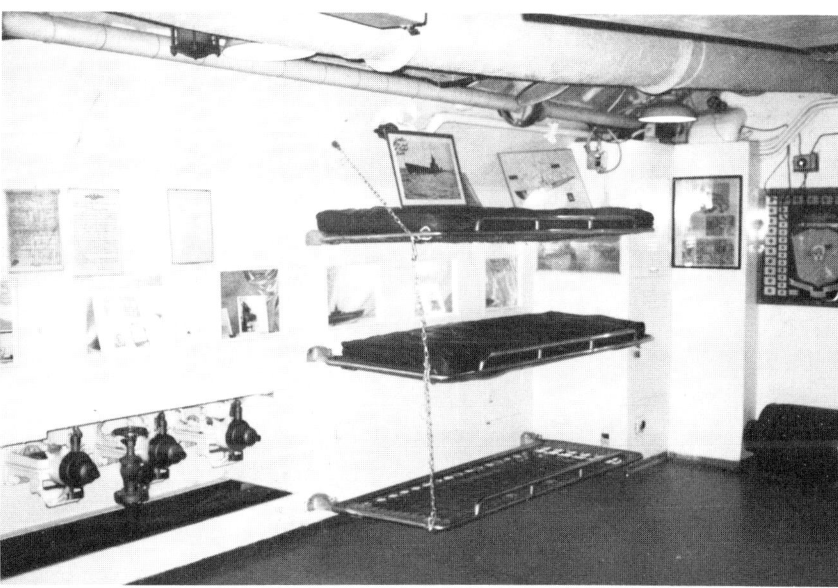

The *Cod* (SS-224), like *Drum*, is in near-perfect wartime configuration and is very clean. This sub, moored on Lake Erie in downtown Cleveland, Ohio, had the unique distinction of having all seven of her war patrols designated successful. The interior of the *Cod* is completely open to the public (most are not, especially the torpedo rooms) and several spaces are used for exhibits honoring *Cod* and her sisters. Author's Collection

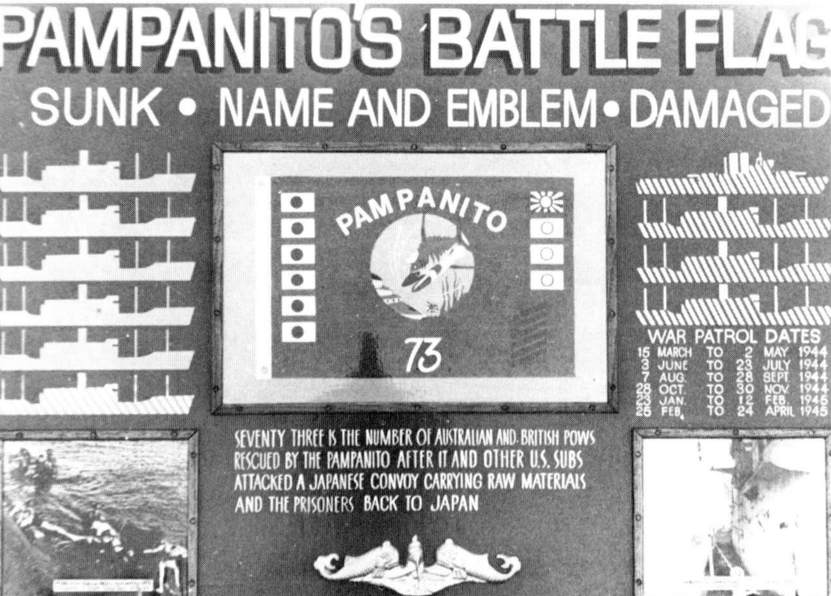

Pampanito (SS-383), preserved in San Francisco, sank five enemy ships in World War II and was one of the submarines that caught a Japanese convoy carrying British and Australian POWs to Japan in September 1944. Pampanito's warflag calls attention to the rescue of 73 prisoners who managed to escape the sinking enemy ships. Winner of six battle stars, *Pampanito* is one of very few preserved World War II vessels on the West Coast. Courtesy of Dean Schumacher and Stan Cohen

Lionfish (SS-298) at Battleship Cove, Fall River, Mass., was a latecomer to the war and she won only one battle star. Although *Lionfish* did not have a war record equal to that of *Croaker* (two hours away on I-95), *Lionfish* still carries a World War II configuration; *Croaker* does not. Author's Collection

Cobia (SS-245), which won four battle stars during World War II and was credited with 16,835 tons sunk, is presently memorialized in Manitowoc, Wis. Twenty-eight fleet submarines were built here during World War II; four were lost in action and one Manitowoc sub – *Rasher* (SS-269) – compiled an outstanding war record. *Cobia* was not built at Manitowoc, but she does retain her wartime configuration and serves admirably as a remembrance to this city's contribution to the war effort. Courtesy of Manitowoc Maritime Museum

river, enjoying a magnificient, quiet setting.

A Presidential Unit Citation winner for sinking three Japanese submarines in four days, this famous sub was credited with 10,558 tons and nine battle stars. A short distance behind the sub is a building containing a small but interesting museum. Just outside the museum building are a number of guns that were used aboard submarines (and some that were not), and several monuments, including one dedicated in 1985 to the memory of *Shark* (SS-174), which was lost in February 1942. On board *Batfish*, which presently has no guns mounted, a 15-minute tape informs visitors where they are inside the sub, what they are looking at and gives historical facts about the "sub killer."

While *Batfish, Bowfin*, battleships *Massachusetts* and *Alabama* as well as the other preserved World War II vessels have tapes, wands or phone-like devices to instruct a visitor, the *Drum* at Mobile, Ala., informs a visitor with metal identification plates and plaques that are attached to nearly every piece of equipment on the sub. Moored inboard of the battleship *Alabama*, the *Drum* – decommissioned in 1946 and therefore still possessing most of her wartime configuration and equipment – is exceptionally well maintained. Except for a sign in the officer's wardroom claiming a Navy Unit Commendation for *Drum*, the vessel is the most effective memorialized submarine conveying 1945 ambiance; even the pictures of pin-up girls are original. The "at sea" setting of the *Drum* – looking south, one can see water to the horizon – lends itself to the sounds of the wind and water, and even if an audio tape were available, it could not be heard much of the time because of the wind. All things considered, the sounds of wind and water are more appropriate here.

In the computer age it is quite interesting to wander around inside the *Drum* and some of the other World War II memorialized submarines to inspect the 1945 era state-of-the-art electronics such as radio equipment and the torpedo data computer. Although somewhat amusing now, these instruments helped *Drum* live through the war, sink 15 ships, place eighth in tonnage sunk (80,580) and win 12 battle stars. Naturally, the one "instrument" in 1985 that draws more attention than any other is the periscope. Like most other equipment on nearly all preserved vessels, the periscope no longer moves up, down or to either side. It is frozen in position to attack the Mobile shipyard. Periscopes, guns, buttons, knobs, switches, valves, wheels and all other objects designed to move are currently removed, bolted or otherwise incapacitated in an effort to encourage visitors to look but not touch-and-break. Many parts on preserved vessels that withstood the rigors of war have been no match for curious children on summer vacation. On submarines, anyway, there seems to be some revenge in favor of the vessel as few children (or writers) escape a visit without one or more first-magnitude bumps of the head against a host of steel "somethings." Forget all the Hollywood movies that show men rushing quickly and nimbly to their battle stations. Not even a midget could move rapidly over 300 feet inside a submarine without placing his person in peril.

The setting for *Cod* (SS-224) is quite similar to that of *Silversides* in that it is on the lakefront practically in the center of a city. However, *Cod* does not have quite the same "closed-in" feeling that one has when viewing *Silversides* in Chicago. *Cod*, enshrined on Lake Erie in downtown Cleveland, Ohio, is in very good condition (good condition being defined as how the sub is pre-

Cavalla (SS-244) made her place in history by sinking *Shokaku*, one of Japan's two greatest combat aircraft carriers, 19 June 1944. Preserved as a memorial at Seawolf Park in Galveston, Texas, *Cavalla* rests on dry land beside destroyer escort USS *Stewart* (DE-238). In 1947, *Cavalla*, a *Gato*-class submarine, was modernized and emerged with a streamlined sail (conning tower), and an extended and squared bow containing electronic gear enabling her to track other submarines. In these pictures, one can see Cavalla's placement on Galveston Bay (picture taken from Stewart's bridge), a torpedo room and the main propulsion controls in the maneuvering room. Author's Collection

Like *Cavalla, Croaker* (SS-246) was modernized after World War II. Preserved as a memorial at Groton, Conn., *Croaker* is moored only a short distance from General Dynamics (Trident construction), the U.S. Sub Base, the memorialized *Nautilus* (SSN-571), the U.S. Coast Guard Academy (New London) and the conning tower of *Flasher* (SS-249) – the national submarine memorial enshrined by the Sub Vets of World War II. *Croaker* earned fame in her own right by sinking 19,710 tons of enemy naval and merchant shipping and she received a Navy Unit Commdendation. Author's Collection

Torsk (SS-423) had the unique distinction of recording the last sinking of an enemy warship in World War II, and won two battle stars for World War II service. Currently preserved as a memorial in Baltimore's Inner Harbor not far from the enshrined USS *Constellation, Torsk* has long since lost her World War II configuration. The picture seen here shows *Torsk* in her wartime appearance. In 1985, she resembles *Cavalla, Croaker* and *Becuna.* USN

sented to the public, not how ready she is for sea). Although *Cod* had the unique distinction of having all seven of her war patrols declared successful (seven battle stars), she did not win either of the two major awards a ship or sub could win. Still, there is something magnetic about this submarine that commands respect. This perspective is offered after visiting the sub, but it seems to come through even in the picture presented in the Color section.

For a time *Cod* had her deck guns beside the sub instead of onboard. The United States and Canada have an agreement concerning "fortifications" along their borders, and this includes the lakes. Happily, Canada does not consider *Cod* a threat, and several guns are now mounted on deck.

Cod's conning tower is adorned with a colorful scoreboard. The champagne glass symbolized the party in Perth, Australia, given in honor of Cod's crew for rescuing the crew of the Dutch submarine *0-19.* Inside the *Cod* there is a small museum (see picture) and attention is called to the wartime practice of having a bunk in use 24 hours a day with men on different watches sharing the same bunk at different times of the day. Unlike most of the other preserved submarines, two world War II submarine veterans were on hand into 1985 to greet visitors and to provide a narrative of first-hand experiences that no audio tape could hope to match.

Pampanito (SS-383) in San Francisco sank five enemy ships for a total of 27,288 tons, and was one of the submarines that caught a Japanese convoy carrying British and Australian POWs to Japan in September 1944. Pampanito's war flag (see photo) calls attention to the rescue of 73 prisoners who managed to

The enshrined conning tower of the *Sailfish* (SS-192) within the Portsmouth Navy Yard evokes many memories and emotions. Life began for SS-192 with the name *Squalus,* but the name was changed after SS-192 sank in May 1939 taking the lives of nearly half her crew. Raised, rebuilt and recommissioned with the new name *Sailfish,* SS-192 went on to win nine battle stars and a Presidential Unit Citation. Continuing to be star-crossed, she sank a Japanese escort carrier containing 21 survivors of *Sculpin,* the sub that located *Squalus* in May 1939 and assisted in rescue operations. USN

The conning tower of *Flasher* (SS-249) was selected by the Sub Vets of World War II to be the national submarine memorial to the 3,505 officers and men of the "Silent Service" who were lost during the war. Note the monument in front of the conning tower; thereon are plaques listing the 52 lost submarines. *Flasher* led all U.S. Navy submarines in tonnage sunk, sank two destroyers and several tankers, and received a Presidential Unit Citation. Author's Collection

The conning tower of *Balao* (SS-285) rests in the Washington, D.C., Navy Yard a short distance from the Navy Memorial Museum, the Potomac River and the destroyer *Barry*. This *Barry* inherited the name of a famous World War II destroyer (DD-248). *Balao* was the class leader of 132 "thick-skinned" subs, and she was featured in a Hollywood movie. For portions of the movie, she was painted pink. In 1985, the conning tower is again gray. Author's Collection

Inside the Navy Memorial Museum in the Washington Navy Yard is a room completely devoted to submarines. Numerous plaques and parts of submarines fill the room. The periscopes are in working condition and a visitor can track vessels in the Potomac. Note the upper portions of the periscopes protruding through the roof of the museum. Author's Collection

escape the sinking enemy ships. Winner of six battle stars, *Pampanito* is one of very few preserved World War II vessels on the West Coast.

Lionfish (SS-298) at Battleship Cove, Fall River, Mass., was a late comer to the war and she won only one battle star. Still, she is an excellent addition to the other ships, boats and exhibits at Battleship Cove. Although *Lionfish* did not have a war record equal to that of *Croaker*, which is less than two hours away, *Lionfish* better "looks the role" as she retains her World War II configuration whereas *Croaker* does not.

Considering the significance of Groton, Conn., Manitowoc, Wis., and Portsmouth, N.H., in World War II submarine construction, it is most fitting that all three locations have major memorials to World War II submarines. Groton and Portsmouth open directly to the sea but Manitowoc is a long way from any ocean. During World War II, 28 submarines were built in Manitowoc and many had to travel the Mississippi River before touching the ocean. Presently in Manitowoc is the memorialized World War II submarine *Cobia* (SS-245) which won four battle stars during the war and was credited with 16,835 tons sunk. Unfortunately, *Cobia* was not one of the subs built at Manitowoc (she was built at Groton), but she does appear in wartime configuration and she succeeds in honoring the city's historic contribution to the war effort. Happily, the city of Manitowoc is almost as proud of *Cobia* as they would have been had they been able to have obtained one of their own. Unquestionably this would have been the ideal location for the most successful submarine built at Manitowoc, *Rasher* (SS-269). But,

Rasher was greatly modified after the war and served on into the 1970s. Consequently, *Cobia* perhaps better serves to capture remembrance of the wartime subs.

Four World War II submarines that won battle stars exist in memorial status with their present configuration considerably different from their 1945 appearance. Obviously, these four--*Cavalla* (SS-244), *Croaker* (SS-246), *Becuna* (SS-319) and *Torsk* (SS-423) – served the Navy in the post-war years and were modernized to meet new challenges in technology. Just as changes in configuration have diminished the World War II historical authenticity of *Yorktown, Intrepid, Little Rock and Laffey*, so it is with these four submarines.

Resting entirely on dry land only a few feet from the memorialized destroyer escort USS *Stewart, Cavalla* and *Stewart* appear to be "keeping watch" over the entrance into Galveston Bay at Seawolf Park. Those not well informed on World War II history, particularly children, will often spend more time on the *Stewart* as it has numerous guns and other topside attractions to investigate. Cavalla's deck now has no guns, and in place of her former wood and steel deck is concrete – just like that of the battleship *Texas* only a few miles north. And, the "Guppy" conning tower does not lend itself to climbing in the manner allowed by subs still carrying wartime configuration. Still, diminished authenticity or not, one familiar with World War II naval history cannot but stand in awe when visiting the *Cavalla*. This is the submarine that sank *Shokaku*, one of the six Japanese carriers to attack Pearl Harbor, and with the possible exception of sister ship *Zuikaku*, Japan's greatest combat carrier. *Cavalla* won a Presidential Unit Citation for sinking *Shokaku* (19 June 1944) and a total of four battle stars. On 18 September 1978, she was honored with salutes from the crew of a new *Cavalla* (SSN-68) when the nuclear submarine crossed her bow while entering Galveston harbor.

The conning tower of Presidential Unit Citation winner *Pintado* (SS-387) is located on the grounds of the Nimitz Museum in Fredericksburg, Texas. The conning tower is not in as poor condition as this picture portrays; nonetheless, it was scheduled for attention soon after the picture was taken in the summer of 1985. Author's Collection

Inside the superb Nimitz Museum is a display devoted to submarines. In this picture, which shows only a portion of the exhibit, one can see the bell of the *Hake* (SS-256) and a torpedo door from the famous *Seahorse* (SS-304). Adm. Chester Nimitz was no stranger to submarines during his long, distinguished career. Author's Collection

Pearl Harbor survivor *Narwhal* (SS-167) (pictured) tied *Thresher* (SS-200) for most battle stars awarded to a submarine for World War II service (15). The two 6-inch guns of *Narwhal*–the largest ever placed on U.S. Navy submarines–were used to good advantage on several occasions. Into 1985, the two guns stand in front of Morton Hall on the sub base at Groton. Seaman Bill Spellman of Kentucky stands beside one gun to provide perspective. Author's Collection

One sincerely hopes that the nuclear *Cavalla* will never be called upon to match the record of her famous predecessor.

Like *Cavalla*, *Croaker* at Groton, Conn., has a streamlined sail (conning tower) and an extended and squared bow containing electronic gear to track other submarines. And, like *Cavalla*, there are no guns on deck. But, *Croaker*, too, earned her place in history by the sinking of a Japanese cruiser (*Nagara*, 7 August 1944) and several merchant vessels for an official total of 19,710 tons. Recipient of the Navy Unit Commendation, *Croaker* was awarded three battle stars for World War II.

Croaker is particularly fortunate to be located where she is today. Within walking distance up Thames Street is the memorialized conning tower of the USS *Flasher*, and only a hundred yards from Croaker's berth is General Dynamics, construction site for Trident nuclear submarines. Only minutes away is the U.S. Coast Guard Academy (New London), the U.S. Submarine Base (Groton), and just outside the sub base is the now-memorialized *Nautilus* (SSN-571), the world's first nuclear-powered submarine. Easily seen from the Interstate 95 bridge, Croaker's greatest

This large monument was placed in honor of *Seawolf* (SS-197) and the 17 Army Rangers lost when this submarine was mistakenly sunk by U.S. Navy air and surface units in October 1944. The battleship *Texas* is out of the photo at left, but the San Jacinto Battlefield Monument is visible beyond the *Seawolf* memorial. The plaque on the *Seawolf* monument lists Seawolf's unofficial claims in number of ships and tonnage sunk. Officially, *Seawolf* sank 18 ships for 71,609 tons. The great fighting sub was the only sub to win two Navy Unit Commendations. Author's Collection

In 1985, a new monument was dedicated to the memory of *Shark* (SS-174), lost in 1942. The monument stands on the grounds of War Memorial Park in Muskogee, Okla. In this picture, a monument honoring Roosevelt's Rough Riders stands at right and submarine *Batfish* is visible in the background. Author's Collection

fortune is its location in a city that despite its size and industrial importance has retained its village atmosphere.

Anyone interested in visiting George Dewey's flagship, USS *Olympia* (C-6) of Spanish American War fame, must also visit the submarine *Becuna* because the submarine is inboard of the *Olympia* and must be crossed to get to the cruiser. *Becuna* won four battle stars for World War II service. *Torsk*, preserved as a memorial in Baltimore's Inner Harbor, is also resting quite near another famous ship of older vintage, the USS *Constellation* which was the first ship commissioned into the U.S. Navy. *Torsk* won only two battle stars, but had the distinction of recording the last sinking of an enemy warship during World War II.

Flasher (SS-249), *Squalus/Sailfish* (SS-192), *Balao* (SS-285) and *Pintado* (SS-387) were famous submarines that have been memorialized by having their respective conning towers preserved. Only a few blocks from the enshrined *Croaker* is Flasher's conning tower, set in concrete and representing the national memorial for the Sub Vets of World War II. This very appropriate memorial is comprised of the conning tower with guns fore and aft of the bridge, a large monument containing 52 plaques honoring the subs lost during the war, and an attractive wooden sign placed near a large mast with colors atop. Facing the Thames River on a gentle sloping hillside, *Flasher* continues to serve. During the war *Flasher*, which sank several tankers and two destroyers, was the only submarine officially credited with more than 100,000 tons of enemy shipping sunk as she placed first in this category. She was fourth in ships sunk with 21 and she earned a Presidential Unit Citation.

The ironic relationship between *Squalus/Sailfish* and sister ship *Sculpin* was related earlier in this chapter and therefore is not repeated here. However, attention must be drawn to the fact that the conning tower of SS-192 has been enshrined within the Portsmouth, N.H., Navy Yard (see picture in this chapter and in the Color section). It is appropriate here to note again that this submarine sank in May 1939 while making a test dive, lost 26 men but had 33 saved by use of a rescue chamber, was raised four months later, recommissioned under the new name *Sailfish* and went on to win nine battle stars and a Presidential Unit Citation for sinking the Japanese escort carrier *Chuyo*. Whereas most of the preserved ships and submarines from the World War II era cause one to remember one particular event, the conning tower of *Squalus/Sailfish* evokes an unusual mixture of emotions and memories of both sacrifice and success.

On the grounds of Battleship Park in Mobile, Ala., are several monuments placed by the U.S. Submarine Veterans of World War II. *Herring* (SS-233), lost in 1942, is remembered as is Lt. Cmdr. Howard W. Gilmore, a Selma, Ala., native who sacrificed his life in combat while CO of the submarine *Growler*. In the background of the *Herring* monument is the enshrined *Drum* while the battleship *Alabama* appears behind the memorial to Gilmore. Author's Collection

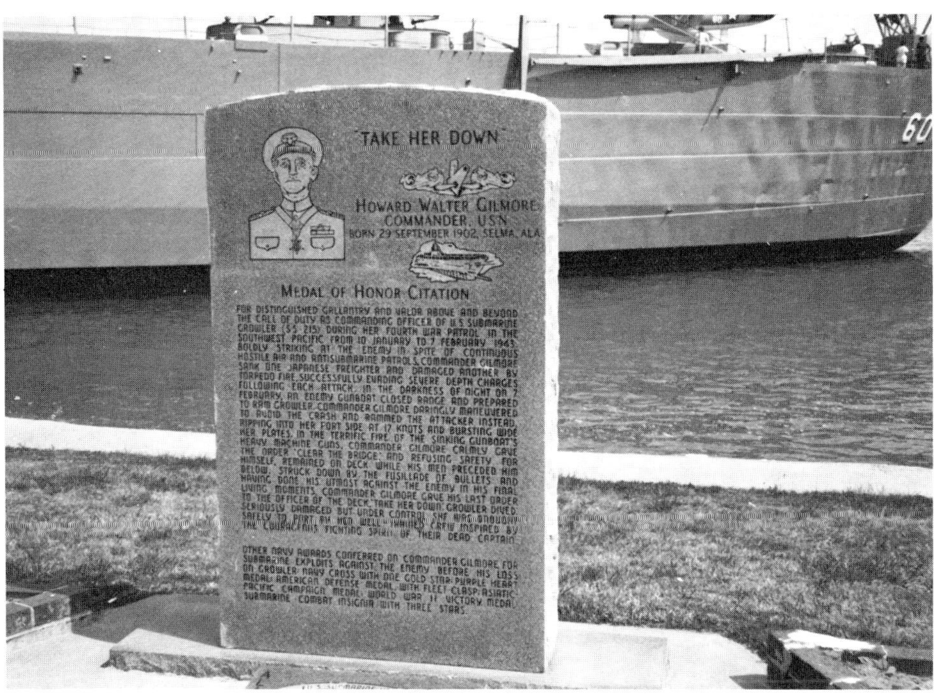

Balao's conning tower, within the Washington, D.C., Navy Yard, will remind some of the fact that she was the class leader of the "thick-skinned" class that followed the *Gato* class. Able to dive to 600 feet, members of this class arrived late in the war but several made outstanding contributions and earned enviable war records. Other observers of this conning tower will recall that *Balao* was the "star" of a Hollywood movie in which a portion of the script called for her to be painted pink. The movie success led to a television series featuring a pink submarine. The story is told around the Washington Navy Yard that soon after the conning tower was brought to the yard to be prepared for enshrinement, several thought it would be a note of high humor to paint it pink. Higher authorities, however, failed to grasp the humor. In 1984, the conning tower was painted with a yellow primer and no evidence of pink was apparent. In 1985, a coat of gray was applied and the tower rests beside the Potomac in the dignified appearance it deserves.

The conning tower of Presidential Unit Citation winner *Pintado* (SS-387) has been preserved, and in the summer of 1985 it was located on the grounds of the Nimitz Museum in Fredericksburg, Texas. The picture accompanying this chapter reveals a need for paint on SS-387's conning tower, but this should not detract from anyone's opinion of the superb Nimitz Museum. Not everything can be done at once, and the staff of this museum is committed to quality exhibits. Most likely, by the time the ink is dry on the final copy of this book, so too will a new coat of paint be dry on Pintado's conning tower.

Before leaving the subject of the Nimitz Museum, it should be noted that Admiral Nimitz himself was at one time a submariner, and the museum named for him in his hometown devotes considerable space to subs. Embedded in the memorial wall is a plaque honoring Cmdr. Samuel Dealey and *Harder*; pictures and narrative dominate a submarine exhibit which features a bell from *Hake* (SS-256) (the bell was broken loose during a depth charge attack, but was still on deck when *Hake* surfaced) and a torpedo door from high-scoring *Seahorse* (SS-304). Of course, the usual "Still on Patrol" plaque is here, evidence again of the continuing concern of Submarine Veterans for their lost friends.

Access to the submarine base at Groton, Conn., is not easy, but a wealth of history is there for those privileged to enter. Near the small base museum and library are several large outdoor exhibits. Within a block one will see captured Japanese and German midget submarines, and in front of Morton Hall are the two 6-inch guns that once went to war on the deck of Pearl Harbor veteran *Narwhal* (SS-167). These big guns, like the two on sister ship *Nautilus* (SS-168), were put to good use on special missions including an assignment to create a diversion in the Kuriles in mid-1943. The largest guns ever carried on an American submarine, they now call to remembrance a submarine that tied for first with *Thresher* (SS-200) in battle stars (15) awarded to World War II submarines.

Happily, there are a multitude of monuments across the country honoring World War II submarines. The large monument honoring *Seawolf* near the battleship *Texas* has already been mentioned as has the 1985 dedication of the monument honoring *Shark* (SS-174) near the *Batfish* at Muskogee (see pictures). There are too many to list individually but representative of other monuments (some with embedded torpedoes) honoring lost submarines are those for the legendary *Wahoo* at Wahoo, Neb.; Navy Unit Commendation winner *Swordfish* (SS-193) at St.Paul, Minn.; Presidential Unit Citation winner *Trout* near Falmouth, Mass.; and *Herring* (SS-233) at Mobile, Ala. Only a few feet from the *Herring* memorial and the enshrined *Drum* is a large monument honoring Lt. Cmdr. Howard W. Gilmore. Gilmore, who was posthumously awarded the Medal of Honor for his courageous and sacrificial "take her down" order on *Growler* in February 1943, was born in Selma, Ala.

One applauds the fact that Gilmore has been honored in his home state, but Gilmore, Morton, O'Kane, Dealey, Cromwell, Street, Ramage, Fluckey and all the other brave men of the "silent service" belong first to the nation. It is well that so many memorials have been placed to memorialize these men and their subs. It will be better if their examples of success and sacrifice are emulated by this and future generations. Burdens may be different, but the need for honor, integrity and devotion to duty will not be in any less demand.

Within the Columbia River Maritime Museum, Astoria, Oregon, is part of the conning tower – with operable periscopes – from the famous *Rasher* SS-269. Courtesy of Ed Doss

CHAPTER SIX
VETERANS 40 YEARS AFTER VICTORY

At a destroyer-escort reunion the story is told of a sailor aboard a DE who would not leave his gun during battle to receive attention for his wounds. Finally, his life's blood drained away and only then did he give up his post. At a submarine reunion the story is told of survivors devoting their energy to supporting wounded crewmembers instead of reserving strength for themselves. And, at another reunion, the story is told of a cruiser scout-plane pilot unable to find his ship due to darkness and weather. With only a few minutes of fuel left, he radioed his ship for assistance. No response came from his cruiser as it was under orders not to break radio silence. Shortly afterward came the pilot's last words . . . "I understand . . ."

Forty years after victory in World War II, U.S. Navy veterans gather at reunions to celebrate life, to recall a long-ago victory when they helped chase enemies away from American shores, and to renew friendships formed at a time when the hovering presence of combat forged friendships simultaneously permanent and tenuous. Much of the conversation at these reunions centers on the success of the U.S. Navy in the war. Less conversation centers on the memories of sacrifice (such as those above) because 40 years is still not long enough to remove the pain of such remembrance. And still less conversation is devoted to the thought of whether or not future generations will remember either the success or sacrifice of 1941-1945.

The question concerning the future being unanswerable, the veterans of the cruiser *Columbia* (CL-56) meet annually to visit and discuss how they can continue to serve the memory of their friends who made the ultimate sacrifice. To date, the veterans of the *Columbia* have elected to support a memorial student scholarship fund at the University of South Carolina, and have collected historical records, memorabilia and photographs.

Although the veterans of the *Columbia* have a "natural" place to meet in the state of South Carolina – their 1984 reunion was held in Columbia, S.C. – they have been known to carry their reunions to all points of the compass. In 1985 they met in St. Louis; in 1986 they will return to Columbia.

Whereas *Columbia* veterans gather primarily to honor their own, some reunions are designed to honor all veterans of all services who set aside the security of civilian life to defend that security. In Painesville, Ohio, veterans of all branches meet each 7 December to remember the attack on Pearl Harbor. World War II Navy veteran Bill Kochever hosts the event and entrance is contingent, in part, upon wearing at least one piece of the uniform worn during active duty days. Some of the veterans arrive resplendent in full uniform; others appear to have just lost a Halloween-party contest. "Smokey" Joe Silva, who at age 17 spent some unhappy weeks on Guadalcanal in 1942 after his carrier air group was ordered ashore, also remembers Pearl Harbor anniversaries. In December 1985 this super-patriot put together an elaborate program at Cypress Gardens, Fla., that even included a mock air attack similar to the Japanese torpedo plane attack against Battleship Row. President of the Pacific War Veterans WWII Association, Silva worked with the American Legion to organize "A Day of Remembrance."

Henry (Hank) Pyzdrowski, who spent 47 hours in the water after his carrier *Gambier Bay* (CVE-73) was sunk during the 25 October 1944 action off Samar, is another tireless veteran constantly on the move to ensure that his comrades are not forgotten. On 14 August 1985 Vice President George Bush (a decorated World War II naval aviator himself) and Secretary of the Navy John Lehman hosted ceremonies on board the USS *Enterprise* (CVN-65) in San Francisco Bay to commemorate the cessation of hostilities with Japan: Hank Pyzdrowski was there. In October 1985 annual ceremonies were held on the USS *Yorktown* (CV-10) to honor--in part – the World War II escort carriers: Hank Pyzdrowski was there. And, he was present in 1977 when a hundred survivors returned to the site of the battle off Samar and the location of the sunken *Gambier Bay*. Like those already mentioned, Hank does not meditate long on the ceremonies of the past because he is too busy preparing other memorials.

Rear Adm. John E. Kirkpatrick (USN ret.) does not always have time to travel to reunions he would like to attend. First, he has a business to run in Oklahoma City, and second, the Naval Academy graduate is a veteran of several ships and he could spend much of his time just attending reunions. Still, few are as active in promoting the remembrance of World War II naval veterans as Rear Adm. Kirkpatrick. When the effort was going forward to preserve the *Batfish*, he was instrumental in the success of the project. When Capt. Frank Conlon (USN, ret), director of the battleship *North Carolina* Memorial, needs funds for a special project – like the new orientation center – he calls upon John Kirkpatrick. And, when one visits Oklahoma City, a "must see" in that city is the very large Kirkpatrick Center, a unique cultural center and museum. Within the Kirkpatrick Center is a Navy Gallery emphasizing Oklahoma's contributions to the Navy as well as the Navy in general. In August 1942 then-Commander Kirkpatrick successfully directed the anti-aircraft guns of the *North Carolina* against Japanese planes during the Battle of the Eastern Solomons, the first occasion in which a modern American battleship was assigned the duty of defending an aircraft carrier (*Enterprise*) in battle. Forty-three years later, Rear Adm. John E. Kirkpatrick is still serving.

A number of reunion groups were started soon after World War II ended, but a surprising number have come into being only in the last few years. The long serving heavy cruiser USS *St. Paul* (CA-73) served

Veteran Frank Sheetz stands beside the submarine *Croaker* at Groton. During World War II Sheetz served aboard this Navy Unit Commendation winner, and he continues to serve the memorialized sub into 1985. Courtesy of Frank Sheetz

A modern warship (*The Crommelins*) as well as this monument at Battleship Park in Mobile honors the five Alabama-born Crommelin brothers who graduated from the Naval Academy and then served with distinction in World War II. Two, Charles and Richard, were killed in action. Books, articles, monuments and memorials will long evoke memories of men like the Crommelins who knew both success and sacrifice in World War II. Author's Collection

until 1971 and there did not seem to be a need to form a reunion group until the last active all-gun cruiser was scrapped. News of the famous ship's 1980 dismantling bestirred veteran Frank I. Alliger Jr., who was determined to honor CA-73 and the men who served upon her decks. Beginning in 1983, Alliger set out to find his former shipmates. In 1976 another long serving ship, the carrier USS *Hancock* (CV-19), was sold for scrap. Two years later Edmund Orchowski organized a reunion in Atlantic City and the event was so successful that an association was formed to plan future reunions. At last count the *Hancock* veterans numbered nearly 600 and interest in remembering their ship and shipmates is evidenced by the outstanding *Hancock* exhibit placed aboard the *Yorktown* in 1984. The 70+ year-old battleship *Texas* still exists, but the reunion group of the ship's veterans is less than four years old. In 1982 Vincent Mossucco began organizing a reunion, and in April 1983 veterans of the "Champion of Cherbourg" gathered for the first time since World War II.

Few of the veterans who have been responsible for originating World War II reunion groups were "appointed" the responsibility. In most instances, the originator recognized the fact that the only way such a group could be formed was for him to take up the challenge. If he didn't, probabilities were that no one else would. Such was the case with Ray Kanoff and the USS *South Dakota* veterans. Ray attended the formal ceremonies of the ship's memorial dedication in 1969. Although the event was well attended by the public and a host of governmental dignitaries, only a few veterans of the famous ship were in the crowd. Afterwards, Ray could not rid himself of the thought how great it would be to have a reunion of his old shipmates. Finally realizing that his dream could come true

"Smokey" Joe Silva, who at age 17 spent several unhappy weeks on Guadalcanal in late 1942 and early 1943, put together an elaborate program on 7 December 1985 at Cypress Gardens, Fla., to mark the 44th anniversary of the attack on Pearl Harbor. A highlight of the event was a mock air attack similar to the Japanese torpedo plane attack against Battleship Row. Navy veteran Silva, who is president of the Pacific War Veterans WWII Association, worked with the American Legion to organize "A Day of Remembrance." Courtesy of Joe Silva

only if he were willing to pay the price in time, worry, money and effort, he set out to pay the price. Notices went out to veterans' magazines, letters came in, and in July 1970, 204 veterans of the *South Dakota* celebrated their first reunion in Sioux Falls. In 1985 the *South Dakota* veterans enjoyed their most recent reunion. There is no question that the involvement of South Dakota's veterans has added a greater degree of meaning to the outstanding memorial to the ship, but one wonders how many veterans of this fighting ship took the time to remember the dream of one man that has enriched many lives as well as a memorial and history.

A few men like South Dakota's Kanoff, Samuel B. Robert's (DE-413) Lloyd A. Gurnett, Philadelphia's (CL-41) F.J. Amoroson and Bowfin's Thomas P. Stack, John Bertrand, A.S. Weidner and O.L. Carden are still at the helm of the groups they started, but by 1985 a number of reunion groups had outlived the man or men responsible for originating the group. These groups have been blessed by relative latecomers who have become the driving force of the group and/or a special servant. Al Levesque helped turn the USS *Quincy* Association from an organization primarily interested in continuing the wartime practice of "elbow-bending, thirst-quenching" into a group more dedicated to remembering fallen comrades. Toward this new objective, Levesque has devoted countless hours to establishing a USS *Quincy* (both CA-39 and CA-71) exhibit in the City Hall Building, Quincy, Mass. Travis Price of the USS *Mobile* (CL-63) group, who began writing former shipmates in 1946 while in college, has given countless interviews to the media to help perpetuate the memory of his cruiser, and it was his idea to establish a compartment aboard the USS *Alabama* to honor CL-63. Ideas, however, are not manifested without energy, and Travis Price also provided that.

About an hour after this picture was taken, approximately 200 other veterans arrived at Hellriegel's Inn in Painesville, Ohio, to join host Bill Kochever (far right) for his annual Pearl Harbor Remembrance observance. Admittance to the banquet is for all veterans to wear at least one piece of their uniform from active duty days. Widely acclaimed for his patriotism and community service, Kochever has hosted this event for nearly two decades. Courtesy of Annabelle

Harry Welton and R.W. Gregory kept alive the idea of creating multiple exhibits to honor their ship, the USS *Enterprise* (CV-6), after the disheartening loss of the carrier that Forrestal and Truman slated for preservation. And, John A. Brown of the USS *Washington* (BB-56) Reunion Group is currently serving as executive director after having helped put together the first reunion in 1950. In addition to collecting memorabilia and records for the group, he is currently considering options toward the goal of having the memorial to his ship returned to some place of honor. As mentioned earlier (Chapter One) a "permanent" memorial to BB-56 – the only U.S. Navy battleship to sink a Japanese battleship in World War II – was dismantled and removed from the Washington State Capitol and placed in storage.

The name John Brown appears more than once among the "driving forces" of reunion groups. John R. Brown of the USS *Alabama* Crewman's Association was elected president of an informal group in 1970, and since that time he has headed the association. Under his leadership the association was chartered in the state of Alabama (1975) and he has accepted the annual responsibility of making reunion arrangements. For the past 14 years he has published a quarterly newsletter ("Scuttlebutt"), maintained all records, collected dues, issued membership cards and headed fund raising efforts to purchase large bronze plaques (see photo) which he designed. On 13 April 1985 John R. Brown and his fellow shipmates gathered near the number five dual five-inch gun mount to dedicate another plaque. This one honors the men killed when another five-inch mount accidently fired into number five (see photo) on 21 February 1944.

In the "special servants" category are the secretaries of reunion groups. The strength of a group – whether gathering for reunions, attempting to place memorials, or assembling research materials for books and articles – is dependent upon the effectiveness of an association's secretaries, editors and public affairs officers. Among the more outstanding "servants" of their respective reunion groups in 1985 are Eldon C. Davis (*New Orleans*), Jack Gallagher (*Essex*), Mike Marckese (*Chester*), Ed Doss (*Enterprise*), Don Bovill (*Minneapolis*), Peter Montalvo (*Yorktown* CV-5), Joe Sharkey (*Yorktown* CV-10), Hank Shafman (*Houston*), and Fred Hickman (*Columbia*). With regret, it is noted that 1985 was the last year of official service for Shafman and Hickman; their successors have big shoes to fill.

Much of the success of the men just listed in serving their respective reunion groups is due to their ability to write, and their willingness to write not only outstanding newsletters but also write individual letters of inquiries concerning membership, research, etc. Some groups have been blessed with men who have applied their writing skills to recording the history of their ship. Excellent examples are Thomas A. McMahill's book on the USS *Brooklyn* (CL-40), J. Ed Hudson's book on the USS *Cabot* (CVL-28) and a book in progress on the USS *Sullivans* by Bob Sander. Several articles authored by retired Capt. E.B. Mott (*Tuscaloosa* and *Enterprise*) and Dr. Harold L. Buell (Commander USN, Ret.) were published in 1985.

Not all the "servants" of reunion groups are men. Several women have contributed greatly to the effective administration of groups and even to their establishment. Betty Orchowski was extremely effective in helping husband Ed organize the USS *Hancock* Association just as Mary E. Kramer, wife of Don Kramer, was

Henry (Hank) Pyzdrowski, who spent 47 hours in the water after his carrier *Gambier Bay* (CVE-73) was sunk during the 25 October 1944 action off Samar, is unflagging in zeal to ensure the memory of his former shipmates lost during World War II. In the top photo Hank (second from right) is seen aboard the USS *Enterprise* (CVN-65) in August 1985 during the 40th Anniversary Commemoration hosted by Vice President George Bush. In the bottom picture he is seen with the daughters of the late Vice Adm. Clifton A.F. "Ziggy" Sprague during ceremonies aboard the *Yorktown* in October 1985 at which time Vice Adm. Sprague was inducted into the Carrier Aviation Hall of Fame. Courtesy of Heritage Foundation

instrumental in the establishment of the USS *Chicago* reunion group. When Ed Klopfenstein died in 1982, his wife Pauline took up his duties as treasurer; after three years, the quality of her work has been such that the men of the *Enterprise* Association will not let her quit. The USS *Birmingham* reunion committee is well served by Mrs. Robert L. Jeffreys; Mrs. James A. "Betty" Duff effectively serves the USS *Miami* reunion committee and Mrs. Dorothy McClanahan adds a new dimension to the meaning of the word "service" for the USS *Pittsburgh* Association. In response to a request from this writer, Mrs. McClanahan answered in quick time with pages and pages . . . all hand-written. Such a response makes the word "thanks" totally inadequate.

Forty years after World War II, veterans' reunions abounded in 1985 and at every reunion the favorite pastime was reliving the war years. It will be noted that the consumption of liquid refreshments is the result of such reminiscences, not the cause. Veterans travel to reunions from all parts of the country. They travel by car, plane and bus; one 80-year-old veteran drove a motor home from California to Virginia. Another veteran, attending the Destroyer Escort Sailors Association reunion in Orlando, probably could not fly to the event as he still carries so much shrapnel in his body that he could not pass through airline security gates.

Many groups have a personality; reunion groups are no exception. At first thought it might seem that one gathering of World War II naval veterans would be similar to others, but it is not so. When destroyer veterans gather, there is a feeling of discontent; perhaps this impression is due to the theme mentioned in Chapter Four. The feeling around submariners is – unexpectedly – similar. Gaiety attends battleship and cruiser reunions; debate characterizes most carrier groups. However, personality differences are

In August 1942 John E. Kirkpatrick was gunnery officer aboard the battleship *North Carolina* during the Battle of the Eastern Solomons. The now retired rear admiral operates a business in Oklahoma City, but makes time for the preservation of World War II naval history. Rear Admiral Kirkpatrick helped preserve and place the submarine *Batfish* at Muskogee, helped build a new orientation center for the battleship *North Carolina* and established a Navy Gallery in the Kirkpatrick Center, a large cultural center and museum in Oklahoma City. Author's Collection

noticeable among groups of the same classification.

In the late spring of 1985 veterans of the *Essex* (CV-9) met in Williamsburg, Va., while veterans of the USS *Franklin* (CV-13) met a few miles away in Norfolk, Va. Both reunions were well attended, both were successful, but the two were very dissimilar in tone. Laughter was much in evidence in Williamsburg; in Norfolk, laughs were nearly nonexistent. The atmosphere in Williamsburg was convivial; in Norfolk, it was cordial but solemn. Forty years after World War II, the afternoon of 19 March 1945 still has not lost its impact upon the survivors of "Big Ben."

Interspersed with the veterans of the *Franklin* in Norfolk were family members of the 724 men who died in the fire, smoke and water aboard and around CV-13 that tragic day. Conversations about that day came relatively easy, but only when initiated by a question. While visiting the carriers *Coral Sea* and *Eisenhower*, thoughts of March 1945 were temporarily suspended. Upon returning to the hotel, veterans and visitors again began conversations with the question, "Where were you on the *Franklin* on *that* day?"

No veteran of the *Franklin* appeared anxious to discuss 19 March 1945, especially Reon G. Hillegass Jr. Perhaps he has been asked to tell his story too many times; perhaps he feels – with justification – that anyone interested in the *Franklin* should already know the story. Reluctantly, and with detachment insulating remembrance of great pain, the "Big Ben" survivor related the story of how nearly 300 men trapped on the third deck lived through the flaming afternoon by breathing air admitted by a three-inch overboard discharge vent. Ordinarily, the three-inch opening was used to pump out water from the inside, and ordinarily this vent was well above the waterline. On 19 March 1945, however, *Franklin* listed heavily to starboard and the overboard discharge vent was alternately above and below water. No matter; refreshing salt water was nearly as welcome as fresh air that particular afternoon.

When the *Franklin* was scrapped in 1968, Reon Hillegass asked officials at the Portsmouth Salvage Company if he could have the small vent. It was cut out and given to him. Some day it will find its way to a special place in a museum, but for the time being, this small mass of metal can have no greater meaning to anyone than to the one who presently owns it.

When rockets began igniting and flying around the burning decks of the *Franklin*, Walter Jordan debated whether or not to abandon ship. When one of the rockets severed a portion of the mast, debate ended and Jordan departed. In 1985 Walter attended his first *Franklin* reunion, although his former shipmates have been meeting regularly for years. "I hoped to find someone from my 150-man division at this reunion," he remarked. "I feel so bad; I knew they were all dead from 1945, but still, I hoped to find just one..."

Another *Franklin* veteran, the Rev. W.H. Scoates, stated the obvious in an invocation when he said "...we sense our fallen brethren at our side..." When asked what he believed the fallen would say about 19 March 1945, Scoates replied "they would tell us to live because preservation of life is what they died for."

As if the stories shared at this reunion were not sad enough, there was yet one further unhappy note for many who came to Norfolk in 1985. In 1967 elaborate plans were announced by the city of Norfolk for a naval museum to be built around a significant portion of the *Franklin's* island structure. Newspaper accounts carried detailed stories of the planned museum, and an artist's rendering showed how the *Franklin's* mast and island structure forward of the stack would be placed on the roof of the museum building. So much was publicized about this proposal that many veterans of the *Franklin* came to Norfolk in 1985 fully expecting to see the preserved sections of their ship. And why not? From time to time articles have appeared mentioning the memorial, and one national magazine was planning a major article on the subject even as the veterans traveled to Norfolk. The museum is not there. Sadly, the story was related from one veteran to another how plans to build the museum were delayed

Four veterans of the USS *Hancock* (CV-19) (from left, R. Goedeke, Ed Orchowski, Charlie Boyst and Joe Harmon) stand in front of a newly acquired F4U "Corsair" aboard the *Yorktown* in October 1985. Just below the flight deck the veterans of the *Hancock* have placed memorabilia to perpetuate the memory of their carrier. In the Hancock Room, Capt. James J. Doyle, a chaplain aboard CV-19 in 1944-45, views memorabilia he contributed including a wartime photo and helmet. Author's Collection and Ed Orchowski

Travis Price, seen here with his wife during a *Mobile* (CL-63) reunion, began searching for former shipmates in 1946, helped form the Mobile's reunion group, and championed the idea for a Mobile Room aboard the *Alabama* (see pictures in Chapter Three and section on "Bells"). Courtesy of Travis Price

John A. Brown, executive director of the USS *Washington* (BB-56) reunion group, helped put together the first BB-56 reunion in 1950 and he is still at it into 1985. Note the artifacts from the famous battleship immediately behind the *Washington* veteran. Courtesy of John A. Brown

while seeking money, and how in time even the rusting remains of the mast and island structure were sent on to the scrapyard to be discarded like the rest of the carrier. As sometimes happens when several entities are involved, communication breaks down (sound familiar to anyone who read earlier chapters?) and good intentions result in problems. When the remains of the island structure were sold, the Navy reminded Norfolk that the preserved parts of the *Franklin* were still Navy property, and Norfolk was obliged to reimburse the Navy.

And, as if all this was not enough to add yet another tear to the eyes of a "Big Ben" veteran, the site proposed for the museum that would have included the Franklin's island and mast was the *exact* waterfront location upon which the hotel hosting the *Franklin* reunion was built. Great for irony. Sad for history and a group of veterans who deserved much better.

Beginning in 1985 Alvin Tidwell (chairman), Tom King and Franklin's survivors have begun the research process toward the day they will dedicate the largest plaque to rest in the "Arlington of Naval Aviation." Target date: October 1987.

In Williamsburg, veterans of the *Essex* spent little time reflecting on the effort to have their carrier preserved at Bridgeport, Conn. The effort was made in 1971, it failed, and like the earlier experience of the veterans of the *Enterprise*, it is perhaps too soon for the men of the *Essex* to concern themselves with an alternate memorial. It may be too soon to consider an alternate memorial, but in no way is the "oldest and boldest" forgotten by her men. Robert Fitch served on CV-9 in the late 1950s and early 1960s; when he stepped on board and saw the World War II battle record of the *Essex* on the carrier's island, he knew "I've got something to live up to." Warren E. Potter, chairman of the 1985 reunion, recalled how disappointed the first CO of the *Essex* (Capt. Donald Duncan, who helped plan the Halsey-Doolittle raid) was at not being able to stay with the *Essex* when she began her combat life. Philip Ard remembers seeing a newsreel concerning the launching of the *Essex* in the summer of 1942. Shortly after, he was assigned to the carrier, and as chief yeoman in charge of the captain's office, he saw the war in a manner that would have been the envy of any historian. A.F. Doyle remembers the dangers inherent in working on a flight deck; death and injury were constant companions of flight deck personnel during flight deck operations as well as in combat. And, J.D. Stanlake shared the story of what it was like to land in Japan with engine trouble just before the surrender was signed.

Interesting stories always abound at *Essex* reunions, partially because *Essex* is not the only ship many veterans served aboard. Commissioning on the last day of 1942, many of the original *Essex* crew came to the carrier from the sunken *Wasp* and the heavy cruisers lost off Savo Island. Regardless of when one joined CV-9, all *Essex* veterans are in agreement on one matter. There is a feeling that CV-9's place in naval history has not drawn the attention it deserves: too much discussion of the *Essex* class and too little on the lead ship itself. Unless a major memorial is placed or an excellent book published on the *Essex*, the concerns of CV-9's veterans could become even more justified. *Essex* earned her place in naval history with a well-documented combat career in World War II and Korea. No one can ever be satisfied when a job well done is overlooked or forgotten.

When the veterans of the *Yorktown* (CV-10) Association meet, they all have one very pleasant memory to share: their ship has been preserved as a memorial. *Yorktown* (CV-10) seems to have been blessed with all the good fortune that escaped her famous predecessor, *Yorktown* (CV-5). During World War II *Yorktown* (CV-10) hit the enemy hard, but was hit only once with few casualties. After lengthy service, the "Fighting Lady" was scheduled for demolition. The effort to preserve the *Enterprise* as a national memorial in Washington, D.C. had failed in 1958, and for similar reasons – lack of money – the effort to preserve the *Essex* at Bridgeport failed. The country had several battleship memorials in 1975, but no carrier had been preserved to call remembrance to a "carrier war." While negotiations between *Yorktown* veterans and the state of Virginia were moving slowly, word came that the state of South Carolina was seeking ships for the new Patriot's Point Naval and Maritime Museum. Quickly, a new series of negotiations were completed, South Carolina obtained the first World War II era carrier to be saved from the scrap

Thanks to another John Brown, this one John R. Brown, the USS *Alabama* Crewman's Association is a viable, active reunion group. In the top picture *Alabama* veterans offer a prayer during a brief ceremony in which a plaque (just visible at left) was dedicated to several former shipmates killed in an accident. In the middle picture, Mrs. Doris West admires two of the plaques designed by John R. Brown which are presently aboard the *Alabama*, while the bottom picture is self-explanatory. All three photos were taken during the *Alabama* veterans April 1985 reunion. Author's Collection

In the fall of 1985 the USS *Houston* Association brought its annual reunion to Mobile, Ala. An honored guest was Marine Corps Col. John Grider Miller (at left), author of the book *The Battle to Save the Houston.* In the middle is outgoing secretary Hank Shafman and at right is incoming secretary Don G. Michalak. Author's Collection

Pictured here are several veterans of the *Houston* who were on board in October 1944. Front from left are Hank Shafman, Jim Potter, C.C. York and J. "Ski" Skarzenski; back from left are Jack Santos, Rear Adm. Clarence Broussard, Rear Adm. George H. Miller and R.W. Ramsey. Miller, Broussard and York were particularly instrumental in the effort to save the stricken cruiser. Author's Collection

Fortunately for history J. Ed Hudson has not been content to hold memories of his ship, USS *Cabot* (CVL-28), within himself. Like several other veterans, he has penned a history of his ship. More recently, he and several other former *Cabot* shipmates have investigated possibilities of establishing a museum exhibit for their ship. The old *Cabot* still lives in 1985 in the navy of Spain (see Chapter Two). Courtesy of J. Ed. Hudson

World War II Navy reunion groups owe a healthy portion of their success to women who have served as officers of reunion groups (mostly secretary and treasurer). And, more than one woman has been partially responsible for the origination of a reunion association. Shown here at the 1984 dedication of the Hancock Room aboard the *Yorktown* in Charleston harbor is one such woman, Mrs. Betty Orchowski (cutting ribbon). Proud husband Ed stands immediately to her right. Courtesy of Ed Orchowski

heap, and veterans of the *Yorktown* achieved the seemingly impossible task of saving their ship.

At the heart of the *Yorktown* veterans' most pleasant memory is the remembrance of one man's effort to save their ship. In the wardroom of the now preserved carrier is a large impressive plaque that reads:

USS YORKTOWN CV-10
ASSOCIATION'S ROOMS
Dedicated by Appreciative Members
to
JAMES TAYLOR BRYAN Jr.
Our founder in 1948 and Tireless and
Envisioned Leader the Past 36 Years
The Instigator and Keystone in the
Successful Efforts of Saving From
The Scrap Heap Our Beloved
"FIGHTING LADY"
The Founder and Persistent Developer
Of The U.S. Navy's Carrier Aviation
National Memorial and Hall of Fame
October 6th, 1984

Appropriately, the image of a bomb is at the top of the plaque denoting Bryan's wartime responsibilities as an aviation ordnance officer.

Bryan hosted a *Yorktown* reunion in 1948 and has since dedicated his life to ensuring the memory not only of the close friends he lost but also to the memory of all naval aviators and ships' company who did not come home to enjoy the benefits of the freedom they helped preserve. Once the *Yorktown* was brought to Charleston harbor, Bryan set to work to establish the "Arlington of Carrier Aviation" (see Chapter Two) and to arrange for sections of the ship to be opened to other carrier veterans who wished to have a place for memorializing their ship. Never one to rest on yesterday's accomplishments,. Bryan currently burns up telephone lines (his phone bill approaches the national debt) seeking funds for new projects, encouraging research efforts and asking veterans to assist in the remembrance of their fallen shipmates. In time, James Bryan will be remembered as the man who did more than any other to honor the memory of naval officers and men who made the ultimate sacrifice. Before that time, however, Jim's shipmates demonstrate the depth of their affection and appreciation by lining up behind him in his constant push to memorialize all the World War II carriers and the men who served in them.

All of James Bryan's shipmates hold a special place in his heart and memory, but as it is with all men, a few were particularly significant. The late Vice Adm. "Jimmy" Flatley was one; "Smokey" Stover—who did not come back—was another. Still another, James W. "PoP" Condit, did come back after two years. "Pop," now a retired rear admiral, was shot down in the August 1943 raid on Marcus Island and had the unfortunate distinction of being the first pilot who had flown off one of the new *Essex*-class carriers to be captured by the Japanese. Initially not well treated by the enemy, "PoP" once told a Japanese interrogator "Why do you keep asking me what happened to the *Enterprise*? You've reported it sunk six times!" Moved to a POW camp in Japan, Condit painted his name and air group number on a roof inside the camp in August 1945 when Japanese guards left after the Emperor announced cessation of hostilities. A stunned *Yorktown* aviator spotted the sign from the air—stunned because Condit was believed dead. In one of the more inspirational stories of the war—and one that Condit can tell only half way through—the *Yorktown* air group returned to the carrier, stripped the ship of clothing, medical supplies, food and personal gifts, climbed back into their planes and flew straight for the camp. The ensuing "benevolence bombing" tore holes in the roofs of buildings, demolished a latrine and injured friend and foe alike, but the negatives attending this empathetic episode were totally overlooked by Condit and his fellow prisoners.The enthusiasm and overwhelming concern of his fellow aviators quickly extinguished the agony of imprisonment and his anxiety as to how a POW would be perceived when repatriated. Two weeks later, Condit was ushered aboard the USS *Missouri* to represent Naval Aviation POWs during the Japanese surrender ceremonies.

Death or injury was always a possibility during World War II and veterans of ships that were hit don't forget. Battleship *West Virginia* veterans met in their ship's namesake state for the first time in 1985, and the loss of 105 shipmates at Pearl Harbor was a major topic of discussion. Doug Jacobs, Ray Snapp, Don O'Brien and renowned artist Clarence Tibado take seriously their remembrance of the USS *Pensacola* (CA-24). These men were among two dozen *Pensacola* veterans who gathered at the Nimitz Museum in Texas on 13 April 1985 to dedicate a plaque in honor of their 146 former shipmates lost aboard the Navy's first "treaty cruiser." Don G. Michalak, Byron Harris and Camiel Dhaveloose well remember the fight to save the damaged cruiser *Houston* (CL-81) in 1944, but they also remember that several *Houston* veterans served on the *Helena* (CL-50) until she went down "stack to stack" in 1943. Those who survived Helena's death fondly remember the men of destroyers *Radford* and *Nicholas* for giving up their bunks, blankets, clothes and money to those pulled from the water. Murray C. Flanders, veteran of the cruiser USS *Savannah* (CL-42), notes that *Savannah* reunions are scheduled to coincide as nearly as possible with the anniversary of the bomb hit that took the lives of 197 men on 11 September 1943. James Rodgers remembers the USS *Tennessee* being hit by rifle fire by virtue of being so close

Reon G. Hillegass Jr., survived the fire and explosions aboard the *Franklin* in March 1945. Partially responsible for his salvation was the three-inch overboard discharge vent he holds for the camera during the June 1985 *Franklin* reunion in Norfolk, Va. In the second photo, the vent is pictured with 1967 newspaper articles describing the proposed naval museum which was to have incorporated much of the Franklin's island structure and mast. Author's Collection

The Rev. W.H. Scoates points to the flight deck where he spent a long afternoon on 19 March 1945 aboard the burning *Franklin.* When asked what he thought those who died that day would say about their fate, Scoates replied, "They would tell us to live because preservation of life is what they died for." Author's Collection

to the enemy-held Marshall Islands, while one of the more vivid memories of J.V. Lewis of the USS *Raleigh* (CL-7) is two shipmates cutting a man out of the capsized USS *Utah* on 7 December 1941. G.H. Parkin of the famous destroyer *Hoel* (DD-533) remembers the battle off Samar as "quite an engagement," while cruiser Atlanta's Leighton Spadone admits to "a rough memory of that final night" (Naval Battle of Guadalcanal). And, Vernon Bryan, survivor of the USS *Quincy* (CA-39), states that "the subject of Savo...continues to rankle me as no other subject has or ever can."

Of course, not all memories are centered on sinkings, damage and injury. Ed Arterburn, who originated the USS *England* (DE-635) reunion group in 1981, was delighted to know that his former executive officer and later CO, John A. Williamson, would be the keynote speaker at the Orlando, Fla., August 1985 Destroyer Escort Sailors Association convention. Robert L. Bastian, secretary of the USS *Augusta* (CA-31) reunion group, treasures the memory of holding open an elevator door for President Roosevelt just before one of the president's meetings with Prime Minister Winston Churchill which eventuated in the Atlantic Charter. J.C. Ayers, veteran of the cruiser USS *Pittsburgh* (CA-72), recalls with pride not only the record of his ship but also the recent launching of a new *Pittsburgh* (SSN-720), a nuclear powered attack submarine. T.J. "Jake" Powell will always remember the privilege of participating in the dedication of the USS *Helena* memorial, and Edward J. Ward of the Tin Can Sailors organization not only looks back with satisfaction as to what his group has already accomplished but looks forward to the opening of the National Destroyer Museum on board the USS *Kennedy* at Battleship Cove. Like Ward, Russell E. Brown looks back and

Attending his first *Franklin* reunion in 1985, veteran Walter Jordan hoped to find at least one former shipmate from his 150-man division at the reunion. He didn't; they all died aboard ship in March 1945. Author's Collection

ahead. Some day he hopes to see his ship, the USS *New Jersey*, finally retired and enshrined somewhere along the New Jersey coast.

James F. Murray, whose most enduring memory is that of seeing four Japanese carriers burning at Midway from an *Enterprise* SBD, also recalls being court-martialed for possessing "firewater." The two bottles of evidence in his trial were eventually broken on the bow of submarine USS *Bass* (P-2), thus becoming perhaps the only U.S. naval vessel to be "christened" with bourbon.

Murray was present in October 1984 for the dedication of the Enterprise Exhibit at the Naval Aviation Museum. While there, he had occasion to speak briefly to Capt. Grover Walker, director of the Naval Aviation Museum. Walker, a World War II veteran, left the Navy to earn a degree and play football for some of the most outstanding football teams Southern Methodist University ever put on the field. After graduation, he returned to the Navy for two more wars and then assumed the responsibility of director of the new Naval Aviation Museum. Retiring from active duty, he remained in the same job and has been the driving force in creating one of the finest museums of any kind to be found anywhere.

Forty years ago there was no need for a sailor to think about or define pride: it existed. In 1985, it exists again. Evidence of this pride was constantly apparent at veterans' reunions as many a glass was raised in honor of current Secretary of the Navy John Lehman. There is no question among World War II naval veterans as to whether or not Lehman will become one of the great secretaries of the Navy. To them, he already is. This is no small matter to World War II veterans. They made great sarifices 40 years ago and in their twilight years it is most comforting to know that their spirit of success is manifest in a succeeding generation.

Meeting in Williamsburg, Va., in June 1985, veterans of the carrier *Essex* (CV-9) agree on at least one matter: history speaks too often of the *Essex* class and too seldom on the lead ship of the class. To date, no major museum exhibit honoring *Essex* (CV-9) has been established.
Author's Collection

Is everybody happy? Oh well, 11 of 12 isn't bad. Actually, everybody attending the 1985 *Essex* reunion had a very enjoyable time. *Essex* veterans are as effective in organizing a good party and reunion as they were in organizing pain for enemies during World War II and Korea.
Author's Collection

Instigator and keystone in the successful effort of saving *Yorktown* (CV-10) from the scrap heap was James T. Bryan. An aviation ordnance officer aboard CV-10, Bryan is also founder of the Carrier Aviation National Memorial and Hall of Fame aboard the "Fighting Lady." At top Bryan is seen in Charleston harbor in 1975 as CV-10 is towed toward her final berth. In the bottom photo Bryan and former President Gerald R. Ford view the USS *Monterey* (CVL-26) Room aboard *Yorktown.* Courtesy of Yorktown Association

Many World War II veterans who survived World War II have since passed from this life, but they are not forgotten. In October 1985 an F6F "Hellcat" was dedicated aboard the *Yorktown* in memory of Cmdr. (later Vice Adm.) James H. "Jimmy" Flatley who flew the first F6F into combat in 1943. Pictured in front of the "Hellcat" is the son of the World War II ace, Rear Adm. James H. Flatley Jr., his son and grandson. In the eyes of many, the Flatleys are "the royal family of naval aviation." Author's Collection

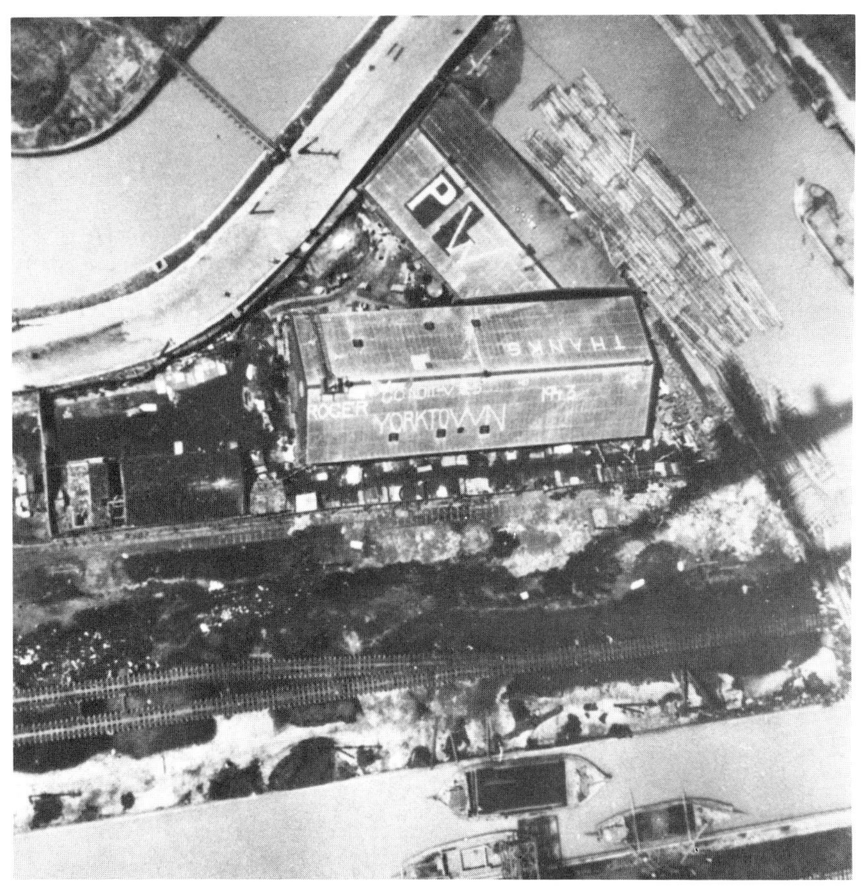

James W. "Pop" Condit and Maj. Gregory "Pappy" Boyington were POWs in this compound in Japan. In August 1945 Condit painted his name, air group and ship's name on the roof of the building seen in this picture. *Yorktown* airmen saw the sign, returned to the carrier to acquire supplies and then "bombed" the camp. Note the "thanks" sign and the shadow of the plane that took this picture. USN courtesy of RADM J.W. Condit

A flight deck accident that put him in the hospital for two years did not discourage David Lister from wanting to fly. Since World War II Lister has been both a charter and test pilot and has been called to testify in numerous court cases relating to plane crashes. The "Corsair" behind Dave is Korean War vintage. Courtesy of Dave Lister

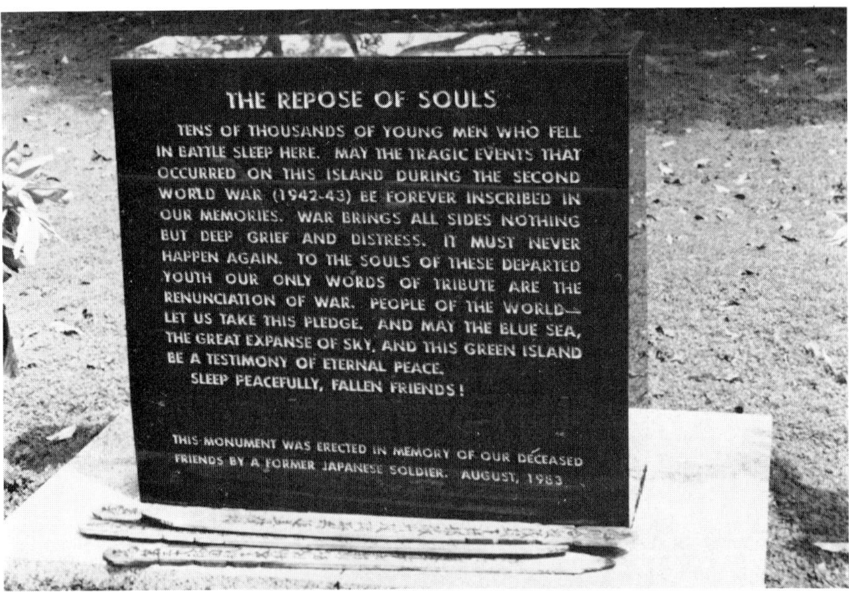

On Guadalcanal is an impressive memorial placed by a Japanese veteran (top photo). American veterans such as Guadalcanal Campaign Veterans vice president Dick Hennig, seen here with his wife while making reunion arrangements with sales director Shirley Kirchharr, plan to equal the Japanese memorial both on Guadalcanal and at a new museum in Michigan. Author's Collection

Capt. John Adams (USN ret.) spends his free time in 1985 on the golf course rather than in the air. Flying off the old *Yorktown* (CV-5), Adams flew F4F "Wildcats" similar to the one behind him in the Battle of the Coral Sea and the Battle of Midway. Despite three enemy planes credited to him, Adams still laments the lack of fuel that kept him and several of his squadron mates from repelling the last air attack on CV-5 at Midway. Author's Collection

One of the very few men to help make history and then preserve it is Capt. Grover Walker (USN ret.), director of the Naval Aviation Museum. Here, Walker (at left) is joined by Rear Adm. Grover B.H. Hall, the late Bob Piper and Rear Adm. Thomas J. Hamilton for ribbon cutting ceremonies during the dedication of the Enterprise Exhibit. Hall and Hamilton were the last two living commanding officers of the "Big E." Walker and Hamilton have more than naval aviation and combat in common; Walker is a former linebacker at SMU while Rear Adm. Hamilton twice coached football at the Naval Academy after starring there as a player. Author's Collection

Too young to even remember World War II, current Secretary of the Navy John Lehman (second from left at ceremony aboard *Yorktown*) is nonetheless extremely popular with World War II naval veterans. From left are James T. Bryan (see text), Secretary Lehman and Supreme Court Justice Byron White. At far right is Rear Adm. J.W. "Pop" Condit (see text), on his right is David McCampbell (Navy's top World War II ace) and on McCampbell's right is Midway survivor George Gay. Over Secretary Lehman's shoulder is Patriot's Point director J.W. Guerry; standing is noted historian/author Clark G. Reynolds. Courtesy of Yorktown Association

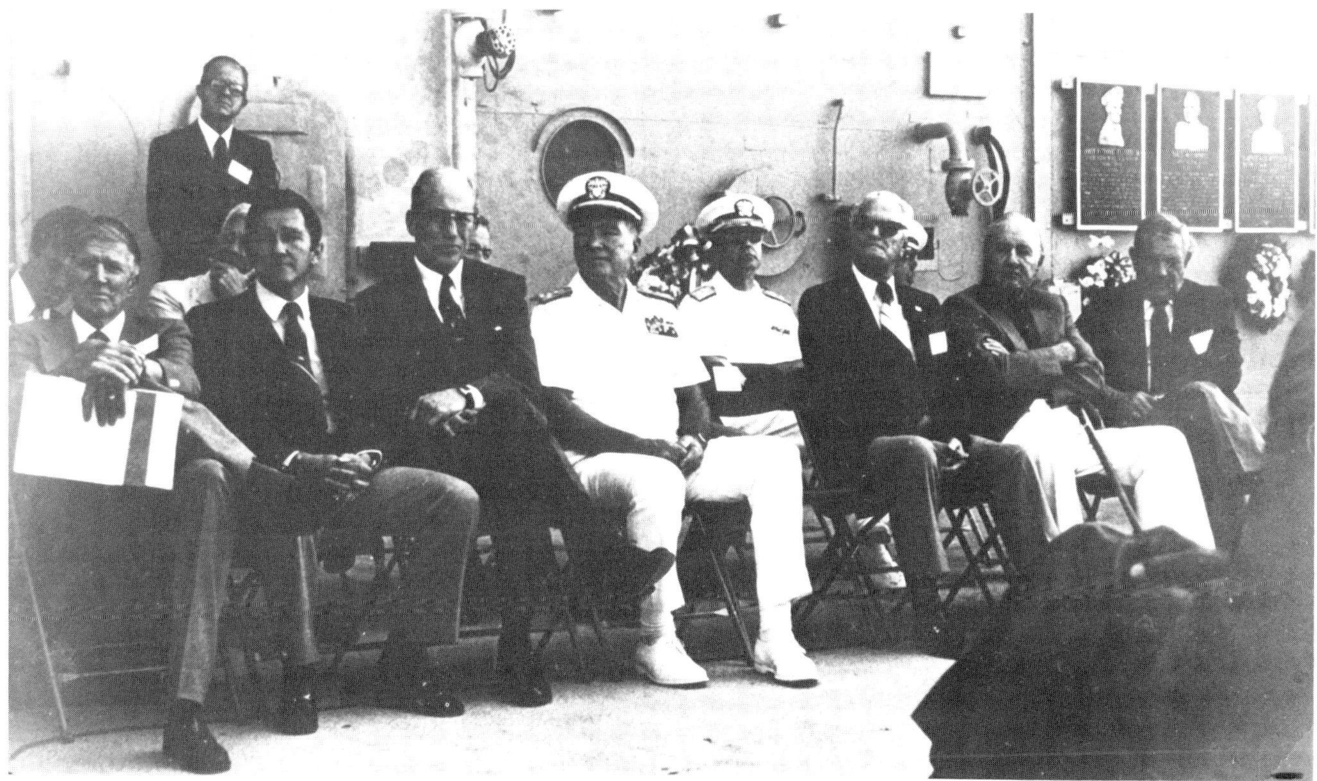

Glen Foster (left) and Glenn H. Parkin (with his wife) had good reason to be happy when photographed in January 1945. Both were among the tragically few survivors from the destroyer *Hoel* DD-533 which was sunk off Samar during the Battle of Leyte Gulf. In October 1985 survivors of the famous *Hoel*, including Foster (middle, standing) and Parkin (second from left, kneeling), gathered in St. Louis for their first reunion. Courtesy of Glenn Parkin

ACKNOWLEDGMENTS

Memories and Memorials: The U.S. Navy 40 Years After Victory began several years and many miles ago. The original concept called for a complete inventory of all artifacts remaining in the Navy's possession. However, Henry Vadnais of the Navy Historical Center wisely offered counsel to limit the scope and concentrate on major existing exhibits.

Like most books concerning naval history, this one began at the Navy Historical Center in the Washington Navy Yard. After the usual consultations with Bob Cressman, Agnes Hoover, Chuck Haberlein, John Vajda and John C. Reilly Jr., it was off across the country to visit World War II memorials and to meet veterans, mostly at their reunions.

Along the way there were unexpected disappointments and unexpected treasures to be found. Among the disappointments – no doubt obvious in the text – were the missing memorials for the carrier *Franklin* in Norfolk and the battleship *Washington* in Olympia. Another was the search for a Midwestern model enthusiast who moved his "fleet" only a few days before my arrival. Among the unexpected treasures was locating the Navy builder's models of several old, famous ships. But, the greatest treasure was meeting the veterans themselves, and meeting members of my generation – a generation born during or just after World War II – who are active in preserving the history of the 1941-45 era.

During World War II men like Stanley Johnston and Eugene Burns wrote stories of the Navy at war. As information from the enemy was not available during the war, parts of books written during that time were later proven erroneous. However, these books are still particularly valuable as they provide unique "I was there" observations and attitudes. In the 1950s and 1960s outstanding books on the war appeared in profusion. Paramount among these was Samuel E. Morison's multi-volume *History of United States Naval Operations in World War II.* In the 1980s a considerable portion of the Navy's 1941-45 history is being preserved by a generation that cannot remember the war. Among these individuals are publishers Stan Cohen and Mike Stevenson; authors Robert L. Lawson, Barrett Tillman, Larry Sowinski, John C. Reilly Jr., Bob Cressman, Col. John G. Miller, M. Jack Smith, Clark G. Reynolds, and John Lundstrom; modeling enthusiasts Larry Sowinski, Tom Walkowiak, James Grigerick, Hal Hague and Tom Arusiewicz; and curators Tim Rizzuto (USS *Kidd*), Wayne Schmidt (USS *Intrepid*), David Clark (USS *Yorktown*), Mike Curtin (Hampton Roads Naval Museum) and Bruce Smith (Admiral Nimitz Museum).

Thanks to the following World War II U.S. Navy veterans, information was obtained concerning the origin and development of reunion associations and the location of existing or planned memorials. Those responding to mailed questionnaires and/or visits and phone calls include: James Boyd, Douglas W. Haward, Warren Potter, Jack Gallagher, Charles Hinn, Philip Ard and Tom Leo (*Essex*); Harold Miller, William Stephenson, Walter Crowe and Father William F. Farrell (*Franklin*); John Larsen (*Iowa*); J. Hawkins (*Tennessee*); Bill Gath (*Kidd*); Perrin Cothran (*Alabama*); Ted Blahnik (*Helena* and Guadalcanal Campaign Veterans); Bill Cunningham and Buhler Glans (*Birmingham*); Roger F. Shurtz (*Chicago*); Frank Leslie, Paul H. Grevencamp, LeRoy E. Ewing, Myron Varland and C.H. Carroll (*Salt Lake City*); Ed Whittler (*San Francisco*); Perry Ustick (*Northampton*); James G. Ross and Glenn H. Anderson (*Washington*); E.W. Rogers (*Mobile*) L.J. Krystynak (*Cleveland*); James E. Tracy (*Chester*); Hugh A. Eubank (*Biloxi*); Cliff Pitts (*Detroit*); G.W.Loveridge (*Omaha*); Louis F. Aurrecoechea (*Reno*); K.P. McDaniel and Frank Clemens (*:Louisville*); Charles A. Cass (*New Orleans*); Bill Bunker (*Helena*); Donald K. Theobald (*Minneapolis*); W.D. McFetrich (*Hornet*); and Jack Collins (DE Sailors). Names mentioned in the text or in picture captions are not repeated here.

The following were equally important to the completion of this book: Isacco A. Valli (Manitowoc Maritime Museum); Dan Harrison (USS *Texas* Memorial); J. Edward Barr and Wanita Cusachs (Louisiana Maritime Museum); Bob Nylen (Nevada State Museum); Derek Valley (Washington State Museum); Mary Lohrenz (Mississippi State Historical Museum); Bill Winberg (*Queen Mary*); Robert Haslach (Royal Netherlands Embassy); K.T. Liem (Erasmus University Rotterdam); John H. Davis (National Park Service); Bobbie Gooch (Naval War College Museum); Dolores Kwiatkowski (Buffalo Naval Park); June Huber (Patriot's Point); LaVerne Luce (Seawolf Park); Capt. William J. Diffley (USS *Alabama* Memorial); Richard Wescott (Augusta-Richmond County Museum); Dr. Jack Rhodes, Louis Michot, R.W. Gregory, Lois Bark; Milton and Kay Osterman; Arlene Kalogeros; Edgar Lewis; Sherman Griswold; Don Wade; Connie Bair; Cynthia Faircloth; Cammie East; Terry Quattlebaum and John S. Blum.

The following were particularly generous in assisting with the acquisition of photographs: Claudia L. Pennington and Agnes F. Hoover (Navy Historical Center); Ruth Dow (Portsmouth Navy Yard); Jim McIngvale and Ron Elias (Ingalls Shipbuilding); Patty M. Maddocks (U.S. Naval Institute); Howard Wedman; Lawrence Seehafer; Julia Von-Wellen; Paul Alburl; Andy Palmer; Cyril A. Jenkins; Marlene Vance; Joe Silva; Dr. and Mrs. Robert King; W.D. Ferguson; James C. Barnhill; Rear Adm. J.W. Condit; J. Ed Hudson; Ed Orchowski; Travis Price; John A. Brown; Henry Pyzdrowski; Barrett Tillman; Bill Winberg;

Alex Ansley, Bill Barr, and Dr. George Smith.

A very special note of appreciation is extended to Dean Schumacher (Dean will perhaps soon begin writing his own books) for his continual assistance in both research for the text and for acquisition of special photographs. A special thanks is also offered to Ron Moreland, director of the Pensacola Naval Air Station Library, for his assistance.

Encouragement is always welcome and acknowledgment is offered to the following for their kind words and sympathetic ears: Rear Adm. Robert E. Riera; Rear Adm. John Crommelin; Rear Adm. Albert Coffin; Capt. John Adams; Frank Albert and Dave Lister (Dave was especially patient as he and I – a test pilot and geography major – were ingloriously lost at road's end in a corn field near Chicago while searching for that city).

Appreciation is expressed to George and Elizabeth Lowry and their children – Catherine, Patrick and Margaret – for the use of their home while in the Washington, D.C., area. And, appreciation is expressed to President Ernest Clevenger and administrators Billy Hilyer, Jimmy Crabtree, Linda Brooks, Donnie Hilliard and Don Earwood not only for their support and understanding but also for declining to accept the suggestion of a Faulkner University colleague that my office be moved to the edge of the campus and be surrounded by barbed wire.

Research assistance and clerical help was provided by Sheryl Sexsmith, Debbie Higgins Argersinger, Dana Bone, Cynthia Boswell, Cynthia Warmack, Beth McKee, Candy Huggins and Mrs. Wilber A. Ewing. Editorial assistance was rendered by publisher Stan Cohen, Karon Hightower, Vicki Pontious and Peter Stark.

THE ART OF JOE CASON

The renderings within this book were drawn by renowned nature and maritime artist Joe Cason. For many years a free-lance artist and designer, Joe was responsible for much of the design work for the Naval Aviation Museum, Pensacola, Fla., before being persuaded to accept a fulltime position in 1981 as chief designer with this magnificient museum.

All of the renderings except one were drawn especially for this book. The exception is the portrayal of an F6F "Hellcat" rising from the deck of *Enterprise* (CV-6), created in honor of the dedication of the *Enterprise* Exhibit at the Naval Aviation Museum in October 1984. The rendering at the front of the battleship chapter portrays the World War II USS *Alabama* (BB-60), her famous Confederate predecessor and the new nuclear submarine *Alabama* (SSBN-731). For the cruiser chapter, a rendering of a *Northampton*-class cruiser was completed to honor the cruiser class upon which fell much of the success and sacrifice of the first year of war. The class included *Northampton* (CA-26), *Chester* (CA-27), *Louisville* (CA-28), *Chicago* (CA-29), *Houston* (CA-30) and *Augusta* (CA-31).

No event of World War II involving destroyers and destroyer escorts captures the essence of success and sacrifice as much as the heroic charge of the "little boys" in the battle off Samar during the momentous Battle of Leyte Gulf. *Johnston* (DD-557), *Hoel* (DD-533), and *Samuel B. Roberts* (DE-413) are honored in Chapter Four for their finest, and last, hour.

Heading Chapter Five is a rendering of the solemn memorial at Pearl Harbor dedicated to the memory of the 52 U.S. Navy submarines lost in World War II, and fronting the veterans chapter is a drawing of four veterans reunited with a "Corsair" on the deck of a memorialized carrier.

As a planned memorial in Norfolk, Va.—which was to have included the mast and a significant portion of the island structure from the USS *Franklin* (CV-13)—was abandoned, Joe has completed a rendering to commemorate "the Lost Memorial." A "permanent" memorial to the battleship *Washington* (BB-56) within the state capitol complex at Olympia was recently dismantled and placed in storage. In honor of the only U.S. Navy battleship to sink one of her own kind, Joe has offered herein a tribute to the great warship and its memorial. And, within the Introduction to this book is a depiction of a memorial to the USS *Trout* near Falmouth, Mass. The solitary setting for this memorial is appropriate, and also seems to call attention to the day when only engraved stones and words on paper will be available to evoke memories of a gallant generation of ships and men.

Previous experience foretells a number of inquiries directed toward acquisition of particular pictures, paintings and/or artistic renderings. Inquiries concerning pictures should be directed to the author in care of the publisher (Pictorial Histories) while inquiries relating to Joe Cason's renderings should be directed to NAVAIR Art, PO Box 34127, Pensacola, Fla., 32507.

APPENDIX I

PRESIDENTIAL UNIT CITATION

Awarded by: Secretary of the Navy in the name of the President

Date established: 6 February 1942 (amended 28 June 1943)

Comparable individual award: Navy Cross
Action required for receipt: ...outstanding performance in action against an enemy of the United States on or after December 6, 1941...

Ribbon description: three horizontal stripes of navy blue (top), gold and scarlet

NAVY UNIT COMMENDATION

Awarded by: Secretary of the Navy with approval of the President

Date established: 18 December 1944

Comparable individual award: Silver Star or Legion of Merit

Action required for receipt: ...subsequent to December 6, 1941 shall have distinguished itself by outstanding heroism in action against the enemy, but not of a degree sufficient to justify the award of the Presidential Unit Citation...

Ribbon description: large wintergreen center stripe flanked on both sides by narrow red, yellow and blue stripes.

Source for recipients of Presidential Unit Citation and Navy Unit Commendation: *Navy and Marine Corps Awards Manual*

Sources for recipients of Battle Stars: *Navy and Marine Corps Awards Manual*; *Dictionary of American Naval Fighting Ships* and direct inquiries to the Navy Historical Center. It should be noted that changes in battle star totals for some ships have been made in response to challenges by respective ship's veterans' associations.

APPENDIX II

U.S. NAVY "AUXILIARIES" MEMORIALS

It would seem that any vessel carrying guns and steaming in a combat zone during World War II would be termed a "combat" ship, but transports, tankers, minesweepers, minelayers, landing craft and others were classified as "auxiliaries." These vessels saw an equal share of combat and won the same awards as battleships, carriers, cruisers, destroyers and submarines. As elementary as this statement is, it is necessary to say that World War II could not have been won without them.

Auxiliaries were not treated herein as doing so would more than double the size of this book. And, a book on auxiliaries deserves to be treated as a separate unit. Still, a few memorials to these ships are noted here to call attention to the fact that auxiliaries have not been totally overlooked.

At San Francisco's Fort Mason one can find the last operational World War II Liberty Ship, SS *Jeremiah O'Brien*. Restored as a memorial to the 2,751 Liberty Ships and their crews, the 1943-built *O'Brien* still

O'Brien. Courtesy of Dean Schumacher

makes two cruises a year around San Francisco Bay. South of San Francisco at Long Beach, Calif., rests another World War II veteran perhaps better known for her peacetime service. Still, the RMS *Queen Mary* recorded a splendid war record carrying 765,429 military personnel to and from combat.

Two World War II minesweepers have been preserved as memorials. The USS *Inaugural* (AM-242) is located on the Mississippi River just below the famous arch in St. Louis, Mo., while the USS *Hazard* (AM-240) rests on dry land in Omaha, Neb. Both are loaded with anti-aircraft guns and one almost automatically begins to search the sky upon a first visit to either vessel.

Although the *Seven Seas* was scrapped in 1979, she is nonetheless pictured here (circa 1971) to note her unique history. After serving as a school ship until 1966, she was purchased by the University of Rotterdam and used as a dormitory for nearly 300 students. In 1971 she was sold to a ship-building firm. This vessel was launched as a merchant ship but in 1941 she was converted into an aircraft carrier and became the USS *Long Island*, the U.S. Navy's first escort carrier (CVE-1). Plowshare to sword and back to plowshare – what a memorial she would have been!

Queen Mary. Courtesy of Wrather Port Properties

Inaugural and *Hazard*.
Author's Collection

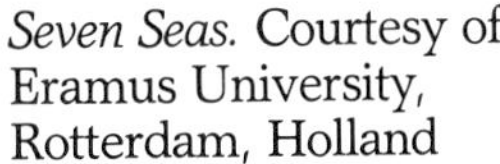
Seven Seas. Courtesy of
Eramus University,
Rotterdam, Holland

APPENDIX III

U.S. NAVY MUSEUMS (1985)

Navy Memorial Museum
Washington Navy Yard
Washington, D.C. 20374

U.S. Naval Academy Museum
Annapolis, Md. 21402

Amphibious Museum
Naval Amphibious Base
Norfolk, Va.

Naval Aviation Museum
Naval Air Station
Pensacola, Fla.

Submarine Force Library and Museum
Naval Submarine Base
New London, Conn.

Naval Supply Corps Museum
Naval Supply Corps School
Athens, Ga.

Hampton Roads Naval Museum
Naval Base
Norfolk, Va.

Naval Air and Test Evaluation Museum
Naval Air Test Center
Patuxent River, Md.

Naval Museum of Undersea Warfare
Keyport, Wash.

Navy/Marine Corps and Coast Guard
Museum of the Pacific
Treasure Island
San Francisco, Calif.

CEC/SEABEE Museum
Naval Construction Center
Port Hueneme, Calif.

Pacific Submarine Museum
Pearl Harbor, Hawaii

Hampton Roads Naval Museum, Norfolk, Virginia. Author's Collection

Naval War College Museum, Newport, Rhode Island. Author's Collection

Inside the Naval Aviation Museum, Pensacola, Florida. Author's Collection

Navy-Marine Corps and Coast Guard Museum of the Pacific, San Francisco, California. Courtesy of Stan Cohen

BIBLIOGRAPHY

GENERAL

Adams, Henry H. *Witness to Power: The Life of Fleet Admiral William D. Leahy.* Annapolis: Naval Institute Press, 1985.

Buell, Thomas B. *Master of Sea Power: A Biography of Fleet Admiral Ernest J. King.* Annapolis/Boston: Naval Institute Press/Little, Brown, 1980.

Cohen, Stan. *East Wind Rain.* Missoula, Montana: Pictorial Histories Publishing Company, 1981.

Coletta, Paolo E. *American Secretaries of the Navy.* Annapolis: Naval Institute Press, 1980.

Costello, John. *The Pacific War.* New York: Rawson, Wade Publishers, Inc., 1981.

Driskill, Frank and Dede Casad. *Chester W. Nimitz: Admiral of the Hills.* Austin, Texas: Eakin Press, 1983.

Freeman, Robert H. *Requiem for a Fleet: The U.S. Navy at Guadalcanal, August 1942-February 1943.* Ventor, New Jersey: Shellback Press, 1984.

Gailey, Harry A. *Peleliu: 1944.* Annapolis: The Nautical and Aviation Publishing Company of America, 1983.

Howarth, Stephen. *The Fighting Ships of the Rising Sun: The Drama of the Imperial Japanese Navy 1895-1945.* New York: Atheneum, 1983.

Hoyt, Edwin P. *Closing the Circle, War In the Pacific: 1945.* New York: Van Nostrand Reinhold Company, 1942.

Hoyt, Edwin P. *The Kamikazes.* New York: Arbor House Publishing Company, 1983.

Jurika, Stephen Jr. *From Pearl Harbor to Vietnam: The Memoirs of Arthur D. Radford.* Stanford, California: Hoover Institution Press, 1980.

Lord, Walter. *Day of Infamy.* Henry Holt Inc., 1957.

Messimer, Dwight R. *Pawns of War: The Loss of the USS Langley and the USS Pecos.* Annapolis: Naval Institute Press, 1983.

Mitchell, Donald W. *History of the Modern American Navy from 1883 through Pearl Harbor.* New York: Alfred A. Knopf, 1946.

Morison, Samuel Eliot. *History of United States Naval Operations in World War II.* Boston: Little, Brown and Company, 1948-1960.

I. *The Battle of the Atlantic,* September 1939-May 1943.

II. *Operations in North African Waters,* October 1942 -June 1943.

III. *The Rising Sun in the Pacific,* 1931-April 1942.

IV. *Coral Sea, Midway and Submarine Actions,* May 1942-August 1942.

V. *The Struggle For Guadalcanal,* August 1942-February 1943.

VI. *Breaking the Bismarcks Barrier,* July 22, 1942-May 1, 1944.

VII. *Aleutians, Gilberts and Marshalls,* June 1942-April 1944.

VIII. *New Guinea and the Marianas,* March 1944-August 1944.

IX. *Sicily-Salerno-Anzio,* January 1943-June 1944.

X. *The Atlantic Battle Won,* May 1943-May 1945.

XI. *The Invasion of France and Germany,* 1944-1945.

XII. *Leyte,* June 1944-January 1945.

XIII. *The Liberation of the Philippines, Luzon, Mindanao, The Visayas,* 1944-August 1945.

XIV. *Victory in the Pacific,* 1945.

Potter, E.B. *Bull Halsey.* Annapolis: Naval Institute Press, 1985.

Prange, Gordon W. *At Dawn We Slept: The Untold Story of Pearl Harbor.* New York: McGraw-Hill Book Company, 1981.

Prange, Gordon W. *Miracle at Midway.* Highstown, New Jersey: McGraw-Hill, 1982.

Scheina, Robert L. *U.S. Coast Guard Cutters and Craft of World War II.* Annapolis: Naval Institute Press, 1982.

Spector, Ronald H. *Eagle Against the Sun: The American War With Japan.* New York: The Free Press, 1985.

Willmott, H.P. *The Barrier and the Javelin.* Annapolis: Naval Institute Press, 1983.

Willmott, H.P. *Empires In the Balance: Japanese and Allied Pacific Strategies to April 1942.* Annapolis: Naval Institute Press, 1982.

Winslow, W.G. *The Fleet the Gods Forgot.* Annapolis: Naval Institute Press, 1982.

Y'Blood, William T. *Red Sun Setting, The Battle of the Philippine Sea.* Annapolis: Naval Institute Press, 1981.

BATTLESHIPS

Friedman, Norman. *U.S. Battleships.* Annapolis: Naval Institute Press, 1985.

Gibbons, Tony. *The Complete Encyclopedia of Battleships.* New York: Crown Books, 1983.

Hodges, Peter. *The Big Gun: Battleship Main Armament 1860-1945.* Annapolis: Naval Institute Press, 1981.

Smith, Myron Jr. *Golden State Battlewagon.* Missoula, Montana: Pictorial Histories Publishing Company, 1984.

Smith, Myron Jr. *Mountaineer Battlewagon: U.S.S. West Virginia (BB-48).* Missoula, Montana: Pictorial Histories Publishing Company, 1982.

AIRCRAFT CARRIERS

Anderson, David A. *Hellcat.* New York: Crown Publishers, Inc., 1981.

Brown, David. *Aircraft Carriers.* New York: Arco Publishing Company, 1977. Bryan, J. III. *Aircraft Carriers.* New York: Ballantine Books Inc., 1954.

Burns, Eugene. *Then There Was One.* New York: Harcourt, Brace and Company, 1944.

Chesneau, Roger. *Aircraft Carriers of the World, 1914 to the Present.* Annapolis: Naval Institute Press.

Clark, Joseph J., with Clark G. Reynolds. *Carrier Admiral.* New York: David McKay Company, Inc., 1970.

Cressman, Bob. *That Gallant Ship USS Yorktown CV-5.* Missoula, Montana: Pictorial Histories Publishing Company, 1985.

Ewing, Steve. *The "Lady Lex" and the "Blue Ghost."* Missoula, Montana: Pictorial Histories Publishing Company, 1983.

Ewing, Steve. *USS Enterprise (CV-6): The Most Decorated Ship of World War II.* Missoula, Montana: Pictorial Histories Publishing Company, 1982.

Frank, Pat and Joseph D. Harrington. *Rendezvous at Midway: USS Yorktown and the Japanese Carrier Fleet.* New York: The John Day Company, 1967.

Friedman, Norman. *U.S. Aircraft Carriers: An Illustrated Design History.* Annapolis: Naval Institute Press, 1983.

Friedman, Norman; Lott, Arnold and Robert Sumrall. *USS Yorktown (CV-10).* Annapolis: Leeward Publications, 1977.

Inoguchi, Captain Rikihei and Tadashi Nakajima. *The Divine Wind.* Annapolis: U.S. Naval Institute, 1958.

Jackson, B.R., and T.E. Doll. *Douglas TBD-1 "Devastator."* Fallbrook: Aero Publishers, 1973.

Johnston, Stanley. *The Grim Reapers.* Philadelphia: The Blakiston Company, 1943.

Johnston, Stanley. *Queen of the Flat-tops: The USS Lexington and the Coral Sea Battle.* New York: E.P. Dutton and Co., Inc., 1942.

Jones, Lloyd S. *U.S. Naval Fighters: 1922-1980.* Fallbrook: Aero Publishers, 1973.

Kilduff, Peter. *U.S. Carriers at War.* Harrisburg, Pennsylvania: Stackpole Books, 1981.

Lundstrom, John. *The First Team: Pacific Naval Air Combat from Pearl Harbor to Midway.* Annapolis: Naval Institute Press, 1984.

Pawlowski, Gareth L. *Flat-tops and Fledglings: A History of American Aircraft Carriers.* London: A.S. Barnes and Company, 1971.

Phillips, Christopher. *Steichen at War: Naval Aviation in the Pacific.* New York: Abrams, 1981.

Smith, Peter C. *Dive Bomber! An Illustrated History.* Annapolis: Naval Institute Press, 1982.

Stafford, Edward P. *The Big E.* New York: Random House, 1962.

Terzibaschitsch, Stefan. *Escort Carriers and Aviation Support Ships of the U.S. Navy.* Annapolis: Naval Institute Press, 1981.

Tillman, Barrett. *The Wildcat in World War II.* Annapolis: Nautical and Aviation Publishing Company of America, 1983.

Tillman, Barrett. *The Dauntless Dive Bomber of World War II.* Annapolis: Naval Institute Press, 1976.

Trumbull, Robert. *The Raft.* Camden, New Jersey: Henry Holt and Company Inc., 1942.

Y'Blood, William T. *Hunter-Killer: U.S. Escort Carriers in the Battle of the Atlantic.* Annapolis: Naval Institute Press, 1983.

CRUISERS

Dorris, Johnathan Truman. *A Log of the Vicennes.* Louisville, Kentucky, 1947.

Ewing, Steve. *American Cruisers of World War II: A Pictorial Encyclopedia.* Missoula, Montana: Pictorial Histories Publishing Company, 1984.

Friedman, Norman. *U.S. Cruisers: An Illustrated Design History.* Annapolis: Naval Institute Press, 1984

Hansen, Chuck. *USS San Francisco: A Technical History.* 1978.

Leach, Raymond. *All the Drowned Sailors.* Stein and Day, 1982.

Miller, John Grider. *The Battle to Save the Houston, October 1944 to March 1945.* Annapolis: Naval Institute Press, 1985.

Newcomb, Richard F. *Savo: The Incredible Naval Debacle Off Guadalcanal.* New York: Holt, Rinehart & Winston, 1961.

Preston, Antony. *Cruisers: An Illustrated History 1880-1980.* New Jersey: Prentice-Hall, 1980.

DESTROYERS, DESTROYER ESCORTS

Becton, Rear Admiral F. Julian with Joseph Morschauser, III. *The Ship That Would Not Die.* New Jersey: Prentice-Hall, 1980.

Calhoun, Capt. C. Raymond. *Typhoon: The Other Enemy.* Annapolis: Naval Institute Press, 1981.

Friedman, Norman. *U.S. Destroyers, An Illustrated Design History.* Annapolis: Naval Institute Press, 1982.

Goodhart, Philip. *Fifty Ships That Saved the World.* New York: Curtis Books, Modern Literary Editions Publishing Company, 1965.

Hara, Captain Tameichi. *Japanese Destroyer Captain.* New York: Ballantine Books Inc., 1961.

Harmon, Scott J. *USS Cassin Young.* Missoula, Montana: Pictorial Histories Publishing Company, 1985.

Johnson, Frank D. *United States PT-Boats of World War II In Action.* Poole, Dorest (England): Blandford Press, 1980.

Lott, Arnold S. and Robert F. Sumrall. *USS Ward—The First Shot.* Annapolis: Leeward Publications, 1977.

Reilly, John C. Jr. *United States Navy Destroyers of World War II.* Annapolis: Naval Institute Press, 1983.

Roscoe, Theodore. *United States Destroyer Operations in World War II.* Annapolis: U.S. Naval Institute, 1953.

Ross, Al. *The Destroyer Escort ENGLAND.* Annapolis: Naval Institute Press, 1985.

Stafford, Commander Edward P. *Little Ship, Big War: The Saga of DE-343.* New York: William Morrow and Company, 1984.

Sumrall, Robert F. and Thomas F. Walkowiak. *USS Kidd (DD-661).* Kresgeville, Pennsylvania: Floating Drydock, 1985.

SUBMARINES

Bagnasco, Erminio. *Submarines of World War Two.* Annapolis: U.S. Naval Institute, 1978.

Cremer, Peter. *U-Boat Commander: A Periscope View of the Battle of the Atlantic.* London, England: The Bodley Head, 1984.

Gugliotte, Bobette. *Pigboat 39: An American Sub Goes to War.* Lexington: University of Kentucky Press, 1984.

Hoyt, Edwin P. *Bowfin: The Story of One of America's Fabled Fleet Submarines in World War II.* New York: Van Nostrand Reinhold Company, 1983.

Lowder, Hughston E. with Jack Scott. *Batfish! The Champion "Submarine Killer" Submarine of World War II.* Englewood Cliffs: Prentice-Hall, 1980.

O'Kane, R.H. *Clear the Bridge: The War Patrols of the USS Tang.* Chicago: Rand McNally, 1977..

Polmar, Norman. *The American Submarine.* Annapolis: The Nautical and Aviation Publishing Company, 1981.

Roscoe, Theodore. *United States Submarine Operations in World War II.* Annapolis: U.S. Naval Institute, 1949.

Stern, Robert C. *U.S. Subs in Action.* Carrollton: Squadron/Signal Publications, 1983.

ADDENDUM

The destroyer-destroyer escort chapter was written in 1985 and in that year the Destroyer-Escort Sailors Association had not placed a memorial such as the one called for in chapter four. However, in the summer of 1986—just after the proofs of this book were completed, but before the final printing—the DE Sailors Association placed a major exhibit aboard the USS *Laffey* at Patriot's Point in Charleston Harbor, South Carolina. Under the direction of Patriot's Point Executive Director J.E. Guerry and Curator David Clark (shown beside the stand and wheel salvaged from the USS *Merrill* DE-392) the exhibit honoring the World War II destroyer escorts is now mostly complete. As more artifacts and memorabilia are donated, the size of the exhibit will increase. Already, however, this exhibit is an appropriate tribute to the memory of great fighting ships.

USS *Indiana* BB-58 memorial at the University of Indiana (1985). Author's Collection

Recommissioning of the USS *Iowa* BB-61, April 1984. Author's Collection

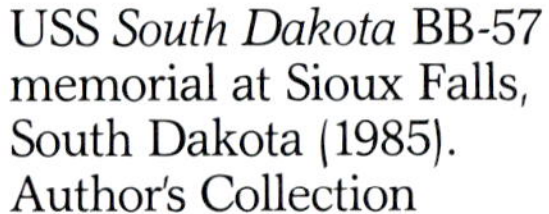
USS *South Dakota* BB-57 memorial at Sioux Falls, South Dakota (1985). Author's Collection

Conning tower of the USS *Squalus/Sailfish* SS-192 at Portsmouth, New Hampshire (1985). USN

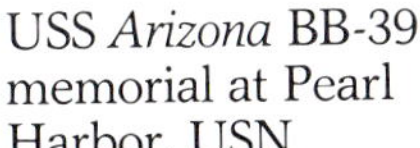

USS *Arizona* BB-39 memorial at Pearl Harbor. USN

Nameplate and mast of the USS *Oakland* CL-95 at Oakland, California (1985). Courtesy of Dean Schumacher

Bow of USS *Stewart* DE-238 and USS *Cavalla* SS-244 at Galveston, Texas (1985). Author's Collection

USS *Cod* SS-224 at Cleveland, Ohio (1985). Author's Collection

Battleship Cove at Fall River, Massachusetts (1985). Author's Collection

Acquired from private sources, the bridge and pilothouse of the Fletcher-class USS *Knapp* (DD-653) is on display at the Columbia River Maritime Museum. Courtesy of Ed Doss

Hatch removed from the sunken USS *Arizona* at the Nimitz Museum in Fredericksburg, Texas (1985). Author's Collection

Memorials, including Presidential Unit Citation's, honoring USS - *Laffey* DD-459 and USS - *Laffey* DD-724 at Patriots Point, Mt. Pleasant, South Carolina. Author's Collection

Top: Blue Angels over the USS *Lexington* CV-16 circa 1980. USN

Bottom left: Mast of the USS *Biloxi* CL-80 at Biloxi, Mississippi (1985). Author's Collection

Bottom right: Scoreboard of the USS *England* DE-635 at the Naval Academy Museum, March 1985. Author's Collection